The
Episcopacy
of
Nicholas Gallagher,
Bishop
of Galveston,
1882–1918

Summerfield G. Roberts
Texas History Series

The

Episcopacy

of

Nicholas Gallagher, Bishop of Galveston, 1882–1918

❧✝❧

Sr. Madeleine Grace, CVI

TEXAS A&M UNIVERSITY PRESS
COLLEGE STATION

Library of Congress Cataloging-in-Publication Data

Names: Grace, Madeleine, Sister, CVI, 1945– author.
Title: The episcopacy of Nicholas Gallagher, Bishop of Galveston, 1882-1918
  / Sr. Madeleine Grace, CVI.
Other titles: Summerfield G. Roberts Texas history series.
Description: First edition. | College Station : Texas A&M University Press,
  [2020] | Series: Summerfield G. Roberts Texas history series | Includes
  bibliographical references and index.
Identifiers: LCCN 2019045106 | ISBN 9781623498337 (hardcover) |
  ISBN 9781623498344 (ebook)
Subjects: LCSH: Catholic Church—Texas—Galveston—History. | Gallagher,
  Nicholas A., Bishop of Galveston, 1846-1918. | Catholic Church—Bishops—
  Biography. | Church work with minorities—Texas—Galveston—Catholic
  Church. | Catholic church buildings—Reconstruction—Texas—Galveston.
  | LCGFT: Biographies.
Classification: LCC BX1418.G35 G73 2020 | DDC 282.092 [B]—dc23
LC record available at https://lccn.loc.gov/2019045106

This work is dedicated to the memory of my parents,
John and Marie Grace
for the example of their deep faith.

Contents

Foreword

The important contributions of Bishop Nicholas A. Gallagher to the development of the Catholic Church in Texas have not received the full attention of historians they merit when the obstacles he faced are thoroughly considered. He came to Texas in 1882 when the Diocese of Galveston was in considerate "turmoil" due to confusion over who was "in-charge" after Bishop Claude Dubuis, thirty-five years as missionary priest and bishop, retired to France but did not resign the administration of the diocese. He assigned to the Vicar General authority over spiritual affairs, and the chancellor was responsible for financial affairs.

It was an arrangement doomed to fail. The priests rallied around one or the other but all were dissatisfied. Rome appointed a bishop to be apostolic administrator while Dubuis retained the title of Bishop of Galveston. The priest appointed S. J. Meyer of New York, first accepted the appointment and then turned it down, no doubt due to stories of dissension among the clergy reaching New York.

In the midst of this confusion, Father Nicholas A. Gallagher of Columbus, Ohio, received unofficial word from a bishop visiting Rome that he would be named the apostolic administrator of Galveston. Aware of the discouraging condition in Galveston, the bishop offered congratulations but urged him to accept the appointment "like a man." When the official announcement arrived a few days later, Gallagher immediately began to receive letters from Galveston that confirmed the general unhappiness, mostly due to a divided clergy.

Archbishop William E. Elder of Cincinnati urged him to accept the appointment "to poor Galveston." One can imagine Gallagher's serious hesitation before giving his acceptance to leave a peaceful priestly life in Ohio for Texas and a diocese with considerable problems.

Gallagher was only thirty-six years old when he became the apostolic administrator of Galveston. He moved quickly to resolve the problem of clerical infighting; he eliminated the office of vicar general and chancellor, and assumed these duties himself. It wasn't long, however, before he faced other problems, some due to his own decisions and others to his reserved personality, which did not easily adapt to the young and developing missionary church in Texas.

The decision to close the Ursuline Chapel to the public misjudged the reaction of Galvestonians, which incurred their disfavors for a long time. Neither did it help him to show special concern for the Dominican sisters who came from Ohio.

The enormous challenge Gallagher faced in the aftermath of the 1900 storm that devastated Galveston and claimed over six thousand lives, including ten sisters and ninety-four orphans, demonstrated his steady hand in the midst of an unbelievable tragedy and his ability to bring hope and courage to the deeply depressed survivors. When the sad memories of the catastrophe were very fresh, he seized the opportunity to begin a seminary in a damaged hotel on Galveston Bay, which fulfilled both a dream and a need.

For thirty-six years Bishop Gallagher was the chief shepherd of the Diocese of Galveston. In those years he brought unity to a divided clergy, rallied the city and the diocese to recover from the great 1900 storm, and made other important contributions to the rapidly growing Catholic Church in Texas. Yet he has not been well known.

Sister Madeleine Grace has helped to lift up this courageous bishop from comparative oblivion to his rightful place among Texas bishops who were responsible for the Church at the beginning of the twentieth century. She has given us a good insight into a rather shy young Bishop who came among total strangers but overcame challenges to be a true shepherd during difficult times and the rapidly changing world of the early 1900s. He promoted Catholic education and increased the number of schools from the two when he arrived in 1882 to thirty-two in 1918. It is noteworthy that one school was established in Galveston for Negro students, which was rare for the South. The diocese had one hospital when he arrived and seven by his death.

I hope this biography of our third bishop will have a large readership. He deserves to be better known for his significant contribution to the development of Catholicism in Texas during challenging and very difficult times. Sister Madeleine Grace has filled a noticeable gap in the history of the mother church of Texas.

—Archbishop Joseph A. Fiorenza

Preface

The germination of this project began with a tour of a refurbished painted church, St. Mary of the Purification, in Plantersville, Texas, in the Diocese of Galveston-Houston. The visitation opened the door of awareness to the struggle of newly habited immigrants in South Texas. The evidence of the beauty of the makeover of the church, under the supervision of Father Ed Kucera, the pastor, made it overwhelmingly apparent how dear the immigrants' Catholic faith was to them. Further study into the history of the parish made it apparent that this nucleus of German Catholics would have had to make many adaptations in living their faith in South Texas. The inexperience of a bishop of Irish heritage, keenly aware of bringing the faith to these people, yet many times without provision of clerics from their native heritage, made the journey rustic, if not at times seemingly audacious.

Bishop Nicholas Aloysius Gallagher served the Diocese of Galveston for thirty-six years, from 1882 until 1918. Whereas unpublished works are found in various archives, especially due to the efforts of Monsignor James Vanderholt, a major published study is not available. These specific perceptions provided the incentive to proceed with the research.

This endeavor would not have been possible without the efforts of the following people.

Monsignor James Vanderholt provided the lion's share of his own research pertaining to Bishop Nicholas Gallagher. The following individuals have brought forth valuable pieces to the work:

Lisa May, archivist for the Archdiocese of Galveston-Houston

Marian Barber and Eric Hartmann, archivists for the Diocese of Austin

Sister Dympna Lyons, CVI, and Sister Brendan O'Donnell, CVI, archivists for the Sisters of the Incarnate Word and Blessed Sacrament

Father George Hosko, CSB, and Dr. Mary Kelleher, archivist and librarian for the University of St. Thomas, respectively

Joanie South Shelley, archivist for St. Thomas High School

Sister Madeleine Munday, RGS, and Sister Joan Spiering, RGS, archivists for the Sisters of the Good Shepherd

Gail Sowell and Adrian Hoffart, archivists, St. Mary of the Purification Parish, Plantersville

Father Edward Udovic, CM, archivist for the Society of the Mission

Sister Patricia Ann Hamiter, CCVI, archivist for the Sisters of Charity of the Incarnate Word, Houston, Texas

Sister Adrian Dover, OP, and Sister Mary Magdalen Hanel, OP, archivists for the Dominican Sisters of Houston

Sister Esther Dunegan, IWBS, archivist for the Diocese of Beaumont

Sister Louise Smith, SSMN, archivist for the Sisters of St. Mary of Namur, Fort Worth, Texas

Michelle Paradis, archivist for the Basilian Fathers, Toronto, Canada

Sister Charlotte Kitowski, CDP, archivist for the Sisters of Divine Providence, San Antonio, Texas

Sister Theresa Kelleher, CVI, and Sister Mary Margaret Rosberg, CVI, proofreaders

—Sister Madeleine Grace, CVI

The
Episcopacy
of
Nicholas Gallagher,
Bishop
of Galveston,
1882–1918

Setting the Stage

The Diocese of Galveston, at its inception, covered the entire state of Texas. This Diocese had been created only in 1847 when Father Jean-Marie Odin, CM, wrote to Bishop Antoine Blanc of New Orleans requesting that Galveston be raised to the status of a diocese. Pope Pius IX responded to the request of the Catholic bishops of the Sixth Provincial Council of Baltimore on May 4, 1847, in raising Galveston to the hierarchical status of a diocese. Seventeen days later Odin was made Bishop of that Diocese.[1]

At the time the Diocese was created, the bull of erection did not define the boundaries of the Diocese of Galveston for no one knew the boundaries of the former Mexican Province of Texas. When Bishop Odin was in Rome in 1851, he informed Cardinal Barnabo, secretary of the Congregation for the Propagation of the Faith, of the difficulties of the limits of his own jurisdiction. He conveyed to the Cardinal that Texas and the territory between the Nueces and the Rio Grande had previously been a part of the Diocese of Monterrey, Mexico, and that the Province of New Mexico had been under the jurisdiction of the Bishop of Durango. When Texas declared independence from Mexico, it claimed the Rio Grande from its mouth to its source as the western boundary. This included on the northern side the major part of New Mexico and on the southern side the area between the Nueces River and the Rio Grande. When the Diocese was created, Galveston was given as its boundaries all of Texas as determined by the settlement of the treaty ending the war with Mexico (Guadalupe Hidalgo, 1848).

There were conflicting claims between the state of Texas and the federal government after this treaty. Odin consulted the Sacred Congregation in 1848 concerning the boundaries he should adopt. He was advised to exercise jurisdiction "over not only that part of the country lying between the Nueces and the Rio Grande Rivers, but also that territory of New Mexico lying east of the Rio Grande considered by Texas to be an integral part of its territory."[2] Odin realized that this territory was too large for one bishop to manage. Since he had received this message immediately prior to his departure for the Seventh Provincial Council of Baltimore in 1849, he presented this matter to the bishops present on May 5 of that year. Odin specifically asked for a vicar apostolic to care for New Mexico. The Holy Father acceded to this request to send Bishop John-Baptiste Lamy as one who would care for the Apostolic Vicariate. The region between the Nueces River and Rio Grande was left within the Diocese of Galveston. Bishop Odin therefore went to visit these areas after returning from the Seventh Provincial Council. The Bull of July 19, 1850, issued by Pope Pius IX, *Ad supremum Apostolicae*, established New Orleans as an archiepiscopal see, named Bishop Blanc as its first archbishop, and designated as suffragans[3] Mobile, Alabama; Natchez, Mississippi; Little Rock, Arkansas; and Galveston, Texas, thus placing Galveston within the Province of New Orleans. The Apostolic Vicariate of New Mexico was created through this document as well as the inclusion of the region between the Nueces and the Rio Grande within the Diocese of Galveston.[4] Bishop Gallagher's predecessor, Claude Dubuis, often told his religious recruits from Lyon and other parts of France that the Diocese of Galveston was larger than the entire country of France. In 1874 Pope Pius IX issued a decree providing for the erection of the Archdiocese of San Antonio and an Apostolic Vicariate of Brownsville.[5] San Antonio was created in 1874, and Brownsville received an Apostolic Vicariate the following year.[6]

Bishop Claude Dubuis, second bishop of the Diocese of Galveston, asked for a coadjutor bishop in 1878; Bishop Pierre Dufal was appointed to the Diocese with the right of succession. Dufal had most recently served as Vicar Apostolic of Eastern Bengal in India and as Superior General of the Congregation of the Holy Cross. In March 1879, Bishop Dubuis was preparing for a trip to France and left Dufal with the power of attorney to transact business while he was absent. Dufal did not like

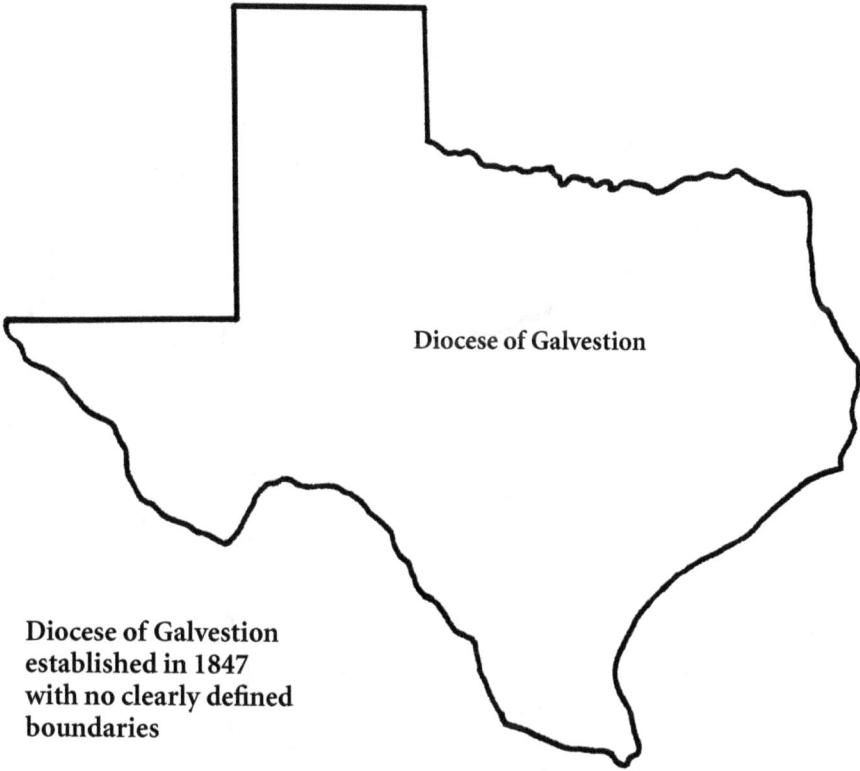

Diocese of Galvestion

Diocese of Galvestion
established in 1847
with no clearly defined
boundaries

Courtesy of Monsignor James Vanderholt.

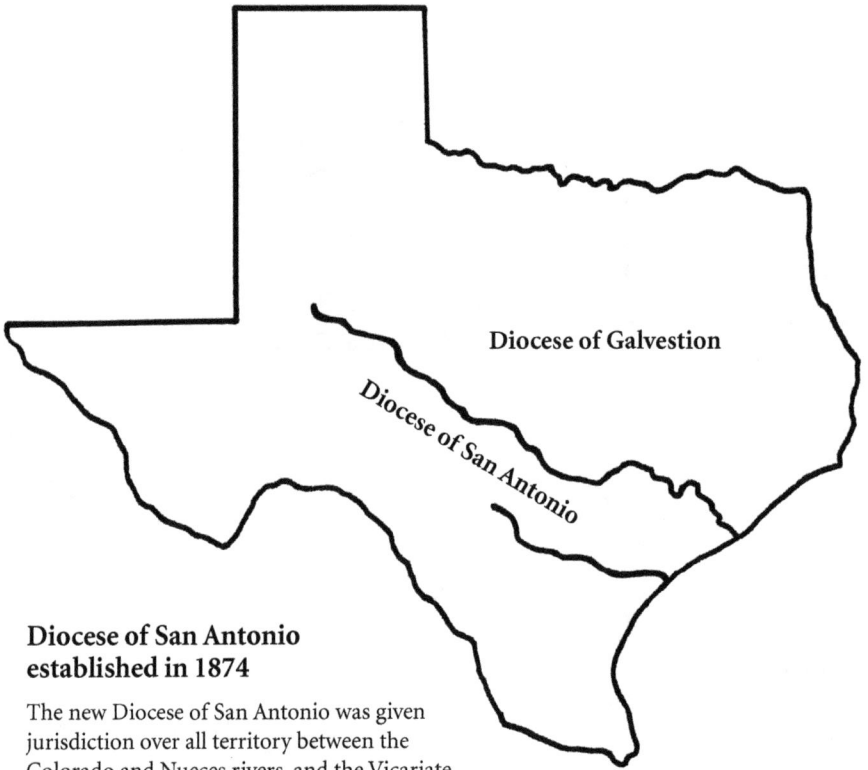

Diocese of Galvestion

Diocese of San Antonio

Diocese of San Antonio established in 1874

The new Diocese of San Antonio was given jurisdiction over all territory between the Colorado and Nueces rivers, and the Vicariate of Brownsville, the present Diocese of Corpus Christi, was assigned the territory between the Nueces and the Rio Grande. These boundary lines were rather vague since the headwaters of both the Nueces and the Colorado were unknown and there was no mention of northern boundaries, but this made little practical difference since most of the land in that section was unexplored and uninhabited.

Courtesy of Monsignor James Vanderholt.

the way the Diocese was being run and pondered how difficult it would be to change it. He decided to submit his letter of resignation to Rome which was accepted in December, 1879. He announced his resignation to the membership of the Diocese in January of 1880, referring to "the interest" of the Diocese and his poor health. In the same statement, in following instructions of Bishop Dubuis, he appointed Father Theodore Buffard Vicar General, as Administrator of the diocese. Bishop Claude Dubuis returned to the Diocese following Dufal's departure; he ordained four men, appointed Louis Chaland as Diocesan Chancellor, reappointed Buffard as Vicar General, and addressed the spiritual affairs of the diocese. He went back to Europe in 1881 and resigned as Administrator of the Diocese in Rome, July 12, 1881, but retained the title. Reverend A. J. Meyer, a Vincentian from Brooklyn was then appointed Bishop of Galveston. Meyer conveyed word to the Diocese that Buffard would administer the Diocese. In the meantime, Meyer heard stories of dissension among the diocesan clergy and of Dufal's resignation. He then asked the Vatican to withdraw his appointment. Buffard began acting as Administrator of the diocese, due to Meyer's appointment and to the chagrin of Father Chaland. The chain of command had to be clarified by the Archbishop of New Orleans, Napoléon Perché. Buffard was Vicar General and Chaland the Chancellor. Yet a number of priests did not like the way Bufford was conducting diocesan business.[7]

Meyer was replaced by Bishop Nicholas Aloysius Gallagher. A. J. McMaster,[8] editor of the *Freeman's Journal*, had his own way of presenting information he had obtained by way of a special cable dispatch from Rome:

The Very Rev. A. J. Meyer, Superior at St. John Baptist's Brooklyn, was named Bishop of Galveston. A most admirable, conscientious, and prudent bishop, he would have been. But the affliction he has suffered for eleven years and more in his eyes,—requiring a dispensation from the recital of the Office-rendering him unable to read twenty minutes a day—was so potently urged by him, on Cardinal McCloskey,—who had been requested by the Cardinal-Prefect of the Propaganda to use his good offices to induce Father Meyer to sacrifice himself and to accept, without delay-that His eminence Cardinal McCloskey *recognized* the painful necessity of supporting Father Meyer's plea. Now, the Very Rev. Nicholas A. Gallagher,

V.G. of Columbus, is appointed *Administrator*, in spirituals and in temporals, of Galveston! Who is Bishop of Galveston? Monseigneur Dubuis resigned his See; and, it was published, his resignation was accepted. If not accepted, *how* could Father Meyer have been named *Bishop of Galveston? Mirabilis in altis Dominus!* But in this case, we must change the first half of the di-phon, and put in place of mirabiles *elationes-depressiones!* "*Mirabiles depressiones* Rome officialis!" It will be a puzzle—till explained—to know who is Bishop of Galveston? But it is no puzzle that Very Rev. Nicholas J. Gallagher, former Administrator of Columbus, while the see was vacant, has been named Bishop of a See in some Infidel place, and Administrator in things Spiritual and Temporal, of the Diocese of Galveston—so grand in its possibilities—and so wretched in fact.

If Dr. Gallagher will accept, and will disentangle a knot on a most beautiful chord, he will not only have a great crown in Heaven, but his success on earth, will render him blessed, very widely. He is not Bishop of Galveston, only Administrator. For reason, he can demand of the Holy See to release him from Administration of a House not his own! And other, less tangled, Sees need self-sacrificing Bishops?[9]

Nicholas Aloysius Gallagher is the first American bishop for the Diocese of Galveston and the first to hail from north of the Mason-Dixon Line. His two episcopal predecessors traveled from much farther, that is, from across the ocean, from France; therefore, they did not carry the embedded antipathies of the Civil War. Even as the first American-born bishop of Galveston, Gallagher's origin in the North so soon after the Civil War[10] was an actuality that would haunt him for many of his initial years as Bishop of the Diocese of Galveston.

Nicholas Gallagher's family came from County Meath, Ireland, to America in 1798 to escape the "vengeance of England inflicted upon the brave, patriotic and liberty-loving sons of Ireland."[11] Edmund Gallagher with his wife, Anna Dorsey, settled in Chester County, Pennsylvania, and began raising a family. The Baptisms of the four oldest children are recorded at St. Joseph Church in Philadelphia between 1801 and 1806. The family moved west to Ohio and settled in Noble County in 1818. They were instrumental in founding the parish of Beaver St. Dominic. Edmund died in 1860, never having seen a steamboat, railroad or telegraph line. Three children in this family brought forth twelve priests and religious sisters, the most well-known was Nicholas Gallagher.[12]

Nicholas Gallagher was the son of John and Mary Ann (Brinton) Gallagher and the grandson of Edmund and Anna (Dorsey) Gallagher. He was born in Temperanceville, Ohio, on February 19, 1846, across the street from what was then St. Mary's Church. The parents of Nicholas sparked the idea of a religious vocation. The Diamond Jubilee edition of the Diocese of Galveston borrowed the description of the future Bishop's father penned by Father John Jacquet of Coshocton, Ohio, on the death of John Gallagher in 1859:

> John Gallagher was a worthy man and true Christian. He frequently spent two or three hours a day in prayer; attended Mass regularly at Washington, five miles distant; and received Holy Communion every month. His house was the home of the priest. It was like a church where the Catholics of the neighborhood fulfilled their Christian duties. It was always open-free of charge-to the orphan, the poor and the afflicted. Many will miss him, I the most.[13]

At the age of ten, Nicholas was tutored by the pastor of Beaver (Coshocton, Ohio), the Reverend John M. Jacquet. This early relationship led to a lasting friendship. Father Jacquet spent the last years of his life with Bishop Gallagher in Galveston.[14] Father Jacquet was described as a saintly man.

The family had moved from Temperanceville and returned to land they owned in Beaver Township; they lived in a house near the rectory. Nicholas entered Mt. St. Mary's of the West[15] in September of 1862. Nicholas's fellow seminarians considered him to be so proper, attentive, and conscientious that they referred to him as "the future bishop."[16] He received tonsure[17] and minor orders on September 20, 1867, from Bishop Purcell[18] and was ordained a priest by Bishop S. H. Rosecrans on Christmas Day in 1868 in Holy Cross Church in Columbus. He was the first priest ordained for the diocese.[19]

Father Gallagher served at St. Patrick's Parish in Columbus until 1871 when he was appointed President of St. Aloysius Seminary in Columbus. He remained in that role until the institution closed for financial reasons. He then returned to St. Patrick's Parish as pastor. When in

1878 the Bishop of the Diocese of Columbus, Bishop Rosecrans, died, Father Gallagher was appointed Administrator of the diocese. The Right Reverend John A. Watterson was made Bishop of the Diocese of Columbus in 1880. Father Gallagher returned to his position as Pastor of St. Patrick's and became Bishop Watterson's Vicar General.[20]

Father Gallagher received a cable on December 26, 1881, in Columbus conveying the message that he had been appointed Administrator of the Diocese of Galveston. As stated by McMaster, Father Gallagher was also named Titular Bishop[21] of Canopus, Africa, on January 10, 1882.[22] He would remain Administrator of the Diocese of Galveston for ten years, becoming bishop only when Bishop Dubuis retired in 1892. The people of Columbus, Ohio desired Father Gallagher to have the ceremony of his episcopal ordination among family and friends in Columbus. However, Bishop Gallagher believed such a ceremony belonged to the people he was called to serve.[23]

In the meantime, the Chancellor of the Diocese of Galveston, the Reverend Louis Chaland, wrote the newly appointed Bishop Gallagher, fearing that he might refuse the appointment after having read the article in the *Freeman's Journal* himself:

Galveston, Texas
January 6, 1882
Rt. Rev. N. A. Gallagher, D.D.
Monsignor:

Having seen in the last number of the *Freeman's Journal* an article likely to make you hesitate in accepting the administration of our Diocese, I hasten to inform you that if we have had difficulties in the Diocese, they have arisen from such circumstances as would have brought about the same results in any other Diocese. For the last eight years or so, Msgr. Dubuis has been ailing more or less with insomnia, nervousness and acute rheumatism that obliged him to spend about half of the time in Europe. Then, a Coadjutor was sent us from Bengal, French by birth, who could not speak English without inciting remark. He also was suffering from various diseases, and he soon found himself not adapted to the work and resigned. Now, we have had and have for Vicar General a priest- the Very Rev. Father Buffard who by his authoritative ways and by his unreasonable denunciations from the pulpit . . . has brought things to such a critical condition that he is the object of severe criticisms and ridicule in many of the best Catholic families in Galveston.

Now, dear Bishop, although obliged to acknowledge all this to be true, I can still assert that all is not lost nor is the difficulty insurmountable. On the contrary, I believe that after your arrival which I hope in the Lord will be in a few weeks—all things will right themselves again with both priests and laity.

As to our financial condition, I can safely say that it is good. We have contracted in the last year or so a debt of some fifteen thousand dollars, but the revenues of the Diocese from rented property and other sources induce me to believe that it can be paid in two years. This debt was made principally in building a wing to our College here, which is a credit to the episcopal city—for it now has eighty boarders and one hundred day scholars.

In conclusion, Rt. Rev. Father, I beg to assure you that for the first few months, we have unceasingly prayed to God to send us a Bishop after His own Heart, and now that the sweet Babe of Bethlehem, who in His birth brought peace to men of good will, has given you to us in answer, I hope that you will hasten to accept, and soon come to us your children bringing peace, because I am confident we have the best of wills, and will prove it to you by our future actions.
Believe me, Rt. Rev. Bishop.

Yours very respectfully,
Louis Chaland,
Chancellor[24]

The letter seemed not to affect the acceptance of the new Bishop, yet it certainly told him that he had his work cut out for himself. He issued a circular letter to the priests of the diocese on March 3 of that year.

To the Clergy of the Diocese of Galveston:

By the Grace of God, and favor of the Holy Apostolic See, having been appointed Administrator of the Diocese of Galveston, in things spiritual and temporal:

We do hereby declare, that we assume entire jurisdiction over the Diocese as granted by the Apostolic Brief, of January 10th, 1882. Therefore, in our absence, until our Episcopal ordination, or until otherwise ordered by us, we delegate to Very Rev. Th. Buffard, the authority to grant Dispensations when required, in accordance with the laws of the Church and particular laws existing, in this Diocese. To him, therefore, all applications for Dispensation are to be directed.

We authorize Very Rev. L. Chaland, to continue during the same time, to take charge of the financial affairs of this Diocese.

We also confirm all the Faculties exercised at present by the Priests of this Diocese as expressed in the printed form.

All other causes which on account of urgency cannot be deferred until our permanent abode amongst you, may be referred to us at Columbus, Ohio, until Easter.

Invoking on you, Reverend Brethren, the blessing of Heaven, and begging God to have you and those entrusted to you in His holy keeping, we ask of you a kind remembrance in your prayers.

Given at St. Mary's Cathedral, Galveston, Texas, this third day of March, 1882.

Nicholas A. Gallagher
Administrator of Galveston[25]

Nicholas Gallagher was consecrated in Galveston on April 30, 1882, by the Right Reverend Edward M. Fitzgerald, Bishop of Little Rock.[26] The sermon was delivered by Bishop John A. Watterson, Bishop of Columbus. This was the first episcopal ordination of a bishop held in that particular region of the country. The happiest person that day was Father Jacquet, Bishop Gallagher's longtime friend.[27] When Bishop Dubuis was promoted to Titular Archbishop of Arca, December 16, 1892,[28] Bishop Gallagher became what he had virtually been since 1882, Bishop of Galveston.[29]

Figure 1. A young Bishop Gallagher. Courtesy of Catholic Archives of Texas, Austin, Texas.

❧ 2 ❧

The Master Builder

Whe hen Bishop Gallagher wrote to Bishop Watterson three months later, he stated that his thoughts often reverted with pleasure to the work and endearing ties that bound him to the Diocese of Columbus.

> I need not tell you my feelings in starting out in my new field of labor, among total strangers, because you no doubt experienced the same on coming to Columbus and therefore can appreciate my situation and it is not for me to say that the condition of things here was any worse than there, nor that I was any more anxious to come here than you were to go to Columbus. Divine Providence has so willed it, and as for me I am here, and with God's help I shall endeavor to do the work I am sent to do.[1]

Early on in his administration, Bishop Gallagher moved quickly to eliminate the infighting among the clergy. Father Buffard remained Vicar General for a few months but then was stationed in Dennison in North Texas where he had served before. Father Louis Chaland remained Chancellor and served at the Cathedral until 1884 and then returned to France. Other reappointments followed. In fact, by 1893, there were no French priests remaining in the administration of the Diocese. Others, like Chaland, had chosen to return to France.[2]

Bishop Gallagher would follow the pattern of his two predecessors in inviting religious orders to minister in the Diocese of Galveston. Apart from that, sometimes diocesan priests followed a bishop south. One of the most unusual cases of a diocesan priest briefly serving in the Diocese of Galveston and then proceeding north was that of the Reverend Thomas McGrady. McGrady's parents were driven from Ireland during the Great Famine. Within the mind of McGrady, the famine represented the consequences of the free market and racism and ushered his thinking onto socialistic ideas. His parents settled in Fayete County, Kentucky and became tenant farmers about 1849. Thomas was the seventh of nine children. His three older sisters became religious. Since the Diocese of Covington did not have a seminary, it is assumed that McGrady did some of his seminary study at Mount St. Mary's in Cincinnati. At that time the seminary was headed by Father Nicholas Gallagher. Five years after Gallagher became Bishop of Galveston, he ordained McGrady to the priesthood on February 10, 1887, in the Cathedral in Galveston.[3]

Father McGrady became Bishop Gallagher's assistant at St. Mary's Cathedral in Galveston for the first year after his ordination. McGrady states of his experience there:

> The labor problem was never mentioned in that sacred abode. The rector [Father James Kirwin] was a good-natured old capitalist, who believed that the toiler should have sufficient coarse food to keep body and soul together, sufficient cheap clothing to cover his nakedness, sufficient money to pay his pew rent, and sufficient time to hear Mass on Sunday. I was then rector of Houston's Irish church, St. Patrick's (1888–1889). There were many toilers in my congregation, but they were all contented as long as they had a job and I never presumed to molest their tranquility. Six months spent in Dallas (1890) did not change the situation. Times were encouraging; activity prevailed in every line of business, and the laboring people seemed to think that they were enjoying the general prosperity.[4]

Some other commentators believe that McGrady was mistaken regarding contentment and tranquility among the parishioners, ascribing to a "vigorous socialist movement" in Galveston and Houston in the 1880s.[5]

McGrady then moved back to his home state of Kentucky, eventually becoming a lecturer and propagandist for the Socialist Party by 1900. He published the novel, *Beyond the Black Ocean*, based on the famine in Ireland in addition to two other volumes and a host of pamphlets. His "unique service" to the Socialist Party was in responding to the Vatican and US Catholic Hierarchy. McGrady was quick to point out what he considered were the shortcomings of Leo XIII's *Rerum Novarum*. He found himself at odds with numerous bishops. Bishop Messner in the Green Bay *Gazette* urged his flock to stay away from McGrady's March 11th lecture in 1902. Sometimes a specific lecture was cancelled if it was to be held in a Knights of Columbus Hall. McGrady was criticized for his $100 fee, while Eugene Debs, who charged twice as much, defended him.

While serving in the Diocese of Covington, McGrady was seen as an eloquent apologist for socialism. He described the early church fathers as socialists and upheld the teachings of Charles Darwin among other "modern" heroes. Bishop Camillus Maes did not approve. McGrady was suspended from ministry and left soon after, retiring from active ministry in California.[6]

In California, the *Los Angeles Herald* in its September 5, 1904 issue, reported that the Reverend Thomas Grady delivered a lecture on "Socialism and Religion" at the local Simpson Auditorium. The reporter went on to state that the term *lecture* should not be applied. Rather, the Reverend Thomas McGrady "talked to his audience." It was a "heart to heart" talk with his hearers. The article conveyed that the Reverend Mr. McGrady was an ex-Catholic priest who severed his connection with the church due to a "discussion" between his bishop and him regarding his tendency to lean toward socialism. McGrady declared that he was not excommunicated. The presentation was given under the auspices of the Socialist Party.[7]

McGrady was only involved in the Socialist movement for ten years, as he met an early death at the age of forty-four in 1907.[8] He died on December 4 of that year and is buried in the Catholic cemetery in his home town of Lexington, Kentucky.[9]

A tribute to Thomas McGrady is found among the speeches of Eugene Debs. Ironically, as Debs stated, "he was denied the right to serve the Socialist movement by Socialists." They accused him of being a "grafter," stating that he wished to "graft on them." He was further accused of making socialist speeches for "the money there was in it." Debs defended his comrade, referring to him as a "great white soul," who had abandoned the "wealth and luxury of the capitalist class" to cast his lot among the "proletariat, the homeless and hungry."[10] One might only wonder how

Bishop Nicholas Gallagher would have dealt with such a "livewire" if McGrady had spent those ten years in the Diocese of Galveston.

Arrival of Religious Orders in Galveston during Bishop Odin's and Bishop Dubuis's Episcopacy

Bishop Jean-Marie Odin, CM (1847–61) and Bishop Claude Marie Dubuis (1862–92) each realized the value of religious orders in serving the vast area of the Diocese of Galveston. Not long after his episcopal ordination in April of 1847 as bishop of Galveston, Odin was in Montreal, Canada, seeking priests and religious for the Diocese of Galveston. While Odin was attending a dinner in his honor in Montreal at the major seminary of the Sulpicians, he met Father Piers Telamon, an Oblate of Mary, who was looking for a missionary assignment. Telamon had previously worked in Canada and Pittsburgh. Father Telamon promised that he would accompany Odin to Texas, would serve in the lower Rio Grande area of the Galveston Diocese and would bring with him other Oblates of Mary.[11] Before returning to Texas, Bishop Odin wrote to Bishop Blanc in New Orleans, exclaiming that two Ursuline nuns would be coming from Quebec and two postulants from Boston. Within a year, Bishop Charles Joseph Eugene de Mazenod withdrew the Oblates from the Diocese of Galveston as he was uncertain of Father Telamon's role as leader of the expedition. He also was not regularly informed of their progress. Bishop Odin failed in that communication endeavor due to his own travels around the Diocese and a fifteen-day siege of fever. The Vincentians were also withdrawn due to an overextension of men. These events led Odin back to Europe where in France he was able to regain the confidence of the Oblates and therefore obtain new recruits in addition to four Incarnate Word Sisters, two Ursulines, four Brothers of Mary and eighteen seminarians.[12]

The Sisters of the Incarnate Word and Blessed Sacrament had come to Galveston at the bidding of Bishop Odin. Bishop Dubuis wrote to Mother Angelique in Lyons seeking Sisters to "take charge of our hospitals and orphan asylums." The three volunteers, coming from the convent at Antiquaille, arrived at the convent in Lyon on September 19, 1866. Bishop Dubuis invested the three Sisters with the habit of the Congregation on September 23. They received their religious names and from then on were known as Sisters of Charity of the Incarnate Word, Houston, Texas. Within a short period of time, they were instructed on the spirituality of Jeanne Chezard de Matel, foundress of the Sisters of the Incarnate Word and Blessed Sacrament.[13] They sailed for Galveston on September 25, 1866. Four more Sisters joined them on December 2, 1867, and then two weeks later, two more. Three aspirants joined the group from Galveston. At that time residents of Galveston were fighting yellow fever.[14] Yet work commenced on a new Charity hospital in Galveston.[15] In addition to these new recruits, the first two Sisters of Divine Providence to come to Texas were on board Bishop Dubuis's ship headed for Galveston.[16] Bishop Dubuis made another voyage to Europe during which he visited France, Italy, and Belgium. He was able to recruit ten priests and fifteen sisters to work in the Diocese of Galveston.[17]

Although Bishop Claude Dubuis traveled to various countries in Europe to obtain priests and religious for the Galveston Diocese, many of his recruits were from just one country, France. This influx of French missionaries ended when Bishop Gallagher took office. He forbade the Sisters of Charity of the Incarnate Word from obtaining candidates in France. He wished for English-speaking candidates only. This thrust for English speaking candidates was seen among other bishops, such as Archbishop John Ireland of Saint Paul, Minnesota, yet it brought with it its own difficulties.[18]

In this case, the Sisters of Charity made an appeal to Bishop Dubuis, asking him to assist them in obtaining new members in Dublin. Bishop Dubuis in turn wrote Bishop Gallagher from Lyons, stating that health kept him, Bishop Dubuis, away from Dublin, yet he would send a letter of recommendation to "prelates and high ecclesiastical authorities" in Ireland so that the Sisters "will be able to manage things every bit as well in my absence."[19]

Arrival of Religious Orders in Galveston during the Episcopacy of Bishop Gallagher
Sisters of the Congregation of the Sacred Heart

One of the first endeavors of Bishop Gallagher in Galveston was to recruit religious Sisters from the diocese of Columbus. While serving in Ohio, then Father Gallagher, became aware that the Sisters of the Congregation at St. Mary of the Springs refused to accept the election of their new Prioress. These two Sisters, Sister Mary Agnes Magevney and Sister Rose Lynch, former prioress, received permission from then Bishop Rosecrans to withdraw from St. Mary's and establish Sacred Heart Academy and Novitiate in Columbus. This School served as a day school for the education of young ladies in the city. In 1879 the Sisters moved this Academy to a rented building in Somerset. The School served students for two or three years with about twenty sisters, twelve or fifteen boarding students, and about sixty day students. They had begun construction on a new school when the opportunity to serve in the Diocese of Galveston came about.[20]

The Sisters of the Congregation of the Sacred Heart had hoped that Father Gallagher would be appointed to the See of Columbus. Initially, the relationship between this Congregation and Bishop Watterson was quite amiable. On a formal visit on October 4, 1880, Bishop Watterson promised Mother Agnes that he would never disturb the Community. However, as time progressed, the relationship simmered. The Bishop would not permit two motherhouses in such close proximity. He furthermore would not permit the Sisters to receive any new members. In time, he planned to unite this Sacred Heart Congregation with the original St. Mary of the Springs Foundation. Mother Agnes, following the unanimous vote of her Sisters, then asked permission to leave the diocese.[21]

Unfortunately, a newspaper clipping in the Columbus *Times* (July 13, 1882) stated that Bishop Watterson had ordered the Sisters to Galveston. This fallacious report caused a furor among the Catholic population. After meeting with a group of Catholic residents from Somerset, the Bishop responded in the *Ohio State Journal* by pointing out that the Sisters had not been dismissed and did not deserve to be dismissed. Transfer to another diocese would require permission of both bishops. The Sisters were free to go to Galveston if they wished.[22]

Bishop Gallagher began the formal process by writing to Bishop Watterson (July 18, 1882) stating that Sister Agnes had received permission to leave the Diocese of Columbus for Galveston. He therefore requested in writing that permission be granted. The transfer of jurisdiction took place two days later in a letter from Bishop Watterson to

Bishop Gallagher. The transfer was complete when Bishop Gallagher wrote to Bishop Watterson (July 23, 1882) acknowledging and accepting the transfer of jurisdiction.

> To Rt. Rev. John A. Watterson, D.D.
> Bishop of Columbus, Ohio
>
> Dear Bishop:
>
> The transfer of jurisdiction, over the Community of the Sisters of St. Dominic in charge of Sister Mary Agnes, made by your Lordship on behalf of the Diocese of Columbus, Ohio, and to the Diocese of Galveston, is hereby acknowledged; and the acceptance thereof is hereby duly made by us on behalf of the Diocese of Galveston, Texas.
>
> Witness our hand and seal this twenty third (23) day of July 1882
> N. A. Gallagher
> Bishop Admin. of Galveston[23]

The Sisters traveled by rail to Galveston. Initially, Mother Agnes had the funds to pay the train fare of the twenty Sisters. However, Bishop Watterson asked Mother Agnes to give that money to him which she did. Thus, on September 8, Bishop Gallagher arrived in Somerset, made all the arrangements and paid all the expenses for the Sisters to travel to Galveston. The Bishop then saw to it that suitable accommodations were provided in Galveston.[24] The Sisters arrived in Galveston on September 29, 1882.[25]

The Sisters were to experience the effects of an outbreak of dengue fever[26] in October 1884. The fever spread through the convent until there were thirteen Sisters suffering from the fever at one time. Most of the priests on the island suffered from it. Bishop Gallagher thought he could survive without going to bed but collapsed at the foot of the altar as he was about to celebrate a Mass of Ordination. He recovered three weeks later.[27]

The Dominican Sisters opened a boarding and day school on October 9, 1882, at the site that became Sacred Heart Convent. They received a state charter three years later. Additions were made to the school in 1888 and 1893. The Academy withstood the effects of the storm of 1900 as it was located on one of the highest spots on the island. It closed temporarily after the storm but reopened again in 1903. After the experience of the storm in Galveston, the Sisters believed the city an impractical site for a boarding school, so they purchased the old Centenary College in Lampasas and named it St. Dominic's Villa Academy. The curriculum of St. Dominic's Villa was so like that of Sacred Heart Academy in Galveston that the Villa was referred to as "Galveston transported from the lowlands to the highlands."[28] However, due to the paucity of students and prejudice against Catholics, the Institution closed in 1925. Unfortunately, the Ku Klux Klan had boycotted and harassed the families, who were mainly farmers, whose children attended St. Dominic's Villa, until these families were forced to withdraw their children from the Academy.[29]

In 1887, at the request of Bishop Gallagher, these Sisters took charge of Holy Rosary School to provide for the education of black children. Mother Agnes Magevney refused compensation for the Sisters who taught in the school. The Sisters of the Holy Family took over this mission in 1897.[30]

The Dominican Sisters experienced various forms of opposition during their initial years in Galveston. Sister Imelda Rosecrans had an uncle, General Rosecrans, who served with the Union forces. It did not help the situation to hear that Mother Agnes' uncle, Colonel Michael Magevney, served with the 154th Tennessee Confederate Infantry. When they opened a school for black children in 1887, the opposition became "more bitter and outspoken."[31]

Three years later, some of the Dominican Sisters were involved in remodeling the Cathedral as well as Bishop Gallagher's parlors.[32] The Dominican Sisters came to administer and teach in a number of Catholic schools in Houston and Galveston in the first quarter of the twentieth century.[33] They were asked to open a free school in Cathedral Parish in 1893. They promptly agreed, but this task reduced their income from fifty to twenty-two dollars a month.[34] By 1900, the Sisters were teaching not only in Galveston but also in Beaumont, Taylor and Houston. In that same year, on August 7, the Constitutions of the Sisters of Penance of the Third Order of St. Dominic were approved by Bishop Gallagher. Through the intercession of Bishop Gallagher, these Sisters became affiliated with the Order of Preachers on June 23, 1902.[35] The Order was approved as a pontifical institute[36] in March 1944.[37]

In the personal correspondence of Bishop Gallagher there is evidence of correspondence with his niece Sister M. Agnes when she was stationed in Brenham and Lampasas. His letter to Sister Agnes in Brenham promises a visit to the convent there soon. He also directed her in the virtue of humility and trust in God. "Pay little attention to the praises of others, . . . Be patient with all under all circumstances. Never be harsh with anyone. Be gentle, charitable and forbearing with all."[38]

While Bishop Gallagher was helpful to the Dominicans in the establishment of the Order, not every Sister was delighted with his service as their regular confessor. Realizing the situation, the Bishop appointed the Jesuits as their confessor when the Society of Jesus came to Galveston. However, the Dominican provincial opposed the change as the spirituality of the two Orders differed. Thus Bishop Gallagher again resumed the role "to the dismay of some and to the delight of others."[39] The second letter written by Bishop Gallagher from Rome gives evidence that he is on church business. He commented that Mother Pauline will soon have postulants from Ireland.[40]

These Dominican Sisters opened St. Agnes Academy in Houston on February 11, 1906. The school was erected at the intersection of Fannin and Isabella and solemnly blessed by Bishop Gallagher. It became affiliated with the University of Texas and was approved by the State Department of Education in 1917. Its enrollment grew from seventy to 270 in the first quarter of its existence.[41]

The National Catholic Educational Association began in 1904. Bishop Gallagher appointed Father John B. O'Leary as diocesan superintendent of schools six years later in 1910. All Sisters involved in education met from December 27 to 29 of that year at the first Diocesan Catholic Institute. The need for accreditation of schools and qualification of teachers became apparent. Because Bishop Gallagher was initially opposed to the attendance of Sisters at universities, they enrolled in correspondence courses from the University of Texas at Austin. Eventually the Sisters were able to attend classes at local universities, or at the Catholic University in Washington, DC, among other institutions of higher learning.[42]

Figure 2. Bishop Gallagher and members of his family. Courtesy of Catholic Archives of Texas, Austin, Texas.

✹ 3 ✹

Spiritual and Material
Innovator

The Society of Jesus

B ishop Gallagher asked the Jesuits of New Orleans to provide aid
to the parishes and schools of Galveston. On June 21, 1844, Father
John F. O'Connor, SJ, became the pastor of a new parish, Sacred Heart,
located on the east end of the city. The Jesuits were also asked to take
control of what was then a struggling St. Mary's University. The Jesuits
celebrated Mass from 1884 to 1892 in a chapel that was set up in one
of the old buildings at St. Mary's University. Sacred Heart Church was
designed by Nicholas Clayton as a French Romanesque edifice. Brother
Cornelius Otten, SJ, directed the project. The Church was dedicated to
the Sacred Heart on January 17, 1892, by Bishop Gallagher. Unfortunately, the storm of 1900 destroyed the building, with the exception of
two stained glass windows and a large crucifix. The Church was rebuilt
on a smaller scale. The Jesuits staffed it until 1924. The land on which
Sacred Heart Church stood was originally given to Bishop Jean Marie Odin, the first bishop of Galveston, on the condition that a school
for boys be erected there. A three-story building was constructed and
served intermittently as a boys' school. The building was demolished
when the Jesuits withdrew. The Jesuits were not able to save St. Mary's
University from closing in 1922.[1]

The Paulist Fathers

The Superior General of the Paulist fathers, Very Reverend George M. Searle, CSP, wrote Bishop Gallagher in May 1907 stating that he had long been considering a foundation for the Order in the Southwest, preferably in Austin. Father Searle was specifically looking toward the education of Catholic students in state colleges and universities. He also hoped to take charge of a parish in addition to the university work. Bishop Gallagher welcomed the suggestion. He did need to check to see if the Holy Cross Fathers would have any objection to a new parish carved from what was then St. Mary's Parish. The Holy Cross Fathers agreed with the project. Bishop Gallagher had two main objectives in mind for the Paulist Fathers.

> I have had in mind not only the spiritual needs of our growing Capital City, but two objects of yet wider importance. These are, first, that your Fathers may make, with the blessing of God, their house a center of missionary activity for Catholics and non-Catholics throughout the Southwest, and especially the diocese of Galveston. But my main and particular object is that your Fathers may exercise a special care and supervision over a very choice portion of our people, the young men and women who are students in the State University. No class of Catholics needs or deserves all the zeal and enlightened interests which the clergy can bestow, more than those who in their youth are far from the healthful environment of their Catholic homes and friends.[2]

Bishop Gallagher's concern was heightened by the encyclical of Pope Pius X, *Acerbo nimis*, which stated:

> In the larger cities, and especially where universities, colleges and secondary schools are located, let classes in religion be organized to instruct in the truths of faith and in the practice of Christian life the youths who attend the public schools from which all religious teaching is banned.[3]

In the document issued on April 15, 1906, the Pontiff urged a special care for the safeguarding of the faith of those students in state schools.

The Paulist Fathers came to Austin on September 7, 1908. Their main objective was the spiritual needs of the Catholic students at the University of Texas. As they desired a new parish, St. Austin's was set up on three lots; the Parish was dedicated to St. Augustine of Canterbury. It served students and parishioners who lived in that area. A three-story brick building was constructed and paid for, largely through the efforts of the Paulists. This building then housed the meeting area for the Newman Club, a classroom, the library, the chaplain's office, the chapel, and living quarters for the priests.[4]

Newman Hall

These two groups, the Dominican Sisters and the Paulist Fathers, actually came together in a common ministry of Newman Hall, affiliated with the University of Texas in Austin. Mother Pauline Gannon, OP, had long desired a Catholic place of residence for women attending the University of Texas. In 1918, she opened Newman Hall, a residence for women attending the state university and likewise for sisters attending summer school.[5] The Paulist priests served as chaplains, as they had been in the locale since 1908 and had built the University Catholic Center in 1913. The cornerstone was blessed and the address given by Monsignor James Kirwin. Bishop Gallagher had died earlier in that year, 1918. Referring to the wishes of the late bishop, Monsignor Kirwin stated:

> Knowing conditions in Texas and realizing that distance and comparative poverty rendered it impossible for our boys to be sent to Catholic universities, he wished to save for God and religion those who come here, forced by necessity to acquire a knowledge of law, engineering, the sciences or to fit themselves as teachers. He weighed all the consequences, he knew that their presence here might be construed as tacit approval of purely secular institutions but he was caught up with the burning desire of the Good Shepherd. And when the occasion demanded and our young women in large numbers were frequenting this institution, he asked the Sisters of St. Dominic to find a way for their protection in the midst of an environment that is necessarily irreligious and materialistic.[6]

The Good Shepherd Sisters

Bishop Gallagher had been attempting to get the Sisters of the Good Shepherd to come to the Diocese of Galveston since 1902. However, the plan did not materialize until May 20, 1914. Bishop Gallagher wrote Mother M. of Loretto on September 9, 1905, to state that due to the unrestrained conditions after the 1900 storm, a house could not be established for the Good Shepherd Sisters. He hoped that the fall of 1906 would bring better news.[7] In September 1906, the Bishop wrote again stating that the grade of the city was being raised seven and eight feet. The place the Bishop had in mind would not be filled in less than a year.[8] The Bishop wrote in July of the following year to state that he would not be able to receive the Sisters for two or possibly three years. He pointed out that the block he had in mind was quite centrally located.[9] When the Bishop wrote in January 1914, he told the Sisters they could select a plot of land.[10] The Sisters expressed joy at this response.[11] In the following month, Bishop Gallagher wrote inviting the Sisters to stay with the Dominican Sisters in Galveston at Sacred Heart Convent or in Houston at St. Agnes Academy while they surveyed possible sites for their convent.[12] In a letter of February 21, 1914, from Bishop Gallagher to Mother Loretto, it appeared that a ten-acre site had been decided on. The Bishop gave the Sisters permission to purchase it and collect funds for the purchase. The Bishop mentioned Father Gaffney as a resource person in managing this affair.[13] A small band of Sisters soon arrived from St. Louis. A furnished house had been established for them. The Bishop came the next day to bless the house. He gave them the ciborium and altar stone for their chapel. He later contributed $1,100 toward the site of a permanent convent. The first convent was actually built on 1511 Chenevert Street. Bishop Gallagher issued a letter on January 28, 1916, to all the priests of the Diocese of Galveston asking them to announce that the Good Shepherd Sisters would be visiting their parish to solicit funds for their mission.

Dear Reverend Father:

As the charitable work of the Good Shepherd Sisters of Houston is for the benefit of the whole Diocese, and as they have not sufficient room to accommodate the many who apply to them and need their care, we hereby give them permission to solicit help in every Parish of this Diocese, in order that they may obtain funds to provide themselves with suitable accommodations. Please announce that the Good Shepherd Sisters will visit your Parish in a few days to appeal to the charity of your good people.

Yours faithfully in Christ,
Nicholas Aloysius,
Bishop of Galveston[14]

Three years later in 1917, the cornerstone was laid for their site on 1410 Richmond Avenue. The institution was on a ten-acre site.[15]

The Basilians

The Congregation of St. Basil attempted to establish an academy for boys in Waco in 1899. Father Robert McBrady, CSB, was assigned to start a Catholic school for boys. Assurances of public support were obtained. The original location of the school was Eighth and Clay Streets, in Assumption Parish where Father Ed Kelly served as pastor. He had paid for the purchase of the land and then transferred the title to the Basilians. The *Waco Evening Telephone* reported on April 5, 1902, that all was ready for the laying of the cornerstone:

> Everything is ready for the laying of the cornerstone and the other exercises which are to take place tomorrow in connection with the new Catholic college which is beginning to loom up grandly from the commanding eminence on which it is situated. The work has been rushed along rapidly since the last start was made, and the structure will doubtless be completed and ready for school purposes within a few months. . . . The school is appreciated by the people here and the laying of the cornerstone formally will be a matter of interest to all.

The *Waco Star Times* reported in its Sunday edition of April 6 that Bishop Nicholas Gallagher celebrated a solemn high Pontifical Mass for the occasion. Many dignitaries were present in addition to a number of Basilians, including the Provincial, the Very Reverend V. Marijon, of St. Michael's College, Toronto, Canada.[16]

St. Basil's was mainly a college preparatory school with some business courses added. The library contained three thousand volumes. The initial enrollment was sixty. New property, about fifteen acres, was obtained at Provident Heights. A three-story building, including a swimming pool with a capacity for one hundred boys, was built. Students attended from several parts of Texas.[17] Boarding was $20 a month. The day students paid $5 a month for the ten-month school year. Father Thomas Hayes, CSB, served as local superior. He was a popular preacher for parish missions around the state. In the spring of 1903, he asked to be relieved of his position for reasons of health. The provincial council reluctantly agreed and appointed Father Francis Foster to replace him. In 1907 Father Michael John Ryan replaced Father Foster. The student enrollment fluctuated due to difficult financial times in Texas. In 1911, Father Thomas Gignac became Superior of St. Basil's College. Growing financial problems clouded the future of the school. The Provincial Council decided to close the school in June 1915 and put the property up for sale.[18] In a letter from the Provincial of the Augustinian Fathers to Bishop Gallagher dated June 24, 1915, it is evident that Bishop Gallagher had requested that they take over St. Basil's College, as the Provincial was asking specific information before approaching his council.[19] Mother M. Albertine of the Sisters of St. Mary of Namur asked permission of Bishop Gallagher, in a correspondence dated July 29, 1915, to buy the property but also to "dispose" of the fifteen acres they held in Highland Place.[20] In a letter dated August 2, 1916, the Provincial of the Oblate Fathers in San Antonio, after hearing of the "trouble between the Parish of Waco and the Basilian Fathers," offered to buy the property for their "apostolic school."[21] The Parish referred to was Assumption Parish in Waco. The property was transferred and sold to the Sisters of St. Mary of Namur.[22] The Sisters began making payments to the Basilians but found they were unable to do anything with the property. Development of the property by way of repair to open a school would have taken too much money. These were the years of the depression. During this time, the city of Waco built a public school across the street. This seemed to seal the fate of the property. The Sisters suggested to the Basilians that they give the property to Bishop Christopher E. Byrne on the occasion of his Golden Jubilee. The transaction would prevent the city claiming back taxes on the property because it would be used for religious purposes. The transference of the land to Bishop Byrne took place between June and September of 1941.[23]

In 1902, the Basilian community, with the consent of Bishop Gallagher, sold their original property and bought property on University Heights for the operation of the School. Unfortunately, a lawsuit, originating with the Diocese, arose over the sale of the original piece of land. Bishop Gallagher chose to institute a suit against the Basilian Order in order to recover damages for the Basilian failure to restore the title to the first property based on the following prescription:

> That if at any time the said community finds that it cannot open and maintain the said school the said community shall surrender and re-transfer the said property to the Catholic Church in Waco, in the person of Rt. Rev. N. A. Gallagher, Bishop of Galveston, or his successor as bishop of Galveston.[24]

The suit was, to a great extent, promoted by Fr. Ed A. Kelly, Pastor of Assumption Parish. It is apparent that the Basilian Fathers and the Apostolic Delegate wished to stay out of the civil court, as evidenced in the following letter from the Apostolic Delegate in Washington, DC, in response to a letter from Fr. Kelly:

> On receiving your letter of March 29th (1916), I wrote to the Basilian Fathers telling them that I would much prefer to see them settle their controversy with you outside the courts by coming to an amicable settlement. Several letters were then exchanged between them and myself until day before yesterday when two of them came to Washington to see me. They explained their side of the case to me, and the arguments, which they gave to support it, which are by no means worthless; so much so that I could no longer insist in the same manner as I had before that they settle with you in a friendly way. They claimed that they would have preferred and that they still prefer to have the question decided by an ecclesiastical tribunal, but that, since you have summoned them before the civil court, they are willing to accept your summons, confident that they will be victorious. A perus-

al of the brief of defense prepared by their lawyer has convinced me that they have a fair chance to win, and I consequently began to fear that you were badly advised when you were told to put the case in the hands of the civil court. The lawyer in fact who gave you this advice, and who has since been retained by them, is said to have afterwards confessed that when he so advised you, he had not studied the case well. This being the condition of things, I would suggest for you to seek further information from competent persons about your rights in the premises, and, if you find that prospects are against you, so withdraw the suit from the civil courts. If you should lose the case after having dragged the Fathers before the civil court, it would be doubly regrettable on account of the scandal and moral effect on the Catholic population.

With expression of good wishes, I remain,
Sincerely yours in Christ,
Most Reverend John Bonzano, D.D.
Apostolic Delegate Washington, D.C.[25]

The Apostolic Delegate wrote Bishop Gallagher in March 1917 expressing great apprehension of the case going to civil court.

Rt. Rev. and Dear Bishop:

I am sending herewith enclosed a letter which I have received from the Very Rev. F. Forester, Provincial of the Basilian Fathers. I shall appreciate it if you will carefully consider the communication and give me your opinion on the matter. At the same time I beg leave to remark that, when a little over a year ago I was convinced that the case be brought into the civil courts, it was only after Your Vicar General and Father Kelly of Waco had represented the affair to me as one of great urgency for which there was no other relief at hand but recourse to the civil courts. Had I been able to study the case more fully, I might not have allowed them to take this course.

I ask you to kindly return the enclosure with your reply and with sentiments of esteem and best wishes, beg to remain

Sincerely yours in Christ,
Most Reverend John Bonzano, D.D.
Apostolic Delegate, Washington, D.C.[26]

Needless to say, Bishop Gallagher did not heed this warning of an unwinnable case.

In the suit, the diocese sought specific performance of the contract, that is, a court-ordered remedy requiring precise fulfillment of the terms of the contract. Since the property had been sold to a third party with the Bishop's consent, this remedy was no longer available to the Diocese. The Provincial of the Basilians, Father F. Forester, wrote Bishop Christopher Byrne in June 1919 explaining the Basilian position in the case, as Bishop Gallagher had died in January 1918. Bishop Byrne and the executors of Bishop Gallagher's will, Father Ed Kelly and Monsignor James Kirwin,[27] chose to go forward with the suit and likewise extend it to an appeals court. The Diocese lost the suit on November 15, 1923.[28] As it turned out, the Diocese of Galveston, which had lost the suit, ended up with the land, for, as previously stated, it was given to Bishop Byrne on the occasion of his Jubilee. St. Louis Parish and Reicher High School are located on this land today.[29]

Even before the Basilians left Waco, Bishop Gallagher urged them to give the young men of Houston a similar opportunity by way of education. Father Thomas Hennessey, Pastor of Annunciation Church, had expressed the desire to Bishop Gallagher that the school be placed within the geographic limits of his downtown parish. According to a letter to Bishop Gallagher, dated January 15, 1900, Father Victorin Marijon, CSB, the Provincial of the Basilians in North America, met with Father Hennessey and discovered that he was "very anxious to have a Catholic school for boys in Houston." He also thanked the Bishop for his hospitality in Galveston.[30] A letter from Father Victorin Marijon, CSB, to Bishop Gallagher, dated February 6, 1900, looked toward the reality of St. Thomas High School.

> Received yesterday from our Superior General a cablegram stating that we are authorized to accept your Lordship' kind offer concerning the opening of a school in Houston. Since we are to start our work there next September, perhaps it would be advisable to let the tenants of the houses on the property know that they will have to leave soon. However, I will not correspond with Fr. Hennessey until I hear from your Lordship, who will be kind enough to tell me what formalities we have to go through to receive from you the property.[31]

Initially, St. Thomas College was a one-room school. There were no electric lights, air conditioning, or indoor plumbing in the Old Catholic Building, which was located at Franklin and Caroline. This one-room structure was originally part of a two-story structure built by Franciscan priests. It had been used by Ursuline nuns and by the Sisters of the Incarnate Word and Blessed Sacrament before they established Incarnate Word Academy in 1873. It had been part of St. Joseph's Infirmary. However, when the infirmary burned in 1884, this one building was spared. Forty-four young men from age nine through sixteen were educated in that one room that year. Bishop Gallagher had transferred the deed of the "Old Catholic Building," valued at $12,000, to the Basilians on June 5, 1900.[32]

Father Nicholas Roche, CSB, was the founding Superior and first Principal of St. Thomas College. He was assisted by Father Vincent Donnelly, the first American Basilian, and Father Albert Hurley, CSB, a Canadian. Classes began on September 4, 1900. An ad in the *Houston Daily Post* on September 17 of that year accompanied the opening. The ad pointed out that private pupils are accepted.[33] Classical courses were provided that prepared students for the "learned professions." All students studied the Catholic faith. Tuition was $3 for grade school and $5 for high school.[34] The City Directory of 1902–3 provides this listing:

> St. Thomas College Day School for young men and boys, 1213 Franklin Ave. Under the auspices of the Fathers of St. Basil Fr. Nicholas Roche, priest and prof. Mathematics; Rev. Father Vincent Donnelly, prof. English literature and classics; Rev. Ernest Pageau, commercial and French; Rev. Thomas Roach classics; Rev. Leo Von Mach, German and Spanish.[35]

Unfortunately, four days later Galveston was hit by the most deadly hurricane in US history. The "Old Catholic Building" suffered severe damage. While this damage was repairable, it was evident that the Old Catholic Building was inadequate for the students. The building was sold to the International and Great Northern Railroad Company for $25,000 in 1902. St. Thomas College had temporarily moved to the Mason Building on Main and Rusk. In June 1903, land was purchased at

2309 Austin Street and Hadley for $13,000. Father Lawrence Brennan, CSB, was directed to work on a Basilian residence and new school and not to spend more than $15,000. Actual expenses amounted to $34,311. The Basilians raised and borrowed the funds, enabling them to open the school in the fall of 1904. The Basilian Provincial Council had some misgivings regarding the Houston Basilians in reference to their ability to carry the remaining mortgages, as there were no savings; yet, the project continued on.[36]

The staff of Basilians was shared with the Seminary at La Porte. In the summer of 1906 Father Nicholas Roche, CSB, who had been so much a part of the establishment of St. Thomas College, was called to administer St. Michael's College in Toronto. He was replaced by Father Thomas Gignac, CSB, who served for one year, and then Father Francis Powell, CSB, who served for three years. Father Richard Drohan, CSB, a teacher at the school, died suddenly during a football scrimmage. He was replaced by Father Michael Pickett, CSB, who had been previously serving at St. Mary's Seminary. Father Donnelly, CSB, would likewise return to St. Thomas from La Porte in 1914 to serve as principal.

As a result of a "terrible storm" in 1915, Father John C. Plomer, CSB, reported $2,000 damage.[37] The enrollment of the school fluctuated over the next few years because there was an impending war and competition from public schools. As Bishop Gallagher approached the end of his episcopate, he found the Basilians he had invited on firm footing at St. Thomas High School. In a short span of time, property was obtained on Austin Street where a new building was erected that served Houston boys for thirty-nine years.[38]

First Ordination Ceremony in Oklahoma

In addition to enriching the Diocese of Galveston by inviting religious orders to come and serve, Bishop Gallagher was responsible for the first ordination ceremony in the state of Oklahoma; it took place at Sacred Heart Monastery in Sacred Heart, Oklahoma, in August 1887. Following a week of retreat, Bishop Gallagher, on August 21, ordained Brother Germanus, Brother Vincent, Brother Louis, and Brother Norbert as deacons. The following day Bishop Gallagher raised them to the level of the priesthood. The Native Americans of the region, eager to witness the ceremony, had pitched their tents. They were quite taken with the music, rich vestments, and colorful procession. Bishop Gallagher spoke in simple terms. His visitors gave signs of being pleased and impressed. The fathers afterward invited the Native Americans to a barbecue. In the afternoon in the chapel of the Sisters of Mercy, several young women received the religious habit of the Sisters of Mercy. Others took vows.[39]

Growth of Parishes and Educational Institutions Carved Out of Annunciation Parish

Reverend Joseph Querat, pastor of St. Vincent's Church, was responsible for the beginning of the Catholic school system in Houston; he had requested the Ursuline Sisters to open a school for girls there in the early 1860s. The school girls were taught in a large house opposite St Vincent's Church that was part of the church property. When these Sisters withdrew from this ministry, Father Querat requested three Sisters of Charity of the Incarnate Word from Galveston to continue the work. They arrived in January 1869. These Sisters lived in what was the old parish house on the corner of Franklin and Caroline Streets. The contract Father Querat had with the Sisters of Charity expired in 1873. Father Querat requested that Bishop Dubuis, then Bishop of Galveston, ask Mother Mary St. Claire of Victoria, Superior of the Sisters of the Incarnate Word and Blessed Sacrament, for a few Sisters to establish a house of the Order in Houston. Sister St. Gabriel, Sister St. Laurente, and Sister Mary Therese Paronnet arrived in Houston on April 25, 1873, taking up residence in the old Franciscan monastery, which had previously been inhabited by the Sisters of Charity of the Incarnate Word. Mass was celebrated in the chapel there on May 5, 1873, and school began. This day is considered Foundation Day for these Sisters in Houston. These Sisters were joined by others from Victoria. Father Querat obtained the half block adjoining Annunciation as the site for the school to be run by the Sisters. The Sisters taught in the "Old Convent" until November 15, 1873, when they moved into the partly finished building. The building they left behind would later become the first St. Joseph's Infirmary in Houston.[40]

The Sisters lived a simple life in the initial years. There was no plaster or ceiling in the unfinished building so they could see the stars through the roof at night. Maintaining any kind of warmth in such a structure was quite a challenge. The only monetary funds they had were from their teaching. It was not uncommon for them to wonder where the next meal was coming from.[41]

Incarnate Word Academy opened on January 3, 1874. The number of students grew, including boarders. The school was chartered by the state in 1878, granting it the power to confer diplomas. By 1888, the main building and left wing were completed. The Sisters' chapel was found in a small building adjoining the sanctuary of Annunciation Church. It was strictly private (curtained off) as required by the Rule. This situation remained until 1923, fifty years later. At that time the chapel was moved into the convent building. Two of the Sisters, Mother Gabriel and Sister Evangelist, made trips to Europe, principally France and Ireland, seeking vocations. The ministry of the Sisters remained with the young girls of Incarnate Word Academy until 1892. The rigor of the French Rule had been previously relaxed under Bishop Dubuis, thus allowing the Sisters to leave the convent and minister in other schools in the city.[42]

While Father Joseph Querat brought the Sisters to Houston, Father Thomas Hennessy, the second pastor (1879–1913) of Annunciation Church, enabled the Sisters to help build the parochial school system. This was through the permission of Bishop Dubuis followed by Bishop Gallagher. The first Annunciation school was in one room built over the Sisters' chapel. Since the girls were taken care of at Incarnate Word Academy, this boys' school opened on November 2, 1876. The school soon became overcrowded. The major purpose of the school was to prepare the boys for First Communion and Confirmation. The school was discontinued briefly in 1880 but then began again in a frame building constructed adjacent to the church. This school was operated and financed by the Sisters. Father Hennessy tore down the frame building in 1903 and put up a brick building in its place. Seven years later the Pastor made the school a parish responsibility, thereby discontinuing tuition. Annunciation became the first free parochial school in the city. When Father Walsh became pastor in 1913, he believed that the girls should profit from the free school. Three years later, in 1916, Annunciation school became coeducational.[43]

In October 1879, St. Joseph's Parish was carved out of a part of what used to be Annunciation Parish. Mother Gabriel had a small building erected that temporarily served as church and school. Three Incarnate Word Sisters traveled daily from Incarnate Word Academy in a cart pulled by mules. The Sisters further had to carry a lunch basket back and forth as there was no cafeteria. It was not uncommon for the mules to stand in a deep mud hole and not budge until the Sisters got out of the cart to get the wheels in motion again. It was at this time that Sister Xavier organized the first sodality in the city affiliated with Rome.[44]

St. Patrick's Church and School was organized in 1880 at the bidding of some Catholics living in the Fifth Ward who approached Father Hennessy. Mother Gabriel was again asked so she purchased land not far from the present site of St. Patrick's Church. The school was opened on September 1, 1880, with two Incarnate Word Sisters traveling back and forth from the Academy each day, usually in a buggy. When the vehicle landed in a ditch, the Sisters ended up walking. By 1890, two school buildings were in operation at St. Patrick's. However, they both went up in smoke on May 18 of that year in one of the many Fifth Ward fires. By September 1893, Father S. Murphy, a new Pastor, erected and put in operation a new school. In all of these schools established during this era, boys and girls were in separate classrooms. St. Patrick's School and Church were again lost to fire in the "Blazing Fifth" Ward on February 20, 1912, but were rebuilt by Father Haughron and back in operation by November 12, 1912.[45]

The Incarnate Word Sisters suffered the loss of Mother Gabriel in 1895. The elections for the Incarnate Word Sisters that year were presided over by Bishop Gallagher assisted by Father Thomas Hennessy. Mother Magdalen Hickey was elected Superior.[46]

Blessed Sacrament Parish was carved out of the east end of Annunciation Parish. Father J. Schnetzer in 1906 built a church and school and then applied to Mother Magdalen for Sisters. Three Incarnate Word Sisters were sent to the east end to further the cause of education.[47] In each of these educational endeavors, the pastor and Incarnate Word Sisters had the full support of Bishop Dubuis in the early years but more readily the support of Bishop Gallagher as Catholic education became dominant in Houston. Bishop Gallagher set the parish limits in 1909 and named the parish in honor of the Blessed Sacrament. The tuition-free parochial school was opened in September, 1910.[48]

In these early days, Father Hennessy was the spiritual advisor of the Sisters living at Incarnate Word Academy. In many ways he was also the director in regard to secular affairs. Father Hennessy believed that new material comforts such as electric lighting weakened religious discipline. The Sisters therefore survived with gas lights and a wood-burning stove until 1921, when electric lighting was installed.[49]

Even at the age of seventy-seven, Father Hennessy did not curtail his activities. He was in the confessional each morning at 5:30 a.m. He placed his candle outside the confessional so that parishioners would know he was there. At 6:00 a.m., he was saying Mass.[50]

A newspaper clipping from Monsignor Anton Frank described Father Hennessy in this manner:

> Everywhere he was regarded as a real father and real peacemaker. He was great power for social reform and in this he had the cooperation of the Methodist minister, the famous Rev. George Rankin, who died later in Dallas. The two of them cleaned up Houston. He died pastor of Annunciation Church in 1913. He was a great advocate of temperance, referring to Annunciation's Rectory as Temperance Hall.[51]

Father Hennessy's funeral was the largest Houston had ever witnessed. While the Sisters were quite accustomed to Father Hennessy's monastic discipline, Father George Walsh, his successor, came from a different cloth. The installation of electricity brought about many conveniences including electric irons in the laundry rather than heating irons.[52]

Additional Parishes and Schools

Sacred Heart Parish was carved out of Annunciation Parish in 1897 through the aspirations of Bishop Gallagher. Located downtown on the corner of Pierce and San Jacinto, the new parish included a school. The cornerstone was laid on Sunday, May 16, 1897. The Church was dedicated on November 6, 1897. Father Thomas Keaney was the founding Pastor. He was transferred to the Gulf Coast prior to the 1900 storm. Unfortunately, he lost his life during that storm, the one priest lost as a result of the hurricane. The Dominican Sisters were in charge of Sacred Heart School which opened its doors in 1897. Bishop Gallagher dedicated a new Church on April 14, 1912.[53]

Bishop Gallagher assigned the care of Holy Rosary Parish to the Dominican Fathers of the Province of St. Joseph on March 1, 1913. The Parish actually began in a private home on the corner of Milan and McGregor. By September 1913, the pastor, Father Augustine LaPlante, OP, had moved the parish into a two-story building. The first floor was a temporary church and the second, classrooms. A seventh grade was added to the school in June 1919.[54]

The Oblate Fathers took on the administration of Immaculate Conception Parish at the request of Bishop Gallagher in October 1911. The first church was dedicated a year later by Bishop Gallagher. The school was likewise opened in 1912 under the direction of the Sisters of Divine Providence.[55] Bishop Gallagher was concerned that an "adequate and appropriate ministry" was made available for Spanish-speaking Catholics. The Oblates of Mary Immaculate agreed to provide for Immaculate Conception Parish, established as a diocesan mission in 1911. The Bishop wished the mission would have "charge of all Mexicans in the Diocese of Galveston, not otherwise provided for."[56] Thus, the 1915 Catholic Directory stated that Immaculate Conception Parish of Houston (then Magnolia Park) cared for fourteen mission churches, eight mission stations, four prison camps in addition to the coal mines of Bastrop County, and the coal mines of Rockdale in Milan county, St. Mary of Elgin in Bastrop county, and St. Joseph of Manor in Travis County.[57]

Not long after the turn of the century, the Heights area in Houston became densely populated. Heights Boulevard was referred to as the "most beautiful street" in Houston. Bishop Gallagher commissioned Father G. T. Walsh to begin a parish, All Saints', on January 1, 1908. Commencing with the celebration of Mass in the Knights of Pythias Hall on Twelfth Street, slightly more than a year later, on March 9, 1909, Bishop Gallagher laid the cornerstone for the building of the church and rectory. Six months later, on August 16, the Bishop dedicated the Church. The day school was opened four years later in 1913 with the Dominican Sisters staffing the school.[58] Originally, the two sacristies were used as classrooms. A small two-room school was built in 1914.[59]

Sister Agatha Sheehan, CVI, in calling forth many memories of the Heights commented: "The greatest asset of the new parish was the kindly nature of its first Pastor." Father Walsh possessed the qualities that endeared him to the people. The parishioners were sorry to lose him to Annunciation Church in 1914.[60]

St. Patrick's Church in Galveston was actually built during the administration of Bishop Dubuis. A rather modest building was put up as the parish church. However, it was destroyed by a storm not long after. Nicholas Clayton, a member of this new Parish, designed the rebuilt Church. The cornerstone was laid on St. Patrick's Day, 1872. During the 1900 storm, the tower fell, crushing the church and almost crushing the pastor, Father Clement Lowrey. When the Church was designed by Nicholas Clayton and rebuilt, it was raised five feet to meet the standards established by Galvestonians. The dedication took place February 2, 1902.[61]

A year after the 1900 storm, the Ursuline Sisters opened Villa Maria School in Bryan. In the same time frame, the Dominican Sisters opened the boarding school, St. Dominic, in Lampasas. These religious communities chose to have other commitments in addition to those on the island of Galveston. Unfortunately, the Lampasas school closed in 1925 and the Bryan school closed in 1929.[62]

A small number of Czech Catholic families from Moravia settled in the area referred to as Sealy in 1885. Five years later they had built a small frame church and established a parish cemetery. Unfortunately, the church was destroyed by fire in 1898; it was later rebuilt by the parishioners. The 1900 storm demolished the second church. Bishop Gallagher donated the funds for the new church. In 1901 it was dedicated to the Immaculate Conception of the Blessed Virgin Mary. The first resident Pastor, Reverend William Skocek, came directly from Moravia.[63]

Catholics of Czech origin settled in Fayette County in 1890. Guardian Angel Parish was established two years later. Services were held in the Krasna School building at that time. Three years earlier, Bishop Gallagher had suggested that the congregation build a sanctuary on a site close to the railroad in Wallis. The nearly completed church was destroyed by a tornado during the 1900 storm. Even though the parishioners still owed $1,000 on the destroyed structure, they trusted in the Lord and built again, completing the church in 1904. The Parish had

grown so much by 1912 that a larger church was needed. It was completed by 1915.[64] Guardian Angel Parish in Wallis is one of two of Texas'
painted churches,[65] in the Galveston-Houston archdiocese; the other is
located in Plantersville.

The Sisters of Mercy opened a school in Smithville in 1897. The
school was given the name Villa Maria and the parish was Sacred Heart.
The advent of a railroad line had much to do with the establishment of
the school. The school, however, closed in 1906, and the public school
used the buildings for some time.[66]

Monsignor James Kirwin dedicated the present church, St. Stanislaus Kostka in Anderson on August 6, 1918, yet its history goes much
further back. The Polish immigrants of Grimes county initially had
Mass celebrated in the homes in 1872. The following year they bought
a public school and turned it into a church. In 1897 Father F. X. Pruss
built a church 40 by 60 feet and turned the old public school into a
parochial school. The school was discontinued when Father Pruss left
in 1903. Father Dombrowski remodeled the church in 1912 when he
became Pastor. Bishop Gallagher asked Father Domanski to establish a
parochial school, but he had great difficulty with that project. Rather, he
found the church too small for the faithful. Within a year, he had a new
edifice erected. The parochial school so desired by Bishop Gallagher
never materialized as the parishioners were quite scattered, most times
seven to ten miles away. The economy, further, was not doing that well.
In addition, some parents were not that eager to send their children to
school.[67]

Sixteen years before the 1900 storm, Bishop Gallagher decided to divide his episcopal parish in Galveston. He assigned the east end to the
Society of Jesus on June 21, 1884. While the first Mass was offered in
a temporary chapel, construction of a church was begun in 1889 and
completed with the dedication on January 17, 1892 by Bishop Gallagher. The style was described in the *Galveston Daily News* as "French
Romanesque derived from examples in Province and Normandy of the
tenth, eleventh and twelfth centuries." The *Galveston News* referred to
the Edifice designed by Nicholas Clayton, Sacred Heart Church as the
largest church in Texas. While the people proudly entered into worship
in this magnificent building for eight years, it was demolished in the
1900 storm. Bishop Gallagher gave generously toward the rebuilding of

the Church from funds collected from Catholics in the United States. The Bishop presided over the laying of the cornerstone on June 21, 1903, and the dedication on January 17, 1904. While the new structure was not as large or pretentious as the old, the style was described as Moresque (Moorish style). The "new Church" included a dome 100 feet high and an altar and communion rail made of marble.[68]

Education of Black Catholic Children

The Holy Family Sisters, founded in New Orleans in 1842 for the education of needy black residents, came to the Diocese of Galveston in 1898 at the invitation of Bishop Gallagher. They took charge of Holy Rosary Parish School in Galveston. The Church was blessed by Bishop Gallagher in October 1893. The Church was first provided for by diocesan priests but then the Josephite priests took over the parish on July 1, 1913. This school along with St. Peter Claver Parish in San Antonio were the first to be built for black children. The Dominican Sisters staffed the school for the first ten years and then turned it over to the Holy Family Sisters. A high school was eventually added.[69]

The work among black Catholic children in Houston was actually begun by Father Thomas Hennessy, Pastor of Annunciation Church in Houston. In the spring of 1887, he asked the Sisters of the Incarnate Word and Blessed Sacrament to undertake instruction of the children. The work was successful so a school soon followed. Prior to that time, in August 27, 1872, a plot of ground had been deeded to the Most Reverend C. M. Dubuis. This plot of land was located on the corner of Chenevert and Lamar. It was to be used for educational purposes. Bishop Gallagher built a school on the site in the summer of 1887. He dedicated it under the patronage of his patron, St. Nicholas, in October of that year. Mother Gabriel, Superior of Incarnate Word Academy, sent three Sisters of the Incarnate Word and Blessed Sacrament to teach there. In October 1901 the Josephite Fathers of Baltimore were placed in charge of St. Nicholas. This invitation of Bishop Gallagher came through the efforts of Father Hennessy and the Very Reverend Father Roche, CSB, president of St. Thomas College in Houston. Father Francis Tobin, SSJ was assigned as the first resident Pastor.[70] Father Tobin immediately saw to it that the run-down building was repaired. He was followed by Father Narcisse Denis, SSJ, and Father Joseph Murphy, SSJ. Father Charles Reilly, SSJ, took over in July 1904. He built a convent for the Sisters of the Holy Family[71] who arrived in September 1905 from New Orleans to continue the work begun by the Sisters of the Incarnate Word and Blessed Sacrament.[72] Father John McKeever, SSJ, sold the parish property in 1920 and bought a plot of ground on the corner of Bell and St. Emmanuel. Two frame buildings were erected and later stuccoed. One was a church and school and the other a convent. The new chapel was established on September 19, 1920.[73]

Correspondence between Bishop Gallagher and Mother Katherine Drexel, SBS, in 1916 and 1917 provides testimony that Mother Drexel[74] donated $6,000 for the building of a church and school for the black people in Beaumont. As the Bishop had expressed the desire that the Sisters of the Blessed Sacrament come to Beaumont, Mother Drexel humbly asked in her correspondence of March 17, 1917, "Will your Lordship accept us?"[75] These Sisters would eventually staff Blessed Sacrament School in Beaumont (1917), Sacred Heart School in Port Arthur (1927), and St. Therese School in Orange (1946).[76]

Father Martin Huhn petitioned Bishop Nicholas Gallagher in December of 1888 asking permission to work among black residents within the Diocese of Galveston. Father Huhn had previously worked in a parish and established an orphanage, Guardian Angel, in the diocese of Leavenworth. However, his financial management was brought into question there. Bishop Gallagher gladly accepted Father Huhn's request to work among black residents in the diocese.[77]

Baylor University was established in 1845, in Independence, Texas. The men's college moved to Waco and the women's college to Belton in 1886. Father Huhn moved his orphans from Kansas into these abandoned Baylor buildings. As these original orphans grew up and moved away, few replaced them. There is record of Father Huhn sending out letters in German soliciting support for the orphanage. While the *Catholic Directory* of 1891 listed thirty-five boys in Guardian Angel Industrial School, seven years later, in 1898, the *Directory* listed only the parish of Guardian Angel.[78] Father Huhn made monthly trips to Hidalgo to minister to the people there. He remained as Pastor to Guardian Angel Parish there in Independence until his death on February 15, 1915, at the age of sixty-five.[79]

Few Catholics would know that the original Baylor University in Independence, Texas was actually owned by the Catholic Church and served as a school for black Catholic orphans for approximately a decade. This may never have happened if Bishop Gallagher had not developed a reputation for serving the needs of black Catholics in his Diocese, especially in the arena of education.

Health Care

EXPANSION OF THE ORDER OF SISTERS OF CHARITY OF THE INCARNATE WORD

Genesis of St. Joseph's Infirmary

Father Thomas Hennessy, second Pastor of Annunciation Church (1878–1913), was instrumental in bringing the Sisters of Charity of the Incarnate Word to Houston to establish St. Joseph's Hospital in that city. As a young man, Hennessy had settled in the town of Powderhorne where he married the daughter of a Baptist minister. After her death, he resolved to enter the priesthood and was ordained in June 1863 in Galveston. He was instrumental in the establishment of several parishes near Annunciation Church, including Blessed Sacrament, St. Patrick's, and St. Joseph's.[80]

With the approval of Bishop Gallagher, Father Hennessy, on March 11, 1887, invited Mother Mary Augustine Edwards, the Superior of the Congregation of the Sisters of Charity of the Incarnate Word, to establish a Houston house for the purpose of caring for the sick. The two Sisters from Galveston began Houston's first general hospital at the corner of Franklin Avenue and Caroline Street. This building was actually referred to as the Catholic Building for it had been used by Franciscan priests when they staffed St. Vincent's Parish, by Ursuline Sisters from New Orleans when they staffed St. Vincent's School (1867–1869), and by these Sisters when they likewise staffed the same school (1869–1873). The Sisters of the Incarnate Word and Blessed Sacrament from Victoria had temporarily lived there before moving to Incarnate Word Academy on Crawford Street (April–November, 1873). St. Joseph's Infirmary was opened to the public on June 1, 1887. Two years later the medical officer for the indigent sick was impressed with the methods of caring for the sick. After the county judge toured the hospital, Mother St. Louis was requested to receive the indigent sick of Harris County. There was quite a bit of dissatisfaction with the old Houston Infirmary on Washington Avenue. Mother St. Louis agreed. The Sisters soon expanded their facilities. A new three-story building, St. Joseph's County Hospital, was erected across the street. The Sisters were paid 50 cents a day for indigent patients. Private patients paid two dollars a day. The diagnosis of patients with smallpox led to the construction of a smallpox hospital in an abandoned cemetery. There were three hundred victims of smallpox. Approximately sixty died. All of the Sisters volunteered to help at the "pest house." Four from the growing staff of Sisters were chosen.[81] Unfortunately, Mrs. Flanagan's Boarding House next to the hospital caught fire (October 16, 1894). Before long, the entire block was in flames. This was no match for the one fire engine the city owned. Two Sisters lost their lives, and a third was seriously wounded, though she survived. This was a devastation to the Sisters. In addition to the precious loss of life, only $13,000 of the $47,000 damage was covered by insurance. A building was temporarily rented and furniture was bought for $500. The people of Houston, remembering how the Sisters had gotten them through the smallpox epidemic and had provided for the poor during the difficult winter of 1894, wished to return the favor.[82] An excerpt from a letter gives a flavor of the spirit present:

> St. Joseph's Infirmary [is] not only a credit to the city, but an exposition of the best and highest influences among us. Let us, me and you and our next door neighbor, put our shoulder to the wheel and rescue this glorious charity from the ruins in which it lies today. Women, give up that little pet extravagance of yours, that new gown from the East. Men, smoke a cigar less a day for awhile. Children, save the pennies you daily squander on trifles and let us all have a hand in this work for God and humanity.
>
> A Protestant[83]

Mother St. Louis made a personal appeal in the November 25 issue of the *Houston Daily Post*. In 1894 the infirmary was rebuilt with collateral provided by Bishop Gallagher as seen in the records of early council meetings on the transaction:

On the 29th day of the month of December of the year1894, it was
resolved to purchase a block of ground bearing the number 399 fac-
ing Crawford, [LaBranch], Pierce and Calhoun Streets for the sum of
$7,200. We shall ask Rt. Rev. Bishop Gallagher to mortgage property
in the Sisters' favor, leaving them their own ground so that they may
use it as a security for obtaining loans. The block will be on a main
sewer on Crawford Street and said street will be paved, thus freeing the
Sisters from such expenses for years. A frame building will be erected
on the back of the block. The mills may donate some lumber.[84]

Mother St. John Pradinaud, who served as superior of the congregation's foundation in Temple's Santa Fe Hospital, came to supervise the
construction. She was also known for her care of the poor. Each day a
bread line at 3:00 p.m. appeared in the yard of the Sisters. This charity
helped many to survive the difficult winter of 1895.[85]

Groundbreaking for a one-hundred-bed, three-story building designed by Nicholas Clayton took place in the spring of 1895. The site
was completed by a two-story north annex and a frame building from
the Caroline and Franklin site. The *Houston Daily Post* described the
completed building: "The site of the new Infirmary is an admirable one,
there being nothing to keep the southern breeze from the place. It is
situated far from the noise and dust of the City and is especially adapted
as a place for the sick."[86]

During the administration of Sister Columba D'Arcy, a need to re-
vise the Constitutions came about. By this time the Congregation occupied six houses. Bishop Gallagher gave permission for this endeavor and
actively participated in the task. These documents received the approval
of the Bishop on March 17, 1904. Then they were formally adopted by
the Superior and Council.[87]

The Sisters of Charity experienced a great loss on November 23, 1900,
with the passing of Mother St. Louis, the foundress of St. Joseph's Infirmary in Houston. Bishop Gallagher personally accompanied the funeral
cortege to Galveston, where she was buried in Calvary Cemetery. Mother
M. Columba D'Arcy, CCVI, had obtained permission of Bishop Gallagher to borrow $43,000 for an annex to St. Joseph's Infirmary.[88] Sister
M. Cecilia Coffey, CCVI, added a fifty-bed, three-story annex to St. Joseph's in addition to a convent and chapel for the Sisters. Sister Ignatius

Young, CCVI, established Houston's first training school for nurses in December of 1905. The school was chartered under the laws of Texas on November 13, 1906. The first class graduating from St. Joseph's Training School for Nurses completed their studies on June 15, 1907.[89]

During the early 1900s much of the resources of the Congregation were spent restoring their houses in Galveston after the storm and providing a home for the elderly in Houston. A former patient of St. Joseph's Infirmary, Mrs. Delia Costello, deeded a forty-five-acre farm on Bray's Bayou. Mother St. John Pradinaud, while working at St. Joseph's Infirmary, was appointed as director of the farm. She constructed a two-story building that became St. Anthony's Home for the Aged. By 1904, this home was independent of St. Joseph's Infirmary.[90]

St. Joseph's Infirmary celebrated its Silver Jubilee under the administration of Mother M. Claude Ryan, CCVI (1908–13). Bishop Gallagher presided at the opening services of the Jubilee on March 11, 1912. Father Hennessy celebrated the High Mass and Father Kirwin delivered the eulogy on the pioneers of the Congregation.[91]

For twenty years, from 1889 to 1919, St. Joseph's Infirmary cared for the indigent patients of Houston and Harris County. The indigent patients of the city were transferred to the Municipal Hospital on October 2, 1919. Five years later, when a bond issue was approved, Jeff Davis Hospital was built. The county patients were transferred on April 8, 1925.[92] When the United States entered World War I, Mother M. Teresa offered President Wilson the use of the hospitals through the Red Cross.[93]

During the administration of Mother M. Teresa O'Gara, CCVI, the Congregation, with the approval of Bishop Gallagher, applied for and received permission to become a pontifical rather than a diocesan Congregation. This placed the documentation and supervision of the Congregation directly under the Holy See. Mother M. Teresa and Mother M. Columba met Pope Pius X in a private audience November 22, 1912, where he gave approval of the Institute and its works. The pontiff gave the two Sisters his skull cap, or zuchetto, as a token of his appreciation.[94]

The year 1912 witnessed the expansion of St. Anthony's Home through the generous contributions of a benefactor. Mrs. J. E. Bell, a former employee, recalled the great kindness of the Sisters. In honor of her deceased husband, she enabled the construction of a two story brick building that became known as the J. E. Bell Memorial. When the oldest building on that property was damaged three years later in a storm, she financed a three-story building. This was referred to as the Mrs. J. E. Bell Memorial. Four years after her first undertaking for the Sisters, she enabled the construction of a convent and chapel for the Sisters.[95]

St. Mary's Infirmary in Galveston added a four-story west wing two years later. With the permission of Bishop Gallagher, the Sisters took over the operation of hospitals in Orange and Beaumont, Texas, and Shreveport and Lake Charles, Louisiana, among other sites. They further agreed to the administration of a hospital in Texarkana, Arkansas, which was financed through the estate of Michael Meagher.[96]

The Sisters of Charity of the Incarnate Word, San Antonio, Texas[97] founded St. Joseph Hospital in Fort Worth in 1883, specifically for railroad workers. It remained under their administration until October 5, 1991, when the Daughters of Charity took over the sponsorship.[98]

The Sisters of Charity of the Incarnate Word celebrated their Golden Jubilee in October 1916 in Galveston. The festivities continued for three days. Bishop Gallagher celebrated a solemn pontifical Mass of Thanksgiving, Father Kirwin preached, with many priests assisting who were familiar with the work of the Sisters.[99]

Seton Hospital, Austin, Texas

A charitable association made up of Catholic and Protestant women who visited and cared for the sick and the poor under the patronage of St. Vincent de Paul became the group that convinced the Superior of the Sisters of Charity at Emmitsburg to accept the invitation to come to Austin to build a hospital at the turn of the century. Money-raising events followed. The Sisters took full responsibility for the cost. An open house was held for the 40 bed facility on May 26, 1902. During this open house, their first patient was received. Private rooms were then two dollars a day, but charity patients were taken. One of the early patients, Father P. J. O'Reilly, heard of the needs of the Spanish-speaking people who had been left without care or instruction. He obtained permission from Bishop Gallagher to organize Our Lady of Guadalupe Parish. Although Father O'Reilly was a pioneer in this arena of ministry, this work was eventually taken over by the Oblates of Mary Immaculate.[100]

The Daughters of Charity of St. Vincent de Paul were instrumental in working with the smallpox victims in Travis County in 1917 and 1918. A pest camp was established near the city. While the county was unprepared for the outbreak, Sister Rose, who had previous experience with this illness, took charge, and in a few weeks, the panic was over. The Sisters stayed with the patients ten weeks. While the county wished to pay the Sisters for their services, they could not accept funds, so they were presented with a gold medal in appreciation.[101]

When the Spanish influenza[102] struck Austin in 1918, the military installations suffered greatly. The army asked for aid and the Sisters took in 150 patients in a 125-bed facility. The halls were lined with patients. The grounds then became a tent field with forty-eight tents. A fraternity house in addition to several nearby houses were used. The Sisters worked ceaselessly until the pandemic was over. Unfortunately, one of the Sisters succumbed to the disease.[103]

The Seton School of Nursing began operation in 1902. It is accredited by the State Board of Nurse Examiners and is affiliated with the University of Texas. The hospital incorporated it as Seton Hospital School of Nursing in 1947.[104]

Hotel Dieu, El Paso, Texas

In response to the request of the citizens of El Paso, three Sisters of Charity of St. Vincent de Paul opened the first hospital in El Paso, Hotel Dieu on February 15, 1892. As stated in their charter, their purpose was "to administer to the sick, the helpless, and the afflicted and to nurse and care for them, to alleviate their pain and suffering and restore them to health."[105] A two-story brick ten-bed facility was rented as the first hospital. By 1903 they had expanded to a one-hundred-bed, fully equipped facility. A school for nursing was organized in 1898; it received its accreditation from the state in 1900.[106] The hospital and nursing school continued to expand in the twentieth century. However, by 1987, El Paso, discovered that it had a surplus of eight hundred hospital beds. The Sisters sold the facility on December 5 of that year. Some of the Sisters did stay on to help the less fortunate at the San Vicente Health

Center. The Nursing School became a part of the University of Texas at El Paso School of Nursing and Allied Health.[107]

Other Catholic Hospital Facilities

Providence Health Center was opened in 1903 in Waco. It was Waco's first hospital. The venture was initiated by a group of local businessmen who approached the Sisters of Charity of St. Vincent de Paul in Dallas. These men, C. I. Johnson and Dr. J. W. Hale, had been impressed by the service of the Sisters of Charity of St. Vincent de Paul in New Orleans. The cornerstone was laid on October 11, 1903. Bishop Gallagher officiated at a solemn High Mass. Monsignor Kirwin gave a tribute to the work of the Sisters. Initially there was a great amount of anti-Catholic sentiment. The Klan was active at that time. However, the reputation of the care given to the patients eventually spread. In the early years there were few private patients to cover the cost of the indigents. The Sisters therefore arrived at a contract with the Missouri, Kansas and Texas Railroad to treat sick railroad employees. Over the next seven years, the Sisters treated 3,700 railroad employees. Their reputation flourished.[108] Today, Providence Health Center is a full-service medical facility.

In the thirty-six years of service when Bishop Gallagher occupied the see of Galveston, many aspects of the diocese doubled in size: from forty-three to one hundred priests, from fifty churches and chapels to 109, from one hospital to seven, from 30,000 to 70,000 souls.[109]

The Architect and the Bishop

Many of the building projects of the late nineteenth century in Galveston convey the giftedness of Nicholas Joseph Clayton (1840–1916). Born at Cloyne, County Cork, Ireland on November 1, 1840, he came to the United States in 1848 with his widowed mother, Margaret Clayton.

Clayton served in the US Navy from 1862 until 1865. Prior to that time, he worked as a plasterer in Cincinnati, New Orleans, Louisville, and Memphis. While reliable documentation of the years after the Civil War are not available, he is listed as a stone carver and draftsman in

1866 and 1872 in the *Cincinnati City Directory*. Clayton left Cincinnati in October 1871 for Houston, following the path of his aunt and uncle, Mary and Daniel Crowley. Five months later, at the age of thirty-two, he moved to Galveston where he spent the remainder of his life. Clayton must have gained considerable experience in the office of accomplished architects in the various cities he worked in prior to this time in the north. His first job was that of supervising the construction of the First Presbyterian Church for the Memphis architects Jones and Baldwin.[110]

Nicholas Clayton belonged to the first generation of professional architects, for they restricted their work to the design of buildings rather than the actual construction. The demand for buildings in Texas between 1873 and 1893 was sufficient to make this specialization possible. Further, the compilation of data from the 1906 Bureau of the Census indicates that more than 25 percent of Texans were Roman Catholic. In the state's five largest cities, it was the most dominant religion. Clayton was thus deeply involved in an ecclesiastical building program. Parish work was centralized through dioceses. Most of Clayton's Catholic work in the 1870s was done in Galveston.[111] It was through the Roman Catholic diocese of Galveston and the influence of Bishop Claude Dubuis that his first independent work was attained. He designed St. Mary's Church, now Cathedral, in Austin (1873–84). Two religious orders in Galveston became major clients of Clayton, the Sisters of Charity of the Incarnate Word and the Ursuline Sisters.[112]

During the 1870s, Clayton designed St. Patrick's Church (1874–77) and St. Mary's Infirmary (1874–76). The interior designs of St. Patrick's Church were not completed until 1886. A tower, added in 1899, crashed down on the roof in the 1900 storm. Clayton reconstructed St. Patrick's with few modifications in 1901 and 1902. St. Mary's Infirmary was dedicated in 1876, and Clayton made numerous additions and alterations over the next thirty years. This included a dorm and chapel wing. Everything was destroyed in the 1900 storm. In 1901, Clayton designed a new novitiate for the Sisters of Charity of the Incarnate Word on this site. He added a building to St. Mary's Orphan Asylum that included a boys' dorm in 1879–80 and another wing in 1880. All were destroyed in the 1900 storm. Regarding St. Mary's Cathedral, Clayton made numerous internal alterations including the design of a new altar and bishop's throne (1874–77). He further recapped the west towers (1889–90) in addition to other internal changes. After Clayton drew plans for the chapel of the Ursuline Convent, it was built in several stages. The shell was constructed in 1870 and 71; the interiors were completed by 1877. The chapel was furnished and later repaired after the 1875 storm. Ten years later an extension was added. Clayton redesigned the entire convent to make way for needed repairs after the 1900 storm.[113]

During the 1880s, Bishop Gallagher became Nicholas Clayton's most important ecclesiastical patron. Much of his work during this era consisted of alterations, and additions to existing structures. These included St. Mary's University which was a boys' school operated by the diocese in addition to projects begun in the previous decade. Bishop Gallagher invited the New Orleans Province of the Society of Jesus to Galveston in 1845 to take over St. Mary's University and begin a new parish. Clayton designed Sacred Heart Church which became the largest church in Texas when dedicated in 1892. The church was almost completely destroyed during the 1900 storm. It was redesigned by a Jesuit brother by the name of Jimenez. When the dome for the church was damaged after the 1915 hurricane, Clayton was commissioned. He drew the design for the raising and enlarging of the dome.[114] As Clayton's reputation grew, religious orders commissioned him for their own ministries. These included Ursuline Academy in Dallas, St. Edward's University in Austin, and additions to the Convent and School of the Sisters of the Incarnate Word and Blessed Sacrament in Houston.[115] Clayton was commissioned to work with the structural problems at Annunciation Church in Houston, originally constructed in 1869. Father Thomas Hennessy, the second Pastor, enlisted Nicholas Clayton to draw plans for the repair of the church. Large cracks had appeared. The west wall with the two towers began to lean. The repairs were done over an eleven-year period, from 1884 to 1895.

> The long walls along the north and south sides were braced with masonry buttresses, in the style of brickwork for which Clayton was well known. The tall spire of the tower nearest Texas Avenue was removed. Two new entrance vestibules braced the leaning front wall and flanked a new central tower. Overall, the reconstruction of Annunciation by Clayton was a complete architectural transformation. The new roof

from side to side eliminated the original external distinction of the
tall central nave and the low roofed side aisles.[116]

Clayton added a 175-foot tower, making it the tallest structure in Houston for two decades. He continued to work for the parish for the remainder of his life, designing the three-story parish school building in
1906 and a new tabernacle for the church, in 1914.[117]

One of Clayton's most significant commissions in the 1880s was the
Gresham House in Galveston. It was considered the "most elaborate and
imposing house" built in Texas at that time. It appeared in the centennial publication of the American Institute of Architects in 1961 as "one
of the one hundred important structures of the century (1861–1961).
The railroad magnet Colonel Walter Gresham built it for his wife, Jose-
phine Mann Gresham. It is a large country home built using Victorian
architectural design on a small plot of city land." Clayton himself was
not happy with the location of the Gresham home as he saw the size of
the land as insufficient for so imposing a structure. It was erected for an
approximate cost of $250,000.[118] Due to its location on the main thor-
oughfare of the city, its intricate interior design, the Gresham home has
been described as the best of the "Broadway beauties." The home was
actually bought as the residence for the successor to Bishop Gallagher,
the bishop of Galveston, Bishop Byrne. Since an increasing amount of
diocesan business was being carried on in Houston, the bishop's residence was moved to Houston in the 1960s.[119]

Reconstruction projects as well as commissions outside the diocese
of Galveston engulfed Clayton's attention during the 1890s. The first
few years of the twentieth century found him rebuilding that which had
been destroyed by the 1900 storm. However, the new century proved to
be a financial hardship for him. Economic difficulty was compounded
by the reality that Clayton had married late in life, July 8, 1891, when he
was almost fifty. His bride, Miss Mary Ducie, was twenty years younger.
She bore him five children. Mary Ducie was the daughter of an "art-
ist-decorator" who arranged for the interiors of the Gresham Home,[120]
later known as the Bishop's Palace.

Nicholas Clayton's son states that his father was a great architect.
He was interested in turning out notable buildings, but he was a poor
businessman. Essentially, he left money matters to others. Sometimes he

failed to collect for some of his work. On a number of occasions when the building funds were exhausted, Clayton finished the building on his own. The Clayton family blamed one of his partners, Pat Rabitt, for difficulties leading to bankruptcy. Clayton had won the contract for the county courthouse. His plans and specifications were approved. He put up his personal bond of $80,000 and then went to Florida on business. What happened after that is not fully known. Clayton, however, had to forfeit his bond and went bankrupt. The Clayton family maintains that Rabitt changed the plans. Correspondence from Clayton's architect friends and a former partner, Lynch, provide evidence that builders and county officials "ganged up" on Clayton. Apparently, the courthouse was built with Clayton's plans but without his name on the cornerstone. A lawsuit dragged on for ten years. Unfortunately, Clayton could not obtain work of a "substantial nature" due to his bonding failure.[121]

The new century brought younger and more competitive architects to Galveston. Clayton discovered that he was making architectural plans that were never used. He found that another architect was awarded the contract for the Letitia Rosenberg Home rather than he. Likewise, he had drawn plans for a bank in Victoria, but the contract was won by an architect from San Antonio.[122]

Clayton worked out of a home office for the last thirteen years of his life, basically carrying out ecclesiastical commissions. Reconstruction had much to do with his commissions then in addition to new work. He was asked by Bishop Gallagher to design a new wing for St. Mary's Seminary in La Porte (1906–8). However, a disagreement between Clayton and the bishop led Clayton to resign the commission.[123]

In 1910, Clayton designed the apse and transept of what was to be the second Sacred Heart Church, showing the dome for which he became so well known, a design conveying "remarkable vitality and confidence." Five years later, his daughter Mary Clayton, recalled that, after a three-day storm, her seventy-five-year-old father walked the twenty-four blocks between their home and Sacred Heart Church and then climbed onto the roof of the church to check the dome for any damage or defects. There were none.[124]

In 1916, Clayton was repairing a chimney in his home. In the process, he was severely burned. He died of pneumonia and complications from the burns[125] on November 9, 1916.[126]

After Clayton's death, his widow was musing to Rabbi Henry Cohen about what a proper monument would be to distinguish her husband. The rabbi replied softly, "Oh, you don't need one, my dear Mary Lorena. He's got them all over town. Just go around and read some cornerstones."[127] The architecture in Galveston was so dominated by Nicholas Clayton for over a quarter of a century that the time is fittingly called the Clayton Era.[128]

Figure 3. Gresham Home (1892), later known as the Bishop's Palace. Designed by Nicholas Clayton, Galveston, Texas.

Figure 4. St. Mary's Cathedral ca. 1914, refurbished by Nicholas Clayton after the 1900 storm, Galveston, Texas. Courtesy of Rosenberg Library.

Figure 5. Annunciation Church, refurbished by Nicholas Clayton (1884–1895), early twentieth century, Houston, Texas.

❧ 4 ❧

Erection of New Dioceses

Bishop Gallagher had attempted to visit all parts of the diocese, yet he found it impossible for one bishop to care properly for so many souls scattered over so wide an area. The new Bishop pointed out that "the Diocese of Galveston was too large to be conveniently and properly attended from Galveston which is at the southern extremity of the diocese."[1] However, Bishop Gallagher did not seem to have considered the position of El Paso in the creation of the Diocese of Dallas.[2] He petitioned the Provincial Council of New Orleans, pointing out that some parts of the Diocese were 800 miles from Galveston. Bishop Gallagher suggested Dallas as the hub of the next diocese. At that time, the Catholic population in North Texas was about 15,000. There were twenty-five Catholic churches, seventeen priests, three hospitals, five academies for girls, three boarding schools for boys, one orphanage and eight convents. The total population was over a million, the majority claiming a Protestant denomination. The Bishop further pointed out that some Catholics were generally not as fervent or zealous as they might be. They were widely scattered within the area. Many were indifferent and had fallen away from the faith. Gallagher submitted this matter to the bishops of the province of New Orleans who joined with Bishop Gallagher in presenting the matter to Pope Leo XIII in 1889.[3] The Pontiff responded in his brief *Romani Pontificis* on July 15, 1890:

> We most willingly accede, and paying heed to what the prelates of the
> Province of New Orleans have urged for the greater spiritual welfare

of the faithful. . . . We hereby divide or dismember the Diocese of Galveston to form a new Diocese which shall bear the name of Dallas, it's See and most populous city, wherein are found two churches with adjoining dwellings.[4]

This new diocese was to consist of that part of Texas lying north of the counties of Lampasas, Coryell, McLennan, Freestone (Lime Stone), Anderson, Cherokee, Nacogdoches, and Shelby.[5]

The first bishop of the Diocese of Dallas was the Most Reverend Thomas Francis Brennan. Born in Tipperary County, Ireland, his parents moved to America when he was only eight. His family prized education, his father being a teacher of the Classics. As a teenager, he entered St. Bonaventure College in Allegheny, New York, to prepare for the priesthood. He traveled to Europe in 1873 to complete his studies, obtaining a doctor of divinity at the University of Innsbruck and studying a year of Canon Law in Rome. During his initial years as a cleric, he served in country parishes in the diocese of Erie.[6] Brennan represented the Diocese of Erie at the Jubilee of the episcopal ordination of Pope Leo XIII in Rome. Brennan was then raised to the dignity of papal chamberlain. When Father Brennan met Bishop Thomas Heslin of Natchez, Mississippi, while in Rome, Bishop Heslin was impressed with his linguistic abilities: "He speaks German as fluently as English, French like an educated Parisian, and Italian as correctly as English; as a linguist he has few superiors."[7] Two years later, he nominated the young prelate for the appointment in Dallas. This new Diocese was under the authority of the Congregation for the Propaganda of the Faith in Rome, the ministry of the Holy See that cares for mission churches.[8] He was consecrated Bishop at the cathedral in Erie, Pennsylvania, on December 22, 1890, and was installed as Bishop of Dallas in May of 1891 in St. Patrick's Church. Barely thirty-six years old,[9] Bishop Brennan called on the assistance of the Bishop of Galveston in a letter to Bishop Gallagher dated January 12, 1891: "at least in the beginning. The new diocese has been a portion of your solicitude for a long time and therefore I will be glad to go under your instructions for some time."[10] Writing to Archbishop Francis Janssens of New Orleans, the new Bishop stated: "They put me down for being somewhat young. Still I have had many experiences, and hope with God's help to prove myself worthy of the confidence placed

in me."[11] He found in the new Diocese in debt, so he called on his Irish
wit to move beyond the destitute situation of creditors at his door:

> I am but a man as yourselves and you must bear with me in my failings,
> knowing that I have your best good at heart. A priest may be removed,
> but a Bishop is wedded to his church and must abide with it until
> death. You have spoken of me as a young man; if you want to keep me
> perpetually young, you will all help in our financial difficulties.[12]

The people responded warmly to the situation of debt in addition to
plans for a new cathedral. "No place was too far away for him to visit;
no struggling village too insignificant for him to notice; no audience
too poor or illiterate for him to address."[13] He would establish the *Texas
Catholic,* the first newspaper of this kind in the state of Texas. The new
Bishop was attracted by the "simple, abiding faith" of the Mexican
population. He became known for his restless energy in building the
Diocese of Dallas.[14] Unfortunately, the financial problems of the new
Bishop continued. Father Joseph Blum, Pastor of Sacred Heart Church
in Dallas, had borrowed $30,000 to relocate Sacred Heart Church. This
Pastor thought the sale of the current property would cover the debt.
Bishop Gallagher approved of the transaction. Bishop Brennan trans-
ferred Father Blum to Muenster and told Bishop Gallagher he was try-
ing to refinance the debt. Soon after, Bishop Brennan began to chastise
Bishop Gallagher for approving of this loan for property for the Church.
In a letter written July 10, 1891, he stated:

> All would be pleasant with us were it not for the Ross Avenue deal.
> You should have never signed either of the notes for Father Blum.
> Very fine for Maroney [the creditor], - now, they seem to have little
> sympathy for you. However, a building and loan association has been
> forward and I believe money will be had soon.[15]

Each Bishop made a counter financial claim. Then Brennan wrote again
six months later (January 15, 1892) to Gallagher in seeming exasperation:

> As I am making out a list of the annual collections, please send me
> an account of the collection of the first Sunday of Lent, for the Indi-

ans and Negroes. . . . Also please explain how Mr. Ketcham could be transferred to the Indian territory after he had been paid for by Dallas as well as Galveston. Half of the students paid for by diocesan funds are also demanded. If you can write to Fr. Martiniere, [that] you paid $1000 for Dallas since the division; and if you could write last summer demanding that I should assume immediately the foolish bargain contracted by you [the Ross Avenue property]; if you take away $600 from old Fr. Moore and then send him to Ennis; if you hold all the rented property of the diocese and use all collections hereto fore taken in, for Galveston and Houston; if you refuse the demands of Fr. Martiniere for orphans of Paris and Marshall and state there was an orphanage in Dallas before I came, while I paid more than $2000, to finish building it—not yet ever having the deed of it, I justly protest.[16]

Regardless of the matter, this was hardly the prudential tone a junior prelate should adopt toward his senior. Archbishop Janssens of New Orleans referred to him as an "impudent letter writer, lacking the least idea of delicacy of sentiment."[17]

St. Patrick Church was formally dedicated and opened on July 10, 1892. Bishop Brennan was present, assisted by Archbishop Janssens of New Orleans. Archbishop Janssens used the occasion to inquire about the discontent regarding Bishop Brennan. The Archbishop wrote in his diary: "Left today for Dallas where I stayed one day with the Bishop, and assisted the following day at the dedication of the new, fine, stone church at Fort Worth. Among the clergy, sisters and laity there are signs of much dissatisfaction on account the arbitrary and uncanonical actions of the Bishop."[18]

Bishop Brennan needed collateral on the diocesan debt. He listed the Ursuline school and other property as belonging to the diocese. The local banker asked Mother Evangelist, the Ursuline Superior, if the property belonged to the Bishop. When Mother Evangelist objected to the Bishop, his first response was that according to the Councils of Baltimore, all the Catholic schools were owned by the Diocese and the Bishop was guardian and superior of all other church property, referring to other property that the Ursulines owned. Mother Evangelist referred to the Constitutions of the Ursulines, pointing out that only the Vatican could change that document. The Bishop responded that he was only joking. Mother Evangelist did not appreciate the interaction and, after consulting with her own Superior, and on the advice of the clergy of Dallas, wrote Rome about the sufferings of her community and asked that the Vatican protect them from such dangers.[19]

Bishop Brennan enlisted the support of Governor James Hogg to write a letter to the Cardinal Prefect of the Propaganda (July 28, 1892), promoting the notion of an archbishopric in Texas with Bishop Brennan appointed as archbishop: "As a citizen of Texas and its Executive, I feel desirous of seeing its progress acknowledged and its growth promoted by the governing bodies of the various Christian churches. Hence, I would rejoice to see a Catholic Archbishop in the person of the Right Reverend Dr. Brennan named for this State."[20] Brennan further sought out the support of James Gibbons, Archbishop of Baltimore, the highest-ranking prelate of the American hierarchy. Gibbons responded with support of the idea but that it was a matter beyond his own realm.[21] Brennan opposed the idea of San Antonio as the first archbishopric as New Orleans was French and Santa Fe was Hispanic. As he stated, this would create a triangle that would bring about "the foreignization of the Southwest."[22] Neither should it be Galveston as he stated to Bishop Gallagher:

September 20, 1892

Dear Bishop Gallagher:
    The Holy Father, *motu proprio*, has ordered the Propaganda to ask the bishops of the New Orleans province why Texas should not be made a separate province and what they may have against Dallas. As you are only administrator apostolic of Galveston, your see will scarcely be put in the field. Now I am sure next to your own, Dallas is dearest. Please consider the matter without prejudice and with a view to the future and the great impetus it would give to advancement.

Yours truly,
Thomas J. Brennan
Bishop of Dallas[23]

In the meantime, Bishop John Neraz, of San Antonio, wrote Bishop Gallagher stating that he had read in the newspaper that Bishop Brennan had been appointed archbishop. Bishop Neraz asked Bishop Gallagher if it were true. Bishop Neraz expressed the belief that San Antonio would not like to be separated from New Orleans. "At present we have a good Metropolitan in New Orleans. If it were the will of the Holy Father," Bishop Neraz stated, "then Galveston should have the preference." Bishop Neraz then asked Bishop Gallagher to express his opinion on the issue, and to bear in mind that this was confidential matter.[24]

Bishop Gallagher, meanwhile, began to push the idea of Galveston as the Metropolitan of Texas. Brennan went to Rome, hoping to make his ad limina visit.[25] Realizing that this was not going to happen during the August holidays, he made a pilgrimage to the Holy Land and was back in Rome by September 20 when he composed the above letter.[26] He then wrote to Archbishop Janssens of New Orleans stating that he had personally urged the Pope to establish this new province. When Archbishop Janssens received his inquiry from Rome regarding the possibility of Dallas as an archdiocese, he informed Bishop Gallagher on October 6, 1892 that he was indifferent to a see, but if there was one, it should be San Antonio. Further, the archbishop and bishops of the province of New Orleans believe that it was a mistake in making Brennan a bishop and "may the Lord preserve Texas from ever having him as its Archbishop." Archbishop Janssens urged Bishop Gallagher to write Rome on the matter. A week later (October 13, 1892) Archbishop Janssens wrote Bishop Gallagher again. "I have had so many and such serious charges against him, that I have felt compelled in conscience to bring them to the notice of the Propaganda."[27] Many of these charges came from Dallas clergy. How many is uncertain. The letter, signed by Father Joseph Blum, included twelve charges, which are excerpted here:

1. The Bishop plays with ecclesiastical penalties as an infant with grownups. Without cause and for the sake of money, he inflicts suspensions on the best priests. . . .
2. His disposition is unworthy of a bishop. His anger most vehement, so much so that many fear him as a man, because he would stop at nothing. . . . Even with the Blessed Sacrament in his hands he has been unable to control his anger.
3. His speech has often been rude and scandalous.
4. He has given approval to irreligious schools, . . .
5. By way of insinuation he spoke of the election to the episcopate as something which others seek to attain by means altogether adverse to the holiness of the Church.

6. His pride is limitless, and most of the difficulties of the diocese can be reduced to this pride as the cause.

7. He has founded a paper whose sole reason for existence seemed to be . . . to praise the bishop and his vicar general . . . so that the whole matter has everywhere become an object of ridicule. . . .

9. He has granted dispensations for mixed religion without demanding those formalities required by the Church, . . .

10. It is always very difficult to have confidence in what he says

11. He has been shown to be greatly lacking in virtue. . . .

12. Almost all, clergy and laity, especially in the City of Dallas, are opposed to him as one not loved, and this certainly is not for the good of the Church. In him is to be seen the greatest detriment to the Church. He will never be able to recover the love and the affection of his people. The same can be said with regard to the reverence due to the bishop on the part of the religious families. He has done much to create disturbance in the religious houses (as they by private letters can easily show.)[28]

How many clerics were alienated from their bishop is unknown. There is no doubt that Father Blum was. Regarding the approval of non-Catholic schools, Bishop Brennan's sermons convey that he had sympathies for the "Americanist movement" led by Bishop John Ireland of St. Paul. Bishop Ireland believed that Catholic children could attend public schools provided they received catechism classes in their local parishes.[29] Brennan was also accused of using money he had borrowed from a parish in Corsicana to pay a personal debt. When the pastor of that parish heard of this, he wrote Propaganda.[30] Bearing in mind the complaints from the Diocese of Dallas including the letter of Mother Evangelist, Bishop Brennan offered his resignation from the episcopate of Dallas, November 17, 1892.[31] While Pope Leo XIII reserved the case for himself to consider, he did accept the resignation. In a certain sense Brennan is a tragic figure. He lacked the experience of judgment to take on such a role. The Vatican saw in him a man of zeal, charisma and learning yet his areas of vulnerability prevented him from becoming the shepherd needed in the Southwest or in Newfoundland. [32]

Bishop Edward Fitzgerald of Little Rock was appointed administrator of the Diocese of Dallas until a new bishop was chosen. This was a more prudent move than putting Gallagher in charge due to Gallagher's relationship to Brennan. Father Joseph Blum was reappointed to Sacred Heart in Dallas and as Vicar General. When the new Bishop, Edward Joseph Dunne, was appointed, ground was broken for a new cathedral on Ross Avenue. The loan approved by Bishop Gallagher was not foreclosed. The Cathedral, so ardently desired by Bishop Brennan, was designed by the architect Nicholas Clayton, and dedicated by Bishop Dunne October 26, 1902. In spite of all the controversy surrounding Bishop Brennan, Bishop Dunn, who would serve for sixteen years there, was able to build well on the foundation Brennan established for the diocese.[33]

While the transition in Dallas went smoothly, one may ask what went wrong? Bearing in mind that Brennan came from an atmosphere of elegance and learning, certainly from a different tradition, one may wonder whether he was ready for a growing Texas town, the people, including the clergy occupying it, located on the mud flats of the Trinity River. Bishop Brennan was familiar with an attitude established by what was then generations of Irish clergy, which may, at least in the eyes of some historians, have been too "royal" for a frontier town.[34]

The early part of the twentieth century was a time of significant growth for the Church in Texas. While the creation of the dioceses of Corpus Christi and El Paso came about apart from the administration of Bishop Gallagher, they each illustrate the need for more shepherds in the vast area of Texas.

Diocese of Corpus Christi

Bishop Pedro Verdaguer, who had served as bishop of the Vicariate of Brownsville for twenty years, passed away on October 26, 1911. While Bishop Verdaguer had described the region as very poor, it had grown to such a point that erection of a diocese could no longer be postponed. The bishops of the Province of New Orleans voted to suggest to the Holy See that the vicariate be raised to the level of a Diocese. Pope Pius X issued a Bull on March 23, 1912 raising the Apostolic Vicariate of Brownsville to the status of a Diocese with the see at Corpus Christi. The Holy See appointed Most Reverend Paul J. Nussbaum, a Passionist from Philadelphia. The 83,000 Catholics were scattered over 88,000 miles.[35] Bishop Nussbaum introduced various devotions to the diocese, including the

"holy hour" and "forty hours" Eucharistic devotions. He invited the Pas-
sionists to visit every city and town to give lectures, classes or missions as
the situation warranted. The Bishop further sought to increase the number of Catholic schools in the area.[36] The Sisters of the Incarnate Word
and Blessed Sacrament were asked by Bishop Nussbaum to seek permission from Rome for the abrogation of the cloister. This permission was
readily granted. This change gave the teaching Sisters the opportunity
for professional training and academic degrees.[37] Bishop Nussbaum was
in a railroad accident January 25, 1918 during which he was seriously
injured. He found the traveling in the diocese extremely arduous. On
making his ad limina visit to the Holy See in January 1920, he submitted
his resignation which was accepted by the Holy Father. Although times
had been difficult in the Diocese, Bishop Nussbaum managed to create
a fund for the building of a new cathedral which became a reality after
his tenure. Further, the number of Catholic schools and the student population within the schools doubled during his tenure. This was in spite
of a three-year drought, a hurricane in 1916 and a major storm in 1919
and an influenza epidemic that took the lives of his chancellor, Reverend
John Scheid, and the rector of St. Patrick's Cathedral, Reverend Paulinus
Doran, CP.[38]

Diocese of El Paso

The creation of the Diocese of Dallas left the position of El Paso County
in doubt. As Carlos Casteñada has pointed out:

> That the Bull of erection of the Diocese of Dallas intended by impli-
> cation to comprehend El Paso County in that section designated as
> "North Texas" was born out by the Bull of 1897 elevating the Vicariate
> of Arizona to the Diocese of Tucson, for it included no part of Texas.
> The bull of erection of the Diocese of El Paso in 1914, furthermore
> stated clearly that the "counties of El Paso and Culberson, belonging
> to the Diocese of Dallas proper," were to be in the jurisdiction of the
> Diocese of El Paso.[39]

In 1914, there were three churches in El Paso serving 10,000 Catholics. At least these Catholics did not have to go across the border to

get to Mass.[40] All parochial work in the city of El Paso was carried out by Jesuits, so it was appropriate that a Jesuit be made its first bishop. While the see remained vacant for eighteen months, Most Reverend Anthony Schuler was appointed Bishop in 1915. He became known for establishing churches and schools and inviting religious orders. He was influential in establishing two publications, the *Catholic Weekly* and the *Western American.* The Jesuits moved the office of *Revista Catolica* to El Paso, enabling Catholic literature to be published in English and Spanish. Bishop Schuler led a campaign to clean up dance halls, was one of the founders of Associated Charities and was admired by Catholics and non-Catholics alike.[41]

❧ 5 ❧

Early Difficulties
within the Diocese

Bishop Gallagher served thirty-six years as Bishop of Galveston. While in his later episcopal years, his flock showed great appreciation for the services of this third Bishop of Galveston, this was not evident in his initial years.

It must be recalled that Bishop Gallagher came to Galveston seventeen years after the Civil War. He was therefore perceived as a Yankee in an area that had been occupied by federal troops. Members of his flock could recall the occupation of troops and likewise the battles that preceded the occupation.

The clergy were predominantly from France. Some desired another French bishop following Bishop Dubuis. This group found leadership in Father Anthony Truchard, who served on the staff of St. Marys' University in Galveston, and Father Jean Louis Bussant, who was Pastor of St. Patrick's in Galveston. Father Truchard expressed this view:

> There is no room for me in the Diocese for which I was ordained twenty-one years ago. Yet, meanwhile, the lowest tramps, the scum of the country are received with open arms. They will destroy in a month the patient work of the banks of early missionaries. One by one, the older priests are leaving Texas, with the very Reverend Louis Chaland leading the way. . . . I will try and forget the petty jealousies,

mysterious and uncalled for persecution which has almost made life unbearable for me the last five years. I yield to the inevitable. The Klan said it several years ago. . . . The last priest must leave Galveston.[1]

This view was seen among some, not all, French clergy. Father Louis Chambodut, the first priest ordained for the Diocese of Galveston,[2] rector of the cathedral in Galveston, actually led the group seeking an American bishop.

Visit of Cardinal Francesco Satolli, Apostolic Delegate

The matter of an appointment of an Apostolic delegate for the United States was an issue frequently discussed among the American bishops. Due to the issue of Americanism[3] among other issues of the day, Leo XIII, ignoring objections of leading American prelates, appointed in 1893 Cardinal Francesco Satolli as Apostolic delegate to the United States. Cardinal Satolli was elevated to the Cardinalate three years later, on November 29, 1895. Before leaving his post, in the fall of 1896, he chose to make a tour of southern and western states so that he might meet with the faithful and arrive at solutions to some ecclesiastical difficulties in a few dioceses. When Bishop Gallagher heard of the tour, he invited the Cardinal to Galveston. Father Alexis Orban, secretary to the Cardinal, accepted the invitation on February 3 of that year. The Cardinal actually delivered his first public address in English in Galveston. Following formal greetings at the Cathedral, Cardinal Satolli visited the following convents: the Sisters of St. Dominic, St. Mary's Infirmary, St. Mary's Orphanage, and the Ursuline Convent where the students presented a program.

The following day, Sunday, the Cardinal celebrated a solemn pontifical Mass at the Cathedral. Several receptions followed during the day. A number of non-Catholics were in attendance. Before leaving Galveston, the Cardinal sought to address the issue of the Ursuline Convent Chapel, which was then closed to the general public. No changes took place regarding the status of the chapel.

An Unwelcome Petition

While Cardinal Satolli was visiting New Orleans, he was presented with a petition on February 21, 1896, written by M. J. Z. H. Scott and several other laymen, dated February 15, 1896. The document included twenty-two points against Bishop Gallagher. Beginning with the history of the Church in Texas, the signers complained that the unkindness of the Bishop had run off some of their priests. The places of these priests were filled by "arrogant self-seeking substitutes who came to reap where they had not sown." The Bishop and these priests came from an area of the country "where a large class of the people are prejudiced against us." The Bishop's manner of treating the people is "offensive and oppressive." If an attachment arises between a pastor and his people, he is removed at once. The people learned that "to love a pastor is to lose him." His arbitrary regulations regarding mixed marriages generally led to rigid prohibitions. Many Catholic families left the Church, and others were grievously offended. He placed hardships on Christian burials. He dealt "spitefully" with the Ursuline convent as he assumed they would appeal to Rome against him after he had closed the convent chapel to the laity. He was further jealous of them in favor of his (the Dominican) convent. He gave preferential treatment to the Dominican Sisters where he was practically chaplain. He was accused of mishandling funds. This included the accusation that he had deprived the Sisters of Charity of the Incarnate Word of $8,000, which they had intended on spending on their orphanage in Galveston.[4]

In regard to the above issues, Cardinal Satolli wrote Bishop Gallagher on March 20, 1896, stating that the Bishop was correct in not showing the list of complaints to anyone. "I promise you that no one shall ever see it from me, and it is my desire that the matter should go no further." The Cardinal went on to state that he had nothing to say about diocesan regulations, "leaving it to your own prudence and that of your Vicar General and Consultors to make such rules as your experience teaches you are wise." However, the Cardinal insisted that the Ursuline chapel remain open "for the good of religion and the glory of God. . . . This I hope you will do at once, overcoming any sensitiveness you may feel for the good that will surely come from it."[5]

Initially Bishop Gallagher, in a letter dated March 25, 1896, to Cardinal Satolli, refused to open the Ursuline convent "because I think the good of religion requires me to maintain the Episcopal authority in this Diocese." The Bishop went on to ask the Cardinal to carry on a thorough investigation of the matter. He further asked the Cardinal that the Bishop of Little Rock or New Orleans conduct the investigation.[6]

While he was in Galveston, Cardinal Satolli obtained the written and oral promise of Bishop Gallagher that the chapel, closed to the public since February 1894, would be reopened. The Cardinal made this promise known to the laity of Galveston. Archbishop Satolli asked Bishop Gallagher to respond to other charges of the laity of Galveston. They agreed that the material would be reviewed by Archbishop Francis Janssens of New Orleans.[7]

In a letter dated April 2, 1896, Archbishop Janssens wrote Bishop Gallagher stating that he regretted that Bishop Gallagher mentioned his name for such an "unpleasant, delicate and ungrateful duty." The Archbishop pointed out that the charges were written in a bitter spirit. He then wrote to Bishop Gallagher that it would be better to open the Ursuline Convent Chapel in keeping with his promise. The Bishop's authority would not suffer from it. "Your word is sacred." Further, "if the people imagine you may resist a higher authority, then the people may disregard yours." Archbishop Janssens proceeded in stating that "the regulations for the city parishes just now will embitter feelings and do harm to religion. It would be better to think of that when this whole matter is settled."[8]

In a letter dated two days later, Archbishop Janssens asked Bishop Gallagher about certain financial transactions: the purchase of wild lands, the management of moneys entrusted to him for charitable institutions, the loan of Sisters. Archbishop Janssens further maintained in this letter that he himself should not come to Galveston, for it would give too much importance to the affair. He went on to say that those who were complaining about a judgment on a mixed marriage may have turned on the Bishop in regard to the Ursuline Chapel. With the opening of the chapel, the opposition that inspired the charges would fall to the ground.[9]

Cardinal Satolli wrote to Bishop Gallagher April 15, 1896, asking why the Ursuline Convent Chapel was not open to the public. "You promised me twice that it should be re-opened and have failed to keep your word.

You must know that it was only out of regard for you that I did not use my authority and command its re-opening. The matter is however now in the hands of the Archbishop of New Orleans, and I sincerely hope that everything will soon be settled for the best interests of religion."[10] Two weeks later, Bishop Gallagher responded to Cardinal Satolli that there was no alternative but to compromise his episcopal authority in opening the Ursuline Chapel. He further pointed out that the charges made against him were made by supporters of the Ursuline Sisters.[11] However, the chapel was not yet opened.

In a correspondence of May 2, 1896, Archbishop Janssens asked Bishop Gallagher what the debt of the Diocese was. "They stated that there is a debt of $50,000 on the Cathedral parish. Is this so? The Sisters stated you were willing to give the management of the Asylum to them, provided they would hold no fair, nor solicit contributions. Is their statement correct?"[12]

The Ursuline Convent Chapel

The issue that took the greatest length of time to resolve was the re-opening of the convent chapel to the laity. Bishop Dubuis, Bishop Gallagher's predecessor, had urged the Ursuline Sisters to build a large school and chapel. Bishop Dubuis had an understanding with the Sisters that the chapel would be available for a public oratory. The funds from the collections would be used to defray expenses the Sisters had incurred. Bishop Gallagher had ordered the chapel to be closed in an effort to encourage attendance at the local churches. Catholics and Protestants alike objected as the Sisters had been helpful to the populace during storms and yellow fever epidemics. Bishop Gallagher had closed the chapel to the general public in February 1894. In a letter to the Sisters he stated:

> Please close your convent gates against all outsiders who attend your Chapel, as many neglect their duty to their own Church thereby, You may open your chapel to the public on occasion of Receptions, Professions, Paternal Feasts.
>
> Yours faithfully in Christ,
> N. A. Gallagher
> Bishop of Galveston[13]

A number of laymen objected to the closing of this chapel and sent him a petition on January 25, 1895, requesting that the chapel be open to the laity.[14]

Galveston, Texas
January 25, 1895
Right Reverend N. A. Gallagher
Bishop of Galveston

Dear Bishop:

The undersigned, your petitioners, Catholics of Galveston—having the welfare of our Religion uppermost, and actuated solely by a keen desire for justice in the matter herein alluded to, do respectfully submit the following facts for your Lordship's consideration, and earnestly request you to give us an early affirmative reply.

We submit first, that prior to the month of February, 1894, the Ursuline Nuns of Galveston had in connection with their "Time-honored Institution of Learning" a small but beautifully arranged Chapel, where numbers of our devoted Catholics were wont to repair for the purpose of attending Divine Services.

Not only was the little Ursuline chapel a great convenience for the worshippers residing in this section of our city, but it was the pride and joy of the good Sisters to see the forms and faces of their former pupils and constant friends kneeling in silence before the Altar, which they had been so zealously reared to remember and revere.

Much labor and expense had been bestowed in making this perhaps the most inviting place for religious solitude in all the Diocese. ... Here our families loved to linger where they felt so free from all distraction while offering up their prayers. Here the aged, the delicate, and the overworked could easily find access when, to reach the distant Churches of our city would have been to them impossible.... Here, in time of heavy rainfalls so frequent in the spring and summer seasons, the Catholics of this portion of Galveston could come with more convenience than to any other Church.

We furthermore submit that, on or about the month of February, 1894, this little chapel, this quiet little place of worship was *closed* by your Lordship—and to this day remains so closed to outside worshippers to the great sorrow of the Ursuline Nuns, and to the greater inconvenience of a large number of our Catholic population.

For them, and for ourselves we now present this humble request in the interest of Catholicity in Galveston, and ask of you to permit this chapel, our Ursuline convent to be reopened.

When you consider the long and valued services rendered by the Ursulines to society and the Church in Galveston, when you reflect that this Chapel was the pride and glory of these noble Ladies, and that its closure has inflicted actual hardship upon many Catholics who were wont to attend Divine Services there, we feel assured that you will speedily withdraw your order and once more restore happiness to the Catholics of Galveston, and to the undersigned.

Your Respectful and Faithful Petitioners
47 Signatures follow.[15]

In responding to a note from Sister M. Joseph, Bishop Gallagher stated that *all outsiders* were to be excluded, including societies and sodalities.[16]

The Superior of the Ursuline Sisters in Galveston at that time was Mother Mary Joseph Dallmer, the former Mary Dallmer. As a youngster, she had traveled by ship with her widowed mother and siblings on an eighty-two-day voyage from Germany; the family had rested briefly in New Orleans and then sailed again for another fourteen days to Galveston. There the family reunited with Mary Anne's oldest married sister, Maria Eva, and brother George. The married sister had a home waiting for the five children and their mother. Mrs. Dallmer had to take in washing to provide for her children in those lean years, for her lack of knowledge of English closed the doors to most other employment. While this kind of work was readily compared to slave labor in a slave-holding state, Mrs. Dallmer proclaimed that this would not hurt her and that she already had several orders. St. Joseph knew how to work well and would help her. In addition to hard labor, the family had to endure the yellow fever epidemic of 1858.[17]

However, it was a time during which the children were able to receive a Catholic education, which was pivotal to the vocation of Mary Anne. At the Ursuline school, Mary Anne was drawn to Mother Saint Pierre Harrington, often referred to as the second foundress of the convent. During the Civil War, Mary Anne and nine other girls became boarders at the Ursuline Convent. When federal troops began the bombing of the city, General Bankhead Magruder, commander of the Confederate forces, told the Sisters to hoist a yellow flag, signifying that the building was being used as a base hospital. A yellow winter petticoat became that flag. The Battle of Galveston turned the convent into a bloody hospital, but the Sisters chose to remain. In the midst of the turmoil of the war, the young boarders were prepared for and received their First Communion.[18]

Cardinal Satolli, in a letter written March 15, 1896, to Mother Joseph, stated that the conditions for the reopening of the chapel "seem to me to be reasonable and I hope that the re-opening will result in great good to all concerned."[19] The reopening did not take place, for on April 9, 1896, Cardinal Mazzella, prefect of the Congregation of Rites, responded to Mother Joseph:

> No answer can be given before summoning the Bishop who being interested on the matter, must be heard according to justice before any decision.
>
> It is therefore necessary to wait patiently for some time as well as confidently, because it is certain that the Holy Congregation, after having heard both parts, will decide the question with justice and equity.[20]

This letter was followed by another from Cardinal Satolli to Mother Joseph, dated April 15, in which he also urges the Sisters to be patient in the re-opening of the chapel, "for the good Lord will, in His own time, and way, arrange everything." The Cardinal pointed out to Mother Joseph that the matter at that time was in the hands of the Archbishop of New Orleans.[21]

In correspondence of May 5, 1896, Archbishop Janssens wrote Bishop Gallagher begging him to reopen the Ursuline convent to the laity "if for no other reason, do it as a favor to me; and if you hesitate to do it because you fear to compromise your dignity and authority (which in my opinion is by no means compromised) assign it as reason, if you desire to do so, because I have begged it of you as a favor." The Apostolic Delegate was growing impatient.[22]

After much study of the matters brought forward in the petition, Archbishop Janssens, in a correspondence of June 5, 1896, made several recommendations to Bishop Gallagher. First, "Place at the Cathedral a trustworthy priest, who may possess the confidence of the Bishop and the people." Bishop Gallagher's choice of Father Kirwin, although very young to the priesthood, would ultimately alleviate and disintegrate many of the areas of tension. This priest would have the responsibility of paying off the debt there and to "keep the people together." Second, "Appoint a Chaplain for the Dominican Sisters, also a Confessor." Bishop Janssens wrote that it was "unbecoming" for the Bishop to have this role. This is especially true if "a public disorder had to be corrected." The Archbishop went on to state that the bishop is the father of all religious institutions. The reality of taking on these roles "shows a preference and favor to that and to the detriment of the others."[23] Father Hennessy, Pastor of Annunciation Church in Houston, wrote Bishop Gallagher on June 13, 1896, urging him to reopen the Ursuline Convent Chapel. He encouraged the Bishop to state that the opening was the wish of Cardinal Satolli.[24]

A letter followed from the Bishop, addressed to the Superior in the Ursuline Sisters in Galveston:

> June 15, 1896
>
> Reverend Mother Superioress of the Ursuline Convent, Galveston, Texas:
> Permission is hereby granted that the Chapel of the Ursuline Convent may be open to the public every day on occasions when the Holy Sacrifice is offered or the Benediction with the Blessed Sacrament is given therein.
> Jurisdiction over outsiders within the precincts of the Convent, is not granted to any priest.
> Outsiders cannot fulfil their Easter duty in the Ursuline convent.
>
> Faithfully in our Lord,
> Nicholas Aloysius,
> Bishop of Galveston[25]

A second letter was written by Bishop Gallagher on the same day, stating that Cardinal Satolli wished the chapel to be opened without delay, presuming the conditions of the previous letter.

June 15, 1896
Rev. Mother Sr. Joseph
Ursuline Convent, Galveston, Texas

Cardinal Satolli, whom I promised, when he was here to open your chapel, wishes me to do without delay; and with his wish I gladly comply. I am glad to have no further responsibility in the matter. The conditions added are known to His Eminence, I trust that you will have care that these conditions be complied with, insofar as you are concerned.

With best wishes to you all, I remain faithfully
Yours in Christ,
N. A. Gallagher, Bishop[26]

Thus, permission was finally granted by Bishop Gallagher for the opening of the Ursuline Chapel.

A week later, Cardinal Satolli wrote to Mother Joseph in response to a question,

Dear Rev. Mother:

I have received your letter of June 16. In reply to your questions I would answer that the condition of which you call attention evidently means that parochial jurisdiction is denied to priests officiating in your convent and chapel as far as persons and members of your community are concerned. With regard to other doubts, it will be best that you ask all explanations of the Bishop through your Chaplain.
With sincere esteem, and wishing your community all peace and blessing, I remain,

Most faithfully yours in Christ,
Cardinal Satolli,
Apostolic Delegate[27]

Orphanage of the Sisters of Charity
of the Incarnate Word

St. Mary's Orphanage opened in 1867[28] under the episcopate of Bishop
Claude Dubuis and the direction of the Sisters of Charity of the Incarnate Word. Bishop Dubuis had made an agreement with the Sisters of
Charity in Galveston that St. Mary's Infirmary and St. Mary's Orphanage
would always remain together.[29] Bishop Dubuis had drawn up a written agreement dated March 31, 1875, leasing to the Hospital Sisters the
land on which the orphanage was founded. The Sisters were responsible
for all improvements and buildings.[30] The inheritance of Mrs. Laura
Green in addition to funds borrowed from St. Mary's Infirmary were
used for the purchase of Greens Bayou Property. Twenty-eight orphans
were moved from St. Mary's Infirmary to St. Mary's Orphan Asylum.
At that time all orphans were girls. However, they began to take boys
with additional facilities. By 1883, there were 125 orphans. At that time
Bishop Gallagher decided that the Sisters of Charity in Galveston did
not have a sufficient number of Sisters to run the orphanage. He decreed
that the Sisters of Charity of the Incarnate Word, San Antonio, take it
over. Thus the 1875 agreement was terminated on June 5, 1883.[31] This
arrangement lasted until 1887 when Bishop Gallagher called the Sisters
of Charity in Galveston back to operate the orphanage. On March 16,
1896, the same agreement originally made with Bishop Dubuis was re-
newed with Bishop Gallagher.[32]

On June 5, 1896, Archbishop Francis Janssens wrote Bishop Gallagher
regarding control of the orphanage in Galveston, stating that he was far
too involved in the administration of the ministry of the Sisters:

> Give back to the Sisters of the Incarnate Word the full administration
> of the orphan asylum, to render an account to them and to settle with
> them when possible for all the monies, which now the Bishop controls
> for the Asylum and further to allow the said Sisters to have fairs and
> make collections as in former days. Sisters of Asylums, insofar as I
> know, control everywhere their own affairs, or if not they, a Com-
> mittee of gentlemen with the Bishop or priest as President. You put
> yourself to much trouble and you satisfy neither the Sisters nor the
> public. Leaving it all in their hands, they will work better, be more
> satisfied, the people will not have suspicions, will contribute better;

and it will relieve you from much anxiety. It is not good for a Bishop to enter into all the small details of administration, outside of that which belongs to his department.[33]

Bishop Gallagher then decided to organize a board of directors for the orphanage. Undoubtedly he saw this as a means of carrying out the requisite of Archbishop Janssens: "Consult the consultors about all important matters of the diocese. . . . It is a dangerous thing for any Bishop to follow his own ideas, his own mind, without carefully weighing what others may think."[34]

Bishop Gallagher asked Mother Benedict what recompense she desired for services rendered at the orphanage. The Bishop desired to sell the old place to help in the construction of a new orphanage closer to the city if the community was willing to cancel their claims to the deeds of the property. Mother Benedict consented to the sale of the property on condition that half the value of the property be given to the Congregation for compensation for expenses, improvements, and maintenance of the orphanage since February 21, 1874. She also requested the sum of $1,000 to be paid yearly for the services of ten Sisters at the orphanage. The Sisters received $6,000 in consideration of the community's claim on the property, $1,000 yearly for the services of the Sisters at the orphanage, and an additional $1,000 as interest due the Congregation and any claims it had on the Diocese. Unfortunately, Bishop Gallagher did not carry out his plans of moving the orphanage, probably because he did not have the funds. It remained at the Green's Bay site until the tragedy of September 8, 1900.[35]

Resolution

While Archbishop Janssens was adamant in the reopening of the Ursuline Chapel, he also believed that Bishop Gallagher needed to appoint a rector of the Cathedral who would take on many of the issues stemming from a distance between the Bishop and the laity:

> You need at the Cathedral a priest above all reproach and suspicion, in touch with the people, able to gain their esteem and affections so as to lessen and gradually to pay off the debt, and to keep your people together.[36]

Father James Kirwin would serve as rector of the Cathedral for almost thirty years. During that time period he would become one of the most beloved priests in the history of Galveston. The resolution of this unpleasantness had much to do with the person of Father Kirwin. It is amazing that such opposite personalities would work so well together for so many years.[37]

Archbishop Janssens further issued a personal challenge to Bishop Gallagher:

> Priests and people complain you are cold and reserved and seem unsympathetic. I feel convinced that this lies only on the surface and that your heart beats warm and sympathetic for your priests and people. Could you not relax that reserve a little? Could you not show to the surface a little more warmth for clergy and laity? . . . we should try to do the most good whenever and in whatever manner we may be able to do so. I believe the Lord will in the last judgment day be harder on us for severity than for leniency and mercy shown.[38]

Bishop Gallagher did not appoint the chaplaincy of the Dominican Sisters until 1898, but such did eventually happen. Likewise, other matters within the petition were resolved through the reopening of the Ursuline Chapel and Father James Kirwin's rapport with the people.

❧ 6 ❧

The Vicars General

Two of the most revered and well-known priests in Galveston in the later part of the nineteenth century each served as Vicar General of the Diocese of Galveston in addition to a host of other positions. They were Father Louis Chambodut (1821–1880) and Father James Kirwin (1872–1926). Their gifts and personalities were quite different, yet the effect of their service to the Diocese of Galveston long endured on the island.

The Vicar General was second in command to the Bishop. The people of that era were accustomed to a strong Vicar General. Father Chambodut, in taking on significant roles under the two previous bishops, actually paved the way for Father Kirwin. While the Bishop today is required to appoint a Vicar General for the diocese, this authority[1] is not evident at the time under study.

Father Louis Chambodut (1821–1880)

If a stranger were to ask who was the most popular and beloved man in the city of Galveston after the Civil War, the "unhesitating" answer would have been, "Why, Father Chambodut, of course." He was of French ancestry, from the St.-Just-en-Chevalet Department of Loire, France, and his parents provided the best education at that time, sending him to the Grand Seminaire in Lyons where he was ordained a deacon in December 1845. While he could have become a chaplain to royalty, the missionary spirit was burning within him. When Bishop Odin called on

recruits for Texas, the young Chambodut volunteered. After his ordination to the priesthood on March 25, 1846, at St. Louis Cathedral in St.
Louis, Missouri, he accompanied Father Dubuis to Galveston.[2]

Father Chambodut was missioned to Nacogdoches, Texas, soon after. His life there involved many narrow escapes. On one occasion, he
had lost his way and therefore knocked on the door of a farmhouse
for assistance. The family was surprised to find a young Catholic male
who was "humane and kind-hearted." The elderly lady of the house
stuffed his saddle bags with farm produce after he had spent the night
and partaken of breakfast; she stated, "My dear good young man, I am
going to pray every day that you may be converted and become a good
Protestant minister." Father Chambodut replied, "Stop! Stop! You must
not say that, but pray that I may always do the Will of God." The husband intervened, stating that was a good prayer and that they would
pray it every day. A year later Father Chambodut knocked on the same
farmhouse door and the young priest was graciously received. As Father
Chambodut began the prayer of blessing, all made the sign of the cross
with him. The farmer then pulled two books off the shelf left behind by
Father Chambodut, which the family had been studying, a *Catechism of
Christian Doctrine* and Milner's *End of Controversy*. They had been so
impressed by the priest's conviction that he possessed the truth and his
earnestness when he told the lady to pray that they asked to be received
into the Church and remained steadfast members forever after. The
mustard seeds he planted and watered in East Texas grew into mighty
trees.[3]

Bishop Odin appointed Father Chambodut Vicar General in 1852,
by calling the priest to Galveston. Since Bishop Odin traveled across the
diocese, which encompassed the entire state of Texas, he was in Galveston only a few days several times a year. As a consequence, Father
Chambodut took care of much of the administration of the diocese.
This included the erection of the Cathedral and the episcopal residence.
It was within the episcopal residence that Father Chambodut housed
seven Oblates when they arrived on May 22, 1852. Unsettled conditions
on the Mexican border made it prudent for the Oblates to wait before
going into that country. Thus, Father Chambodut gave them the most
secluded part of the house, where they could carry out their community
exercises and enter into community life later.[4]

In 1861 three Texas regiments joined the Army of Virginia and became known as Hood's Brigade. One of the companies came from Galveston and was made up of French settlers who were descendants of the disabled army of Napoleon. Father Chambodut was a favorite of these soldiers. On August 15, 1861, there appeared "an immense concourse" of the military and civilian population to witness the Blessing of the Colors of the Boys in Gray. Father Chambodut addressed the assembly in an eloquent manner. The people of Texas were kept informed of the happenings of the war through newspapers sent by Bishop Odin and other newspapers by Father Chambodut, who imparted the news to the people. He made the Bishop's house available to General Jeb Magruder for his headquarters. In November 1862, the general was made commander of the Southern forces on the Texas coast. The troops stationed in Galveston attended Mass at the cathedral every Sunday. When the war was over, General Magruder made a gift to Father Chambodut of his sword, which the priest highly prized.[5] During the Civil War he checked each day on the Confederate casualties and then contacted the families. He would station himself at the post office when the mail arrived so he was on hand to "console, comfort and encourage." He was solicitous toward the Galvestonians during the Federal occupation, regardless of flag or creed.[6]

During Reconstruction, Father Chambodut told the people of Galveston that they should not leave a "clear field to the Carpet Baggers," but rather he urged them to take an active part in local concerns, including voting. He, a naturalized citizen, was denied the right to cast his vote as "his sympathy with the Rebels had been too conspicuous." Father Chambodut said that he did not regret the cause.[7]

Father Chambodut, as Vicar General under Bishop Dubuis, met the Sisters of Charity of the Incarnate Word at Galveston. He took them to the Ursuline Convent for lodging, where Father Chambodut served as chaplain. They would lodge there until their own convent was built.[8] Father Chambodut found himself in charge of the construction of the first Charity Hospital opened by the Sisters of Charity in Galveston in 1867. During the yellow fever epidemic in June of that year, Father Chambodut saw to it that hospital facilities were made available to victims.[9]

Bishop Jean-Marie Odin turned in the name of Father Chambodut as a possible successor to the episcopate of Galveston. While he was not chosen, the nomination referred to the high regard of Bishop Odin for Chambodut.[10] Odin appointed Father Chambodut as administrator of the diocese until a new bishop was appointed, which was a time period of approximately a year and a half.[11] Chambodut also served as Vicar General under the episcopate of Bishop Dubuis.[12]

As Vicar General for Bishop Dubuis, Father Chambodut defended the cause of the Sisters of Charity of the Incarnate Word in the absence of the Bishop. For more than a year, beginning on May 8, 1868, five to seven of these Sisters were engaged in the care of patients at the Island City Hospital as their own hospital had few patients. The Vicar General asked the city council for some remuneration for these Sisters. The Sisters had been assured verbally by Mayor Williams that they would receive some remuneration. Seven months after the Sisters began working there, a city council meeting was held on December 8, 1868, at which the chairman of the Hospital Committee listed a donation of $500 to the Sisters of Charity in acknowledgment of their services. This appears to be the only payment they were to receive and, according to Sister Loyola Hegarty, it is doubtful they received this. Father Chambodut petitioned the city council on May 13, 1869, requesting that these Sisters receive $100 a month for their services, stating they had not been given any compensation since going to the hospital and that they were finding it difficult to obtain minimum necessities for themselves. Alderman Moses did not disagree with the statement but responded that the Sisters had been placed there at the request of the authorities of the Roman Catholic diocese, and there was no understanding they would receive remuneration. Action on the matter was deferred. The Sisters continued working at the hospital until the objection of a small group of doctors to the ministry of the Sisters at City Hospital made it seem advisable for them to withdraw.[13]

When the Sisters of Charity reopened St. Mary's Infirmary in the summer of 1869, they needed a steady source of income. They thus made a bid for the care of US Marine patients and began a hospital insurance plan for private patients. The Sisters were awarded the contract for the care of the marine patients at the rate of one dollar a day, beginning July 1, 1869. *Fluke's Semi-Weekly Bulletin* reported the following on August 7 of that year:

The Sisters of Charity have under the direction of the Rev. Father Chambodut, re-opened St. Mary's Hospital or Infirmary, for the reception of such as need the comforts of such an institution. There are in every city a large class of persons not paupers, but self-supporting, and in most cases "well-to-do people" who have no settled home or sympathizing friends to care for them in time of sickness. Some are clerks living in restaurants and lodging in their stores, others live in boarding houses, some are domestic employees, servants in families, waiters in hotels, or belong to some other numerous classes that we have indicated. The Catholic Church, or, perhaps more properly speaking, her benevolent orders have opened St. Mary's Infirmary for the use of such. Any person paying the small amount of 25 cents a week—a dollar a month—in advance during health, or $13.00 a year, is entitled to a bed for himself when ill, with medical attendance, nursing, food and all necessaries. We all know that next to a wife or a mother, the Sister of Charity is the best of all nurses. Those sick and wounded during the war, who fell under their care, were fortunate, and will never forget their self-denial and tenderness. Of course it is not to be supposed that this small sum will pay the bills, but it is hoped that other donations will be given, and that many who subscribe will never have occasion to use the institution until that enterprise may be self-supporting. Housekeepers will make subscriptions for one or more beds that they may have good accommodations for a sick servant. Benevolent individuals will do the same that they may have provision for any poor friend or stranger that may be thrown on their protection. It is an insurance against sickness, and will save many an unfortunate from suffering.[14]

It is not certain how long the plan remained in operation, but six weeks after the announcement the *Bulletin* reported that the plan was working well.[15]

A very personal side of Father Chambodut is revealed in his correspondence. His younger sister, Jeanne Marie, had taken the veil in the Ursuline convent in Galveston in 1856. Mother Aloysia, as she was known in religion, left us a brief biography of her brother. At that time, Father Chambodut's niece, who was only seven, entered as a boarder in the Ursuline convent in Galveston. After the Civil War, however, her uncle sent her back to France. One issue for the return to France was safety, while the other was a story that she had fallen in love with a Protestant. Justine had fond memories of Galveston, spending much time with the Green family. At the age of twenty-four, she was still begging her uncle for a return trip. Father Chambodut would have welcomed her return if there were a religious vocation involved, but the Vicar General did not believe that was the case. Undoubtedly, when Father Chambodut made a trip back to France, he broke the news that Mr. and Mrs. Green were deceased and their home was turned into an orphanage.[16]

Father Chambodut spent ten more years in ministry, gathering funds and supervising the construction of the first buildings for St. Mary's Infirmary, St. Patrick's Church, and St. Mary's Orphanage. When his death came, he had no will but had nothing to pass on as he had been so generous during his lifetime. He had a great love of the Incarnate Word and Mary Immaculate. He had established the Sodality of the Children of Mary in Galveston. His love for the Sacred Heart made way for the Archconfraternity, which was affiliated with Rome. It is stated that he exemplified the truth of the beatitude: "Blessed are the meek for they shall possess the land."[17]

While on a mission with Bishop Dubuis to San Antonio on December 7, 1880, Father Chambodut fell ill and passed away. The *Galveston News* recorded that, "Like a thunderbolt from a clear sky came the announcement yesterday afternoon that Father Chambodut was dead. A few had heard that he was ill . . . but by far the greater number of those that knew him well and loved him dearly had little thought that he was soon to be taken from earth."[18] He was buried at St. Mary's Cathedral in Galveston.[19] At the time of his death, one of his friends stated:

> Not a Catholic institution is there in Galveston but has felt the vigorous force of Father Chambodut's helping hand and influence but scare one is there in the diocese that will not recall some act of helpful kindness. Nor did his charity extend simply to those of his own faith. He never stopped to ask, "In what do you believe?" but wherever he saw suffering or need, he hastened to relieve it.[20]

He was the first priest ordained for the Diocese of Galveston, which, at that time, encompassed all of Texas.

Father James Kirwin (1872–1926)

If one were to ask who the most revered priest was in early twentieth-century Galveston, the response, with little doubt, would be Father James Kirwin. He readily became the "right-hand man" of Bishop Gallagher, serving an invaluable role in that administration. If one were to contrast the two personages of Bishop Gallagher and Monsignor Kirwin, one might note that whereas Bishop Gallagher possessed a far-sighted vision and was a great organizer, Monsignor Kirwin was a well-known orator and had the gift of inspiring people. The two often appeared in public together. Bishop Gallagher would bless the church or whatever the occasion called for and Monsignor Kirwin would give the sermon or serve as master of ceremonies. A case in point is the blessing of an altar given by Mrs. John Goggan to Sacred Heart Church in Galveston for its Silver Jubilee celebration. Bishop Gallagher celebrated the Solemn High Pontifical Mass during which the altar was dedicated. Reverend Father Otis gave the sermon. Father Kirwin served as master of ceremonies.[21] The two, Bishop Gallagher and Father Kirwin, had a great respect for each other.[22]

Father Kirwin filled a necessary role in the diocese originally called for by the Archbishop of New Orleans, Archbishop Janssens: "Place at the Cathedral a trustworthy priest, who may possess the confidence of the Bishop and the people."[23]

James Martin Kirwin hailed from Circleville, Ohio, coming into this world on July 1, 1872. His parents were of Irish ancestry. The practice of the Catholic faith was very strong in the home. There he learned of his faith, patriotism, and Christian virtue. He attended public and Catholic schools, eventually completing his college work at St. Mary's College in Lebanon, Kentucky. He went on for seminary studies at Mount St. Mary's the West in Cincinnati, where he finalized his studies. While there, he became an avid athlete, excellent student, and one of two compilers of the volume of the history of *Mount St. Mary's of the West*. He was ordained on June 15, 1895. Bishop Gallagher then sent him for one year of theological work to the Catholic University in Washington, DC, where he was awarded a theological degree. Bishop Gallagher called him forth to Texas on August 15, 1896, where he was immediately appointed rector of St. Mary's Cathedral.[24]

In the Cathedral, Father Kirwin promoted a higher standard of Christian living and religious principles among the youth of Galveston. He became the spiritual director of the Catholic Knights of America as well as the Young Ladies Sodality and the Children of Mary. During the yellow fever epidemic of 1897, he urged the citizens of Galveston to secure proper sanitation and shield the healthy and the sick. He spent his nights and days consoling the sick and dying. For this work he was endeared to the people.[25]

The discontent of the dock workers in Galveston led to a general strike in 1897. All shipping came to a standstill. Since there was no outlet for grain and cotton in Galveston, the goods went to other places for shipment. The strikers grew angry. Violence was imminent. The Southern Pacific Railroad Company sought to end the strike by bringing in strike breakers. The militia was called in to maintain order. Citizens turned to Father Kirwin, pleading that he might seek a settlement. Father Kirwin went to the strikers and called forth their patience. He then went to the president of the Southern Pacific, demanding that the workers be given their "fullest due." Both sides perceived the priest as a "square man," yielded points, and the matter was settled amicably. He was seen as a person who handled a dangerous situation with rare discretion and a finely tuned sense of justice.[26]

In 1898, when the United States went to war with Spain, the people of Galveston decided to form a volunteer regiment. Father Kirwin gave a patriotic speech, which helped form the regiment. The men chose him for chaplain, and the war department approved, giving him the rank of captain. When he was at Camp Hawly, the people of Galveston presented him with a fine horse and necessary equipment. He gathered the soldiers on Sunday morning for Mass and preached on the Gospel of the day. He was honorably discharged from the army in October 1898.[27]

When the greatest storm in the history of the United States struck Galveston, September 8, 1900, a storm that the citizens were entirely unprepared for, Father Kirwin called a meeting of surviving citizens in Tremont Hall; the citizens stood in several feet of water. He and the mayor, Walter Jones, and the chief of police, Edward Ketchum, formed a triumvirate of absolute power. Father Kirwin wrote an order placing the city under martial law. This declaration saved the city from vandals. They next formed a committee to feed the hungry, clothe the naked, rescue the injured, and bury the dead. A committee for each of the twelve city wards was appointed.[28] Appeals were sent out to all the world asking for aid. These goods were placed in a central warehouse and withdrawn as needed. It was estimated that relief was extended to between 17,000 and 20,000 daily and that the value amounted to $40,000 a day. The committee saw the futility of burying the dead and so ordered the bodies to be sent out to sea, but "the sea would not have them," which meant that the only recourse was cremation. A census bureau to count the living and the dead was established. Transportation to the mainland was provided. Father Kirwin was everywhere during these days. Mass was held on September 16 in the Cathedral. The church was packed. Father Kirwin told them not to lose heart for behind them was the humanity of the world and the Providence of God. He urged each parishioner to trust, to build a greater, better, larger and more secure Galveston. The people acceded to that wish by resolving to build a mighty wall to restrain the sea. The cornerstone was laid in 1902 and completed in 1905. Father Kirwin performed the religious service on the completion of the wall.[29]

In 1902 residents of the city were awakened by fire engines as firefighters fought conflagrations that seemed to threaten the entire city. Thousands of dollars' worth of property was destroyed, and entire city blocks were consumed by flames. Father Kirwin assisted in rescuing men, women, and children from the fires. Unfortunately, he received an eye injury, which remained with him for the rest of his life. His vision was from then on obscured by dancing black spots. The people learned from that fire how inadequate their water supply was. Father Kirwin worked to see that the city had a sufficiently pure water supply and likewise a well-equipped and trained Fire Department. The Fire Department awarded him with a gold medal for his efforts. Father Kirwin had become a friend to every man in Galveston.[30]

In 1909, Father Kirwin wished to purge saloons from residential sections of the city. Those supporting this movement organized the Home Protective League. However, there was much opposition. The city charter did not give the local government the power to pass the necessary ordinance even though efforts were made at the local level.[31] So the matter was brought to the state legislature. Galveston's representatives in the House and Senate opposed the measure. Only after a bitter fight in each house of the legislature was the measure passed. The victory was credited to Father Kirwin. The newspapers supported the measure, describing it as a great step forward in municipal government. They ascribed the valiant service to Father Kirwin. While many might have thought that Father Kirwin made enemies in the battle, that was not the case, for they realized the pure motives in Father Kirwin's struggle.[32]

Father Kirwin was often sought after to entertain dignitaries at the city and state level. He praised the state for its progress in the arts and sciences, yet he condemned it for its exaltation of wealth. He clarified to his audience the evil result of soft living and "unbridled license of the passions." In sum, he spoke against the vices of the age and for the true aspirations of the times.[33] He also addressed various groups on topics of current interest. A case in point is an address given to a packed audience in Dallas regarding the topic of socialism, "Socialism—Its Hopes and Its Dangers," during which he pointed out that socialism is an idle dream.[34]

Another topic well visited by Father Kirwin was that of patriotism, especially during the years of World War I. In an address titled "The Church and the Flag," he pointed out that the dangers from without our country are very few. As he stated, "We have stood by the landmarks. We have fostered no entangling alliances." Yet, he described the major threat as one of indifference to high ideals and patriotic purposes. "We are inclined too much to material things," leading to the reality that "our gravest danger comes from the spirit of selfish indulgence and complacent optimism." In his usual straightforward manner, he said, "We must show by our deeds that we prize honor above comfort and justice above gain and mercy above justice."[35]

Patriotic terminology is often found in Father Kirwin's sermons. In a sermon titled "The Christian Soldier," given October 21, 1917, during World War I, he chose the theme from St. Paul's letter to the Ephesians, "Put on the armor of Christ." We are called to gird our loins with truth. The most insistent demand of the military command is to tell the truth. We are further called to wear the breastplate of justice. The Christian who does not is a hypocrite. The shield of faith is necessary in every action. St. Paul points out that only by faith are we able to extinguish "the fiery darts hurled against us by the world, the flesh and the devil." Salvation depends on the helmet in the trenches. St. Paul calls it the helmet of salvation. "Unless the Christian soldier helmets himself with prayer and the sacraments, he can expect to be 'picked off.'" Father Kirwin referred to the Sword of the Spirit as the Word of God. Written for instruction and guidance, "It is our firm hope when our earthly comfort fails. It is the only sword that can clear the way to the promised land, the hope of victory to heaven."[36]

Bishop Gallagher appointed Father Kirwin Vicar General in 1911. In that same year the Basilians withdrew from St. Mary's Seminary due to shortage of Basilians for staffing. Father Kirwin accepted the position as president and professor of moral theology. He likewise taught Scripture. It was stated that the seminary grew and prospered during his administration.[37] Father Kirwin referred to the seminarians as foot soldiers for Jesus Christ. As he commented,

An army is helpless without the infantry. The air service, the artillery and all the rest are merely adjuncts to it. The infantry makes the charge and holds the places conquered. The diocesan clergy are Christ's own infantry. He established it. We should all be proud of our enlistment in the Apostolic Priesthood of Jesus Christ.[38]

Father Thomas Ryan, one of his students, stated that Father Kirwin possessed a sound knowledge of Theology and a clear simple manner of presentation. He was privileged to have been tutored by Father Kirwin at eight fifteen in the evening as he lacked a particular tract of Theology for the course of study that current year. Prior to his lesson, Father Kirwin coached some students in Spanish, pointing out that the seminarian would never know when it was needed in his ministry. Father Kirwin believed that example is better than precept. "To live under the same roof with him was to know him. To know him was to admire him and to love him."[39]

Father Kirwin accompanied the Fourth Texas Infantry to the Mexican border as their chaplain in 1915. He became a firm friend and spiritual guide for many men in the state militia. He was one of the most popular men at the border.[40] In 1917, General John Pershing cabled, asking him to join the chaplain corps in France. Father Kirwin was able to travel as far as New York. When he heard how frail Bishop Gallagher was, he turned back, becoming the administrator of the diocese on the Bishop's death in 1918.[41]

Father Kirwin celebrated the Silver Jubilee of his ordination on June 23, 1920, in the Cathedral. Four bishops, four monsignors, and fifty-five priests were present. This was followed by a banquet in the Galvez Hotel and then a tribute that evening in the Galveston Auditorium, where many people shared their love and respect for the Jubilarian. A number of patriotic and Irish songs were sung, and then Father Kirwin addressed the group, which was the climax of the occasion.[42]

Father Kirwin was named Monsignor by Pope Pius XI on June 24, 1922.[43] The newly named Monsignor Kirwin continued in his active role in the Diocese until he was called home by his maker in 1926. He was called home as quickly as he was called on to serve in the Diocese of Galveston. One Sunday afternoon, he retired for his usual nap. He had asked a young priest, new to the house, for something for a terrific headache. When Father Louis Joseph Reicher[44] returned from Park Place in Houston, where he had said Mass at St. Christopher's Parish, Monsignor Kirwin had been dead for several hours.[45] The date was January 24, 1926. "A solemn four day funeral service was celebrated for the repose of his soul. A wealth of honor and affection was shown him by the highest dignitaries of the Church and State."[46] The Memorial Chapel at St. Mary's Seminary in La Porte was dedicated to him in May 1928. This chapel later became St. Mary's Parish Church after the seminary was moved to Houston.[47]

It is evident that each of these bishops, Odin, Dubuis, and Gallagher, made excellent choices in their Vicar General. While Bishop Dubuis was on the road, Father Chambodut ably ran the Diocese. He possessed the necessary gifts to enable the Catholics of Galveston to make it through the Civil War and the occupation of Federal troops, showing no partiality to either side, even though he was so accused. He further possessed the speaking abilities to clarify the teachings of the faith as he traveled evangelizing.

Bishop Gallagher wisely recognized the giftedness of Father Kirwin, who related to the people through his speaking abilities. His aptitude in ministering to the people on various occasions readily balanced Bishop Gallagher's gifts in administration. Father Kirwin's great love of his country was seen in his service and likewise in his delivery of speeches and homilies. Father Kirwin and Bishop Gallagher were truly dedicated to the building and maintaining of the seminary.

These priests were pastoral, articulate speakers, and dedicated to building the Church in the Diocese of Galveston. Each was an outsider in that he hailed from a different country or region of the United States. Yet their dedication to their priestly ministry left no room for thoughts of prejudice toward their origin. The grace of the Holy Spirit certainly guided each of these Bishops in their choice of Vicar General.

Figure 6. Grave of Father Chambodut, CLM, St. Mary's Cathedral, Galveston, Texas.

Figure 7. J. M. Kirwin as Chaplain First U.S. V.I., Spanish-American War. Courtesy of Rosenberg Library.

Figure 8. Monsignor James Kirwin as Vicar General. Courtesy of Rosenberg Library.

❧ 7 ❧

The 1900 Storm

The first inhabitants of Galveston were the Karankawa Indians, who came to hunt and fish but did not maintain a permanent residence. They were followed by explorers, Cabeza de Vaca in 1528, among others, looking for riches. The viceroy of Mexico, Count Bernardo de Galvez ordered Jose de Evaca to map the area in 1785. The latter named the bay "Bahia de Galveztown." When Stephen F. Austin received permission from the Mexican government to bring settlers to Texas from the (then) United States, many of them settled in Galveston. Austin is reputed to have said that it was the best natural harbor he had seen. Galveston became a Mexican port of entry in 1825. A customhouse was constructed in 1830. The Texas Navy during the Texas Revolution was based at this port. After the victorious fight for Texas independence, local businessmen built wharves and warehouses to handle shipping in the young town. Galveston became the best place on the Texas coast for shipping until dredging of channels became commonplace in the latter part of the nineteenth century and early twentieth century. The Civil War disrupted Galveston's growth temporarily as many in the town left with the imposition of the Union blockade. Confederate troops recaptured the area on January 1, 1863. When the South surrendered in 1865, the city again turned to economic growth. Galveston and Houston had engaged in economic rivalry, even prior to the Civil War. Galveston worked hard to maintain its dominance.[1]

The lifeblood of Galveston was her port. In 1889, the federal government acknowledged the need for a single deep harbor west of New Orleans. The US Army Corps of Engineers determined that would be Galveston. In ten years Galveston was second in the nation in cotton exports and third in wheat. While the port brought wealth, it also included risks, for most of the city was barely above high tide sea level. The highest elevation on the island, nine feet, was Broadway, the boulevard that ran east to west. Most of the residents were unaware of the threat that could come from the Gulf waters. When Galveston's seashores attracted more and more visitors, the salt cedar trees were removed to provide greater access to the beaches. As builders moved west, they took sand from the dunes to fill in shallow areas where they might build. Toward the end of the nineteenth century, these trees and dunes that had initially provided natural barriers to protect the interior of the island no longer prevented the waves from coming in from the Gulf. In addition, there was an openness to flooding from the bay side of the island. Water from Galveston Bay rose when there was a strong wind from the north or when nearby rivers flowed into the bay. While there was discussion of building a seawall, businessmen did not wish to make the investment to bring it about.[2]

The 1900 storm has often been called Isaac's storm, due to the weatherman who attempted to warn people of the impending danger at the last minute. Isaac Monroe Cline was the head of the weather bureau in Galveston. Very early on the Saturday morning of September 8, he realized that something dangerous was approaching:

> The storm swells were increasing in magnitude and frequency and were building up a storm tide which told me as plainly as though it were a written message that a great danger was approaching. Neither the barometer nor the winds were telling me, but the storm tide was telling me to warn the people of the danger approaching.[3]

Isaac Cline worked with the two other men at the weather bureau: his twenty-nine-year-old bachelor brother Joseph Cline and a third temporary employee, John Blagden. They attempted to warn people of the impending storm. The *New York Evening Sun*, twelve days after the storm, credited Isaac Cline with saving thousands of lives.[4] News of an impending storm had come as early as Tuesday, September 4, from the Washington Weather Bureau. By Friday, September 7, the storm was located "south of Louisiana . . . moving slowly northward. . . . Storm warnings are displayed from Pensacola to Galveston."[5] However, hurricane warnings and accurate predictions were only in an infancy stage. The warnings were not specific enough to urge Galvestonians of the approaching danger. The three weathermen traveling around the island had to beg people to move to higher ground. Isaac Cline lost his wife in the storm. Her remains, identified through her wedding ring, were not found until September 30. Fortunately, his three daughters survived. He and his brother were hospitalized. After the storm, Isaac Cline was transferred from Galveston the following year to New Orleans, where he worked for the Weather Bureau until he retired more than thirty years later.[6]

The Angelus rang at 6:00 p.m. at St. Mary's Cathedral the night of September 8. For Father James Kirwin, it sounded "not like a salutation of praise but a warning of death and destruction."[7] The Cathedral tower, built by Nicholas Clayton, swayed and the two-ton bell, which had just tolled, came crashing to the floor. The statue of Mary, Star of the Sea, placed at the Cathedral as a source of protection in prayer, threatened to crash through the ceiling of the cathedral rectory. Bishop Gallagher told Father Kirwin to tell clergymen waiting in the room to prepare for death. The statue of Mary, Star of the Sea, remained on the Cathedral Tower to continue her protection while many in the parish were invoking the Mother of Sorrows to comfort those in distress. The Celtic cross, inlaid with gold, perched on the spire of St. Patrick's Church, was 220 feet off the ground. It had just been completed twelve months earlier. It was the highest structure in Galveston and had withstood the wind all day. At 6:30 p.m. the steel-lined tower came crashing to the ground, taking part of the roof with it. When the storm quelled, all that remained were four small stained glass windows out of twenty-two, two altars, and a few statues.[8]

Sacred Heart Church, located east of the Cathedral, was staffed by the Jesuit Fathers of New Orleans. The priests had just imported fourteen stained glass windows from Munich for the Church. St. Mary's University adjoining it and the rooms of the University Club occupied one city block. They became a refuge for over four hundred people. In the end, the Church became a "complete wreck." The university building, with the exception of the new west wing, was badly damaged, and the rooms of the clubhouse were out in the street with the interior furnishings ruined, yet each of the four hundred people survived.[9]

> The Sacred Heart Church before the storm had in the right aisle, near the altar erected to the Mother of Christ, a large crucifix affixed to a pillar. Now all the sides of this church are demolished save where this pillar with the crucifix stands and the crucifix untouched. It is a sight not to be forgotten to see the image of the Man of Sorrows looking down upon the ruins everywhere.[10]

Immediately prior to the storm, some of the Dominican Sisters had just returned from a few relaxing days in Lampasas. Their community had bought an abandoned Methodist convent there. By Friday morning, Mother Pauline Gannon had gathered the Sisters, expressing her fears of the danger approaching. She advised the Sisters to collect their belongings and go to Houston, but there is no record that any Sisters actually did. Between four and five in the afternoon, the waters were rushing eight to ten feet into the convent. Windows and doors were blown in on the north side. The roof on the chapel blew off. The east end of the building was destroyed. Sister Augustine spent the night singing "Queen of the Waves."[11] The Dominican convent, occupying three-fourths of a block, contained Sisters and thirty children who were boarders. W. P. Stephens reported in the *Globe Democrat*:

> The statue of the Sacred Heart stood in the chapel. The windows blew in and exposed it to the fury of the storm. It was not clamped to the altar. In front of it the Sisters and their charge of children gathered. The Mother Superior was leading them in the singing of hymns. "As long as the statue stands," the mother said to them, "we are safe."
>
> The Sisters tell me that those who were present remained almost motionless, their eyes riveted on the statue, and although the walls and windows were demolished the band of sisters and children, seventy in number, were uninjured.[12]

That statue was later moved to the motherhouse grounds of St. Dominic Villa in Houston. The Dominican convent actually became a place of refuge and hospital for hundreds of homeless. After the storm passed, the Sisters evacuated the boarders from Galveston as soon as possible. They went to Bolivar and then Houston by train; their destination was Sacred Heart Convent on Pierce Street in Houston.

The Ursuline Convent and Academy with its adjacent buildings made up four blocks. The grounds were surrounded by a ten-foot brick wall, but after the storm, most was "a crumbled mass of bricks." No one was refused admittance that night. The school was supposed to have opened that Tuesday with forty-two boarding students from many parts of the state. In addition, there were forty Sisters.[13] The Ursuline Sisters, led by Mother Joseph Dallmer, were credited with saving thousands of lives. They stood at the windows, doors, and porches, pulling people off floating wreckage into the greater safety of the building. These Sisters gave the refugees whatever dry clothes they could.

It was not uncommon to find a man lying in a bed in a nun's cell clothed with a shirt and skirt given him by the Sisters. It was also recorded that four babies were born at Ursuline Convent the night of the storm. Each was immediately baptized.[14] Mother Mary Joseph saw to it that the large bell in the convent tower was kept tolling continuously so that those driven nearby through the wind and rain might recognize this site as a place of refuge. The convent could be seen as a place of last refuge as it was located so near to the water.[15]

The frame buildings collapsed at St. Mary's Infirmary. Most windows were shattered. Part of the roof in the new annex blew away. All day long streams of refugees continued. Destruction was total at the orphanage. Mother M. Mechtilde asked Zachary Scott, a medical student, to go down to the orphanage and bring news. When he came back he would not speak to the young Sisters who greeted him. He went straight to Mother Mechtilde to report that there was not a trace of the ten Sisters or the ninety-four orphans. Later it was learned that three boys survived and were brought to the infirmary.[16] The boys told the story of the rapidly rising water, which forced everyone to the second floor. The Sisters brought up the Blessed Sacrament from the first floor chapel. The Mother Superior, Sister Camillus, had dispatched the workman, Henry, for the clotheslines. The Sisters tied the children together and attached them to their cincture. When the three boys found themselves in water, they got hold of a large tree that had ropes attached. They remained on this tree until they were rescued. A doctor took them to the Bishop's residence. The remains of one Sister were found with nine children attached to her cincture. One Sister was holding a child in her arms. Since it was the feast of Mary's Nativity, the Sisters had all received Communion that morning, not knowing it would be their last.[17] The orphans who survived told the story of the Sisters tying four to six orphans to their waist with rope. They thought they would be strong enough to pull the small children to safety.[18]

At one point, St. Mary's Infirmary had over six hundred sick and injured men, women, and children.[19] The Reverend J. B. Gleissner of St. Joseph Church in Bryan, Texas, on the morning of September 8, had just finished celebrating Mass for the first time in six weeks; he had been recuperating from an illness. He returned to the Infirmary and saw the waves ten to fifteen feet high. He recorded his own memories. The Sisters remarked that they had never seen water get to their gate. Father Gleissner asked about the Blessed Sacrament in the Chapel. A young doctor brought it to him. The Sisters were pulling people who were floating by to safety. The Sisters kept praying for help. Father Gleissner asked the Sisters to sing. They responded with "Queen of the Waves." Every hour Father carried the Blessed Sacrament through the crowds, with people yelling, "Lord, save us else we perish." Part of the wall crashed in. The roof of the building was partly destroyed, but then the water began to recede. While the patients wanted water, there was none to drink until it arrived from Beaumont and Houston, in addition to bread.[20] Between 10:00 and 11:00 p.m. the worst of the storm had passed. The water levels began to fall. The areas near the beach and the center of the island drained more slowly than those areas in the north. The winds continued to blow water on the shores. The debris prevented the water from receding rapidly.[21]

The job of gathering the dead bodies and carrying them out to sea was so abhorrent that recruits had to be gathered at bayonet point and given whiskey. As Father Kirwin stated: "It soon became so that the men could not handle those bodies without stimulants. . . . I am a strong temperate man . . . but I went to the men who were handling those bodies, and I gave them whiskey."[22] When the bodies floated back to shore, cremation was the only solution.[23] Clara Barton would personally come to Galveston with the Red Cross to supervise the rehabilitation efforts.[24] Dr. Wallace Shaw from Houston pointed out the dire need for water when he related that there were two hundred people at St. Mary's Infirmary without water. They had been making coffee with saltwater, which was all they had to drink.[25]

Not long after the storm Bishop Gallagher issued an official estimate of losses to the Catholic Church on the island. More than a thousand lives were lost. Eight thousand were homeless. Three churches were totally destroyed: St. Patrick's, St. Joseph's, and Sacred Heart, at an estimated cost of $361,000. The damage to St. Mary's Infirmary was estimated at $80,000, and the total loss of the orphanage property was $45,000. Bishop Gallagher purchased property on Fortieth and Q Streets. The orphans moved into a large frame house. Nicholas Clayton drew up architectural plans for a brick building. The cornerstone was laid by Bishop Gallagher on the first anniversary of the storm. In December 1901, ten Sisters and ninety orphans moved into their new home. Temporary immediate repairs were made to St. Mary's Infirmary. The cornerstone for a new convent and chapel at St. Mary's Infirmary was laid by Bishop Gallagher on April 9, 1901. The postulants who had been invested with the habit in Houston on September 27, 1900, by Bishop Gallagher were able to return to Galveston when the convent was complete.[26]

Father Kirwin believed that the value of property owned by the Catholic Church in Galveston had been cut in half, from one million to half a million dollars, in the matter of a few hours. Bishop Gallagher did receive $195,000 in contributions to repair and rebuild the churches that had been damaged and destroyed.[27] He further stated that of the 15,000 Catholics living on the island, one thousand had lost their lives and one thousand left to seek their livelihood in other places. He pointed out that after the storm people were in a state of numbness. He referred to a man looking for the remains of his wife. Every time a body was found, he would open the mouth to look at the teeth. When he realized the corpse was not the remains of his wife, he went back to work "as if nothing had happened." As he recalled, "You will hear people talk without emotion of the loss of those nearest to them. We are in that condition that we cannot feel."[28]

Soon after the disastrous storm, the citizens promised to return and rebuild. They wished to resume their place as the great port of the Gulf.[29] In order to do that, the city would have to be safe. Thus, the people of Galveston decided to build a seawall. While the idea of a seawall had been talked about by local businessmen in 1886, it was considered far too expensive and difficult to implement.[30] Father James Kirwin was asked to offer the prayer for the laying of the cornerstone of the new seawall in 1902 and again in 1905 as monuments were raised, marking its completion.[31] The process of raising the city began with the addition of levees around one small section of the city at a time. Any structure in an area forty blocks long and two to twenty blocks wide had to be elevated. These additions were tested when hurricanes struck in 1909 and then again in 1915. In each case, repairs were made to the seawall. The loss of life was considerably less than in 1900.[32]

The damage from the 1900 storm was not confined to Galveston.[33] St. Joseph's Parish in Houston, erected in 1880 by Bishop Dubuis, was destroyed. The only thing saved from the original frame structure was a statue of the Sacred Heart. It was St. Joseph's Church that rang its church bell to warn people of the oncoming storm. That bell, originally cast for the old St. Vincent de Paul church in 1843, was given to Annunciation when St. Vincent's closed in 1878. Annunciation gave it to St. Joseph in 1881. When the bell was found in the ruins of St. Joseph Church after the storm, it was brought back to Annunciation and burnished for the Diamond Jubilee of the parish. It was then put on display in the vestibule of the church.[34] Unfortunately, Father Hennessy witnessed the fall of the cross and the tower of Annunciation Church as a result of the storm.[35]

St. Joseph on the Brazos in Brazoria found that its Church was demolished during the 1900 storm. Father Joseph P. Keany was drowned in the Velasco Hotel. He was the only priest lost in the 1900 storm. For thirteen years the people were served through Mass celebrated in homes by missionary priests. In 1913, the church was rebuilt again. This parish is actually older than the Diocese of Galveston.[36]

Since 1971, hurricanes have been classified based on a scale developed by Herbert Safir, an engineer, and Robert Simpson, who had previously served as director of the National Hurricane Center. The scale determines the strength of the storm using wind speed, barometric pressure, and storm surge. According to this scale, the storm that hit Galveston was probably a category four, with the wind speed between 131 and 155 miles per hour, the barometric pressure between 27.17 and 27.88, and the storm surge thirteen to eighteen feet. All four bridges to the mainland were washed away, and also the telegraph, telephone, and electrical lines. The only way in was by boat. Of the nearly 38,000 inhabitants,[37] in the end, the storm would take the lives of six thousand, the largest number of disaster fatalities in American history.[38] Economically, the storm cost Galveston between twenty and thirty million dollars.[39]

Survivors would recount the noise of the wind and rising waters for decades to come, undoubtedly etched in their memories forever.

Figure 9. Sacred Heart Church, Galveston, pre-1900. Courtesy of Rosenberg Library.

Figure 10. Remains of Sacred Heart Church after the 1900 storm. Courtesy of Rosenberg Library, Galveston, Texas

Figure 11. Sacred Heart Church rebuilt after 1900 storm; design of dome credited to Nicholas Clayton.

Figure 12. St. Mary's Orphanage on the Beach, Galveston, Texas, 1897. Courtesy of The Archives of the Congregation of the Sisters of Charity of the Incarnate Word, Houston, Texas. Not to be reproduced without the proper authorization of the Archives

Figure 13. St. Mary's Orphanage. Rebuilt Sisters of Charity of the Incarnate Word on steps of orphanage, Galveston, 1901. Courtesy of The Archives of the Congregation of the Sisters of Charity of the Incarnate Word, Houston, Texas. Not to be reproduced without the proper authorization of the Archives.

Figure 14. St. Patrick's Church, Galveston, redesigned by Nicholas Clayton after 1900 storm; cornerstone laid, 1902.

❧ 8 ❧

Founding Years of
St. Mary's Seminary[1]

The 1900 storm in no way dampened Bishop Gallagher's interest in spreading the word of God through seminary training, a dream he had shared with his people since 1883. This is evident almost immediately on his taking up the episcopate. He issued a letter to the priests and general populace on December 17, 1883, stating:

Rev. and Dear Sir:

Although the Statutes of this Diocese prescribe that a collection shall be taken up in every Church on Christmas and Easter for the purpose of defraying the expenses of educating young men for the Holy Ministry, and supplying the Diocese with good priests, I cannot let this occasion pass without calling your attention to the fact that, in the past, the Diocesan collections for the Seminary have not been at all sufficient to meet these wants of the Diocese; and, therefore, I earnestly request you to make it known to your people their duty in this regard, and to impress them with the importance of contributing generously in the collections of Christmas and Easter. Please announce this collection the Sunday before the Feast, and may you and those under your charge participate in the real joys of Christmas in the sincere wish of

Your Spiritual Father in Christ,
N. A. Gallagher
Bishop Administrator of Galveston[2]

Bishop Gallagher's zeal to obtain seminarians certainly was an abiding goal for him. In his Lenten letter for the year 1892, he points out that "the Easter collection is for the wants of the Dioceses, and expenses of the Bishop." He goes on to relate that since this year was his tenth in his episcopate, he was required to make his *Ad Limina Apostolorum* visitation to the Holy Father, conveying the conditions of the diocese. At that time, this visitation was made every three to ten years, depending on the distance in travel. The Bishop hoped that the collection would provide "sufficient means to defray the expenses of my trip to Rome."[3]

The *Diary of Bishop Gallagher* reveals that his European voyage included vocation efforts, for he stopped at the seminary at Maynooth in Ireland on June 8, 1892, and likewise made several visitations in Ireland: Belfast, Dublin, and Cork on the way back. The Bishop managed to spend some time in France, Germany, Belgium, and Great Britain in addition to Ireland and Italy. His actual audience with the Pontiff, Leo XIII, took place on July 4, 1892.[4]

Bishop Gallagher believed that every diocese should have its own seminary. If that was not possible, a regional seminary should be established. The Bishop had as one of his primary goals the establishment of a seminary, but he was not the first to take on this challenging task. Father Victor Gury established a seminary in Frelsburg as early as 1854.[5] He was assisted by Father Peter Tarrillian. St. Mary's University on the island educated men for the priesthood with the assistance of Father Louis Claude Marie Chambodut. There were also temporary seminaries in Seguin conducted by the Society of Jesus from Mexico and at St. Mary's in Victoria.[6]

Bishop Gallagher's dream was to build a seminary for the entire south. The records of Monsignor Joseph Valente stated that the Bishop expressed this desire at an annual retreat of the priests and asked for their support.[7] When the seminaries were closed in Victoria and New Orleans, no seminary existed south of the Mason-Dixon Line. St. Mary's Seminary actually became the oldest Catholic theology school in the South by way of continued existence. The wish moved to reality when George Pendarvis, an attorney from Houston, in May 1901, brought to the attention of the Bishop that the Sylvan Beach Hotel was up for sale. It was located in La Porte, on the northwest corner of Trinity Bay.[8]

Monsignor James Vanderholt described the hotel in this way:

> The hotel was really a five story structure with a lookout atop. It stood
> high enough to afford a basement. The first two stories had verandas
> all around, but the third only on the East and South side on account
> of the water tank and an octagon tower on the Northeast corner.
> Water was supplied by a hydraulic ram from a spouting artesian
> well somewhat to the southwest of the hotel and spilling into a gully
> further away. The gully in the ground was used as a harbor grounds,
> surrounding the hotel which was landscaped with flower gardens,
> spacious barn with stables, and the gully dredged to deep water. The
> hotel had its own pier, twelve hundred feet long.[9]

Monsignor Vanderholt believed the hotel was one that had all the conveniences of a resort "inside and out." However, the toilets were outside
the main building. Everything was lighted by carbide gas lights. Since
there was no running water, each room had a basin, pitcher, and jar.
Bearing in mind the notion of a resort, the open woods and prairies
provided horseback and buggy rides in addition to hunting. The bay
spread out from the Battle Ground to Anahuac and Galveston, providing opportunity for boating and fishing. The one drawback seen
at the time of the sale was the remoteness from Houston, and the rail
depot was located a mile away from the town. Further, the storm of
1900 eliminated all water facilities and the beach. Rain damaged the
hotel extensively. However, Bishop Gallagher bought the Sylvan Beach
property for $10,000.[10]

The *Galveston Tribune* saw the seminary as a means of teaching the
seminarians in the American way, rather than through ethnic customs
imposed by foreign priests. Since there were no parochial high schools,
the seminary provided education for boys for the priesthood as well as
schooling from fifth grade up. By the 1901/2 school year, thirty boys
were housed there, beginning with fifth grade and including six seminarians in addition to the faculty, sisters, and caretaker. Thus, 1901 was
the official year of the opening of the seminary in La Porte. It was not
uncommon to find an ad in a local newspaper advertising this opportunity for schooling for young male students:

St. Mary's Seminary, La Porte, Texas

Select Boarding School for Young Men and Boys under supervision of the Right Reverend Bishop of Galveston and Direction of the Fathers of St. Basil

Thoroughly complete courses in Theology, Philosophy, Academics, Commercial and Preparatory Work. Beautifully situated on high spacious ground, gently sloping to join the beach of Galveston Bay, liberally supplied with pure artesian water, ever refreshed by never failing salt water breezes, the institution is giving every assurance of health and favorable conditions for study on hottest of days. Next session commences September 8. Apply.

Very Reverend President[11]

It was further not uncommon for Bishop Gallagher to travel to find seminarians for the Galveston diocese. He returned from such travels, which had him from Milwaukee to Boston, in late October 1904. The Bishop visited all of the seminaries, extending an invitation to the men to come to Texas. Bishop Gallagher at that time was interested in young Americans of Polish and Bohemian descent because of the increasing number of immigrants of these nationalities moving into Texas. He wished to have priests to "minister to their religious wants and at the same time Americanize the newcomers."[12] In 1904, it was too early to determine the success of such travels of Bishop Gallagher.

The original faculty members were Basilians. These included Father James Player, CSB, a native of England who was ordained three years before he became Superior in La Porte; Father Vincent Donnelly, CSB, from New York City, known as an eloquent preacher, who served as treasurer;[13] Father James Plomer, CSB, a native of England who served the entire eleven years the Basilians were at the seminary and who taught English, History, Math, Languages, and Science. Father Edward J. O'Neill, CSB, a native of Canada, taught English. Three Dominican Sisters took care of the domestic affairs and Mr. Patrick Fitzgerald, known as Mr. Fitz, a Civil War veteran, was the caretaker. On rainy evenings, since there were no recreational facilities except dominoes, table games, and ping-pong, Mr. Fitz would entertain the seminarians with "yarn upon yarn" regarding Vicksburg, Dick Dowling, and fighting the Indians. An important part of the seminary was the barn or liberty stable. It housed the fast-trotting black mare "Maude," the buggy, milk cows, and chickens, all under the domain of Mr. Fitz.[14]

As the attendance at the seminary began to grow, Mr. Pickett, CSB, arrived and became Prefect of Discipline. Originally, the Basilian came as a student teacher, but after ordination in 1905, he returned to La Porte. Many of the new students came from Europe as a result of the recruiting efforts of Father John Weimer, the Vicar General. The first seminarian ordained by Bishop Gallagher was A. G. Grattan from Canada. Prior to the advent of St. Mary's Seminary, Bishop Gallagher had sent his men to Cincinnati, Baltimore, or Niagara among other places. Each seminarian spent a few months on his Cathedral staff where the Bishop personally supervised him. This responsibility was turned over to the seminary when it opened.[15]

Sporting activities were a regular outlet for the seminarians. The young men at the seminary played baseball against the students of a Houston high school only to discover that the high school students played a better game.[16] Bishop Gallagher was frequently on hand for a number of seminary events, but especially commencement, during which he took an active role.[17] Undoubtedly, the Bishop had a role in obtaining scholarships for students who did not have the funds. The *Houston Post* recorded that another scholarship had been obtained for St. Mary's Seminary in La Porte, covering tuition, room, and board for ten months, valued at $250.[18]

The following years brought an increase in enrollment. Necessary accommodations followed. The attic was turned into sleeping quarters. Bishop Gallagher chose to build a fireproof building for the lay students and maintain the wood building for the seminarians and professors. Nicholas Clayton of Galveston was chosen as the architect. He was nationally known for his work on the Bishop's Palace and Ursuline Convent. This new cement building relieved the student squeeze. A huge dedication was planned for this building on March 25, 1908. Trainloads of visitors came from Houston and Galveston.[19]

Other Basilians served at the seminary while its enrollment increased. Eventually though, the Basilians would have to withdraw. They had opened St. Basil's School in Waco in 1899, St. Thomas High School in Houston in 1900, and, at the request of Bishop Gallagher, St. Mary's Seminary in La Porte. In 1911, on June 15, the Basilian provincial wrote Bishop Gallagher stating they would have to withdraw from their commitment in La Porte as they were overextended.[20] This decision by the Basilians enabled Bishop Gallagher to staff the seminary with diocesan clergy, a desire he had long possessed. As he wrote to each priest in the diocese on July 25, 1911,

> The withdrawal of the Basilian Fathers from the Seminary enabled me to realize my long cherished desire to have the Diocesan Seminary conducted by the priests of the Diocese. At a meeting of the Diocesan Consultors on July 25, the following appointments were made:
>
> Very Fr. James Kirwin, President,
> Very Fr. J. A. Pelnar, Vice-President,
> Fr. Jerome Rapp, Treasurer,
> Fr. John O'Leary, Director of Studies.
>
> At some personal sacrifice these Priests go to the Seminary to conduct it, with one object in view, the success of native vocations to God's holy priesthood; and the thorough preparation of the young men for their great work. We appeal to you to help them. Owing to present conditions it will be impossible for the Faculty to do the personal soliciting of students, that should be done, and we ask you to seek out good students, whether for the Priesthood, the learned Professions, or commercial life, and encourage them to go to La Porte, for the Session opening September 12, 1911.[21]

Each of these priests had other commitments within the diocese, yet they provided exemplary service to the seminarians. The first ordination under the new faculty was on Christmas Eve, 1911.[22] During that year there were seventy-five college students, that is, those in grade and high school, in addition to fifteen seminarians, who were enrolled in the seven years of theology and philosophy courses.

Bishop Gallagher not only traveled to other parts of the United States looking for seminarians, he also corresponded with the rectors of European seminaries, including the following from Ireland:

February 9, 1913
Very Rev. Brosnan, Prest.
St. Brendan's Seminary
Killarney, Ireland

Dear. Very Reverend Father:

Your kind letter to Very Rev. J. M. Kirwin, V. G. Prest. of our Diocesan Seminary at La Porte, Texas, was handed to me to read, and I am
more than pleased that we can hope to obtain some good subjects for
the Holy Priesthood from your Seminary of St. Brendan's.

Please let us know when you have some ready for Philosophy [and]
we will be glad to have them. If necessary we will admit them free to
our Seminary; but it is presumed they will pay their passage over and
their own personal expenses here [viz.] for clothes, books, etc.

Appreciating your kind consideration
I remain
Yours sincerely in Christ
N. A. Gallagher
Bp. Of Galv.[23]

The 1913/14 school year witnessed the second major construction
project: the building of a gym by Louis A. Adoue in honor of his father,
the late B. Adoue of Galveston. Although the family was not Catholic,
they were good friends of Bishop Gallagher and Father Kirwin. It was
constructed of buff brick, had two handball courts at each end of the
building, and included rooms for hobbies and study. Three thousand
people came to the dedication. A gold medal was presented to Mr. Adoue
from Pope Pius X. This gift was arranged through the bishop's ad limina
visit.[24]

In February 1914, the students were visited by Archbishop Jeremiah
Harty, the first American archbishop of the Philippines. He told many
stories of poorly financed and understaffed clergy and the need for
native vocations. Not long after the visit, Archbishop Harty was transferred to Omaha, Nebraska, where he helped Father Flanagan begin
Boy's Town.[25]

Bishop Gallagher's dream of one seminary for Texas or even the South
was never to be realized. The Oblates opened a seminary in San Anto-

nio two years after St. Mary's opened. The Bexar County School took in seminarians. The Sisters of Divine Providence opened a seminary in Castroville for seminarians from Mexico who were being expelled by the government. It lasted only as long as the persecution. The diocese of San Antonio opened its seminary in 1915.[26]

The 1915 hurricane was the worst since 1900. People came from the surrounding area for shelter. The seminary buildings in La Porte were "literally soaked." Books were damaged, bedding was ruined, and ceiling plaster loosened and fell. The barn was half submerged, the pier was completely gone, and drowned animals floated all over. No one was seriously hurt.[27]

The building established in 1907 was then referred to as the high school building. Having survived the hurricane, it was later known as the college or philosophy building. It housed the chapel, which had been redecorated in 1916 by M. Brazanga, a German artist. This chapel's sanctuary was carpeted and had memorial windows of art and cathedral glass. In that same year, 1916, electricity was first installed in the building.[28]

At the end of each school year, Bishop Gallagher combined graduation, awards, First Communion, and Confirmation. A gold medal was awarded each year for conduct.[29]

When the United States entered World War I in 1917, many of the lay alumni entered the service. Father Marius Chataignon was the only ordained alumnus who served overseas in the war. Since patriotism was high in the seminary, a military unit of seminarians and mature students was formed. Colonel Andrew Jackson Houston, son of Sam Houston and future US senator from Texas, had wooden rifles made for each seminarian in the military unit. They drilled twice a week and marched in the Armistice Day parade. Father Kirwin had gone to the Mexican border with General Pershing in 1915 when Pershing was pursuing Pancho Villa. Pershing asked him to serve overseas. As mentioned earlier, Father Kirwin traveled as far as New York but then returned to the Diocese due to the fragile health of Bishop Gallagher.[30]

Bishop Gallagher had ordained to the deaconate John Kearns from Ireland and Max Budnik from Round Rock, Texas, in the Cathedral rectory. They were ordained to the priesthood in the Cathedral on December 23, 1917, by the seventy-two-year-old bishop. They were his last ordinations.[31]

Figure 15. St. Mary's Seminary, 1901, La Porte. Courtesy of the Archives of Galveston-Houston.

Figure 16. St. Mary's Seminary altar, La Porte. Courtesy of Catholic Archives of Texas, Austin, Texas.

Figure 17. St. Mary's Seminary First Class, La Porte. Courtesy of Catholic Archives of Texas, Austin, Texas.

❧ 9 ❧

Ethnic Challenges in the Early Twentieth Century

During his long tenure as ordinary of the diocese of Galveston, Bishop Gallagher had met multiple challenges. One was the role of the foreign born within the local church. Bishop Nicholas Gallagher served as shepherd of the sprawling Diocese of Galveston at a time when immigration was at its peak. Individuals were flocking to this country from many varied cultures. They wished to maintain those cultural practices and languages in this new land. It was overwhelmingly difficult for one bishop to respond to the desires of every ethnic group.

James A. McMaster, the editor of the *Freeman's Journal*, provided a taste of what Bishop Nicholas Gallagher might expect within the Diocese of Galveston. The *Journal* was a semiweekly independent Catholic paper that McMaster had purchased from John Hughes, the Bishop of New York, in 1848.[1] In writing to Bishop Gallagher in January 1882, the editor pointed out that he had "a most lively interest in the future of the Catholic Church in Texas."[2] McMaster called the new bishop's attention to the fact that there were a number of French priests in the Galveston diocese. The editor recommended to Bishop Gallagher that he maintain Reverend Theodore Buffard as the Vicar General until he found reason for a change. "In that way you will show the French clergy that you are their friend, as well as their spiritual father." One of Bishop Gallagher's greatest difficulties would be in working with German priests. A number of German immigrants had moved into the Diocese of Galveston in recent years. Referring to the situation of Bishop Hughes with the German population in New York, McMaster wrote, "You can never have decent German priests till you have a true and good German Vicar." He recommended to the Bishop that he appoint "a good, sensible, German priest," as vicar. "Otherwise, that part of your flock will go to the devil."[3]

While McMaster expressed caution in dealing with the German population of priests in the Galveston diocese, the staunchness of the lay population of German descent was most notable. A case in point is the group that established itself in and around Plantersville, making themselves members of the parish, the Church of the Nativity of Mary. While very firm in the practice of their faith, they were equally firm in desiring a German priest, which created the ethnic tension so common during this particular era.

Settlement of Immigrants from Russia

The term *Russian Germans* is unfamiliar to many. Actually, the ancestors of this group of people had been invited in 1762 by the German-born monarch Catherine the Great to migrate to Russia. Large stretches of fertile land in the south and east had not been cultivated. Only nomads and robbers traveled through the region. They were to bring western culture and industry to Russia.[4] Unfortunately, very little of the "superior husbandry" of the Germans became general practice among the Russian peasants.[5] A second group of Germans migrated to Russia beginning in 1803 under Czar Alexander I. These Germans settled around the Black Sea city of Odessa and became a buffer against the Turks. They were attempting to escape a series of wars in Europe, including the Seven Years' War, the Napoleonic Wars, and the French Wars of Succession. This group considered themselves more advanced than the Russian peasants. The government isolated them in separate villages. They migrated again, to North and South America. They remained strongly religious, whether it was Catholic or Protestant.[6] Catherine had promised these immigrants the free exercise of their religion by her manifesto of July 22, 1763. They are often referred to as Ukrainian Germans. In 1779 Catherine invited Jesuits from Western Europe to come work in

Russia as they were banned in Europe. The Diocese of Tiraspol was created in 1850. However, there was an anti-Catholic sentiment within the Russian government that outlived Catherine.[7]

When plantation owners lost slaves after the Civil War, they began to look for workers. It is commonly thought that the Plantersville Russian-German settlement came about when the schoolmaster, Kasimer Kiefel recruited seven families to work on what was then the Baker plantation, known as "the Cedars." In fact, Kasimer Kiefel made several trips to Russia as a recruiter. It is also possible that St. Mary's pastor, Father Joseph Klein, not only helped these families settle in Plantersville but also may have made a recruiting trip to Russia himself.[8]

When the Germans from Russia arrived in Texas, the evidence that they had been away from their own homeland could easily be seen. They differed from other Germans with their heavy coats, fur hats, and clumsy boots. Their handwriting was quite different from that of the better educated German immigrants who had arrived in Texas. The distinctive iron crosses in the Catholic cemeteries that are usually found in Russian German cemeteries became a familiar site, especially in Plantersville, where some of these Russian Germans settled.[9]

Father Joseph Klein, having completed his education at St. Meinrad's Seminary in Indiana, was ordained in Indianapolis, Indiana, by Bishop F. S. Chatard, DD, for the Diocese of Galveston. Father Klein was initially stationed at St. Patrick's in Galveston in January 1894, and then transferred in July to Plantersville.[10] There he was instructed by Bishop Nicholas Gallagher to buy ten acres of land three miles north of Plantersville[11] to build St. Mary's Catholic Church, officially known as the Church of the Nativity of Mary. The Church was built for approximately $1,700 by the seventy families who had settled in the area, most of whom were Russian Germans, as well as some Poles.[12] Land for this Church was bought from the Baker family, who owned a large plantation. According to the Grimes County records, a tract of ten acres was purchased for $30 from the estate of Jack Baker. This purchase was made on March 5, 1894.[13] Midnight Mass was celebrated in the Church December 31, 1900. Father Klein remained pastor there for thirteen years.[14]

The little mission Church soon was not large enough to accommodate the rapidly growing number of parishioners. This lack of space was complicated by the difference in language groups, for some knew German and some knew Polish. Thus, the sermon was first given in Polish, so the Polish people entered. Then the same sermon was given in German, so the Germans entered. Those who did not understand either stayed in their places to assure a seat during Mass, which followed the two sermons. At one time the crowd was so great, the floor fell in. This little Church was torn down and rebuilt as a school for Catholic children. Father Klein did the teaching until he could procure the services of teachers.[15] Father Klein left St. Mary's Church in 1907. He was succeeded by several other priests, including Father Jacob Schneitzer. Father George Wilhelm became pastor in 1908 and remained until 1910. During this time the congregation was divided. St. Joseph Church was founded in Stoneham for the Polish-speaking population and was dedicated by Bishop Gallagher in 1910.[16]

Father Wilhelm was succeeded by Father Marcus Dombroski in 1910; he served each church and spoke Polish, German, and English sufficiently enough to be understood. Father Charles Weisneroski was appointed the next pastor on September 27, 1911. However, the congregation was not willing to accept Father Weisneroski since he was not German, even though he spoke German. Bishop Gallagher, in reporting back to a parishioner on August 20, 1911, wrote:

Dear Sir:

Your letter of August 16 was duly received and I am pained to see how little regard you have for your Pastor, as to threaten to take him before the civil court. You have not stated anything against him, and as you have stated no charge against him, I cannot consider your request for me to send a priest up there to investigate. You do not seem to know how to treat a priest in a Christian manner and I will not allow a priest to live at Plantersville until you learn to respect him.

Yours truly,
Nicholas A Gallagher,
Bishop of Galveston[17]

In writing to Father Weisneroski, November 9, 1911, Bishop Gallagher stated:

Rev. Father Weisneroski:

Your letter of the third was duly received informing me that the people of Plantersville are not willing to go to Church, unless I send them a German priest. Therefore, you may discontinue going to Plantersville. However, you should attend urgent sick-calls there, as long as there is no other priest there to attend them.

Rev. Father Litwora is so feeble that he cannot attend to the Parish of Anderson. Therefore, I have ordered him to go to St. Joseph's Infirmary, Houston next week. After he leaves Anderson, I wish you to attend sick-calls there, until I make other arrangements.

Wishing you the blessing of God.
I remain
Yours faithfully in Christ
N. A. Gallagher
Bishop of Galveston[18]

Father Weisneroski, in reporting to Bishop Gallagher, January 25, 1912, stated that he was told he had no right to enter "their" church. Bishop Gallagher replied that Father Weisneroski was not obliged to give services in the church in Plantersville, but those parishioners who wished to go to St. Joseph in Stoneham could do so. In a letter of February 7, 1912, Bishop Gallagher informed the people of Plantersville that due to their conduct, they were not worthy of having a priest living in their midst. He also stated that he believed the "good Catholics of Plantersville do not approve the conduct of those who are opposing the Pastor." The 125th Anniversary Edition of the Diocese of Galveston-Houston does mention that Father J. B. Gleissner of Bryan "was appointed to attend to the needs of the faithful in both Churches briefly."[19] In a letter of July 29, 1912, the congregation of Plantersville apologized for the conduct of some members of the parish. They asked for a German priest, and further, that land might be bought from the church to build a school.

Plantersville, Texas
July 29, 1912
The Rt. Rev. Bishop Gallagher,
Galveston, Texas

We the undersigned newly elected trustees of the Congregation of Plantersville beg your Rt. Reverend Bishop's decision in the subsequent matter. We have succeeded through our election of our School district to tax our district and obtain bonds to build a new School, on or near the present site of the old School. Therefore the congregation begs of the Rt. Rev. Bishop to buy 2 ½ acres of ground of the NW Corner of the Church property as the present ½ acres is not sufficient for the new $3,000 building and the State requires from three to five acres to be deeded to the County School authorities. We maintain the School, as near to a parochial School as we can without interfering with the laws of the State and the whole enrollment consists of Catholic children and we employ only three Catholic teachers if possible. Therefore we beg of the Rt. Rev. Bishop to let us know at his convenience if he will grant us the favor. Furthermore we ask of the Rt. Rev. Bishop to please send to our Congregation a German priest. We humbly beg for forgiveness for the past insulting letters the former trustees have sent to the Bishop. It was through *weakness* on their part and the majority of the congregation was ignorant of what the trustees wrote, with the exception of a few.

The Church has been fully repaired of the damage done by the storm and is strengthened with iron rods and put in first class condition again. The whole congregation promises you Rt. Rev. Bishop to meet all the demands, whatever they may be, as far as we are able, to obtain a priest. We beg to remain your humble servants.[20]

The letter is signed by two trustees. A third was absent.

Bishop Gallagher, in a letter of August 6, 1912, responded that he was not interested in selling church property for a school, and they would not receive a German priest until they respected the priest they had.

Dear Sirs:

Your letter of July 29, was duly received, and in reply I wish to say that I will not sell any of the Church property for a Public School. As to sending you a German Priest, that I will consider when you recognize my authority as Bishop, and accept the priest I have appointed in charge of Plantersville, Rev. C. Weisneroski, who speaks the German language fluently, and can minister to all your spiritual wants. If you claim the right to accept, or not, the priest who is appointed by the Bishop, it will be a long time before you will have a resident priest. You must learn to respect your Bishop and Pastor. A Congregation which will not allow the priest in charge, to officiate in the church, disregards the authority of the Bishop, and disrespects their Pastor.

Yours Very Truly,
+ N. A. Gallagher
Bishop of Galveston[21]

Father George Apel replaced Father Weisneroski in 1913 and served as pastor until 1917.[22]

Most of the church was destroyed by fire in 1917. Bishop Gallagher had to deal with difficulties not only of culture but also of location as the residents of Dobbin expressed their wish that the church be rebuilt there.

Dobbin, Texas, July 11, 1917
Right Rev. N. A. Gallagher
Galveston, Texas

Right Rev. and Dear bishop,

We the undersigned Citizens of Dobbin and vicinity, having in mind the rebuilding of St. Mary's Catholic Church of Plantersville Texas, which was burned a few weeks ago, do respectfully beg leave to lay before you the vast advantages this place has for a Catholic church, and since it has become necessary to build a new church in this part of the country, we being only six miles east of the old city and in the same parish being located in a good undeveloped farming country, with two railroads, good first class gravel highways leading to all the best markets of the country and with other and more important natural advantages which lend to secure a wide and more prosperous future for a Catholic parish, giving more room for better and more substantial agricultural developments which is the life and future of our church and people.

With these facts and many more which we hope to set forth in a petition to your Reverence in a few days asking that St. Mary's Church be built this time where it will have a better outlet with double the territory and only six miles from the old church site, and nine miles from the Catholic church at Stoneham.

We have in a radius of three miles of Dobbin about thirty Catholic families already which gives us ample reason for asking to have the church built there.

Thanking you in advance for your careful consideration in this matter, we are respectfully yours.[23]

Father Apel, who had been serving in the parish since 1913, presented his own difficulties to the Bishop from the Dobbin community of parishioners.

July 22, 1917
Right Rev. Bishop N. A. Gallagher, DD.
Galveston, Texas

Your Grace!

Here with I am returning the petitions as you have requested. Plantersville, however, is at rebellion. We had a meeting this morning, the majority of ours is in favor of rebuilding the church at this old place. I am also in favor for the following reasons: priest house and outside buildings are there, graveyard, etc. is there. And the location 2 miles east is not favorable at all, as I believe. . . . There are about 15 families opposed to me and everything else. . . . They and some others believe to have a right to dominate the priest and slander him at liberty. On the west side of the church are twenty-two families about ten within about 1–2 miles east of the church. The majority will start tomorrow Monday in order to clean up the place and start work soon. The idea is to build a church 36 × 72 with a sanctuary 16 × 18 as figured the building would be erected and paid for, without finishing inside, at present. Now I leave it to you to decide if that church shall be built or if a site at Dobbin shall be selected. But I am also willing to resign, as my health is perhaps not strong enough to resist the stubborn people, . . .

If your Grace should decide to accept my resignation, I am not opposed to accept Lott. I am proud of it, to have the mission in a good shape except Plantersville as I am on the missions, and will be back at Plantersville Tuesday. I hope to find your letter.

I am very respectfully in the Sacred Heart.
Father Apel[24]

Father Apel stayed on as pastor until 1924. Within four months of the fire, the parishioners had rebuilt the Church at Plantersville. More recently, Father Ed Kucera, the current pastor, has expanded and restored this edifice to its original beauty as one of the painted churches of Texas.[25]

St. Mary's in Plantersville was not the only German parish desiring a specific priest for pastor. The members of the congregation of St. Roch in Mentz asked for a residing priest, and this time, specifically Father George Apel, who had already agreed to come there.

Mentz, Texas
Colorado Co., Texas
October 23, 1912

R. Rev. Bishop Gallagher:

We, the undersigned patrons of St. Roch' Parish beg Your Lordship again for a residing priest at our church.

Rev. Father George Apel at Marlin had written a letter to us, stating that he would be willing to accept the position here if Your Lordship would kindly favor this. We would do our utmost to have Rev. Father Apel here for our priest, as he has been here before and knows the Parish well, so we would be very glad to have Father Apel here.

Hope Your Lordship will kindly accept our petition, we sign our names and remain,

Yours very respectfully,
Obedient servants.[26]

The letter was signed by forty-one parishioners. According to the Historical Sketch of the Parish in 1920, Father Apel did serve a second time in the parish, arriving in 1912 and staying until June 1913.[27]

Catholic education was also an important element for these German communities. The Sisters of Divine Providence had staffed a Catho-

lic school in Bernardo, Texas, and Mentz since 1872. Bishop Gallagher
wrote the Superior of the Divine Providence Sisters, Mother Florence,
advising that the Sisters be withdrawn from Bernardo Prairie as there
was not opportunity for daily Mass and Communion. The Sisters left in
the spring of 1912.[28] It must be recalled this was at a time when there
was no resident priest. This school had eighty-five students in 1887–88
yet thirty-five in 1911–12. A parishioner representing the Catholic community in Mentz wrote Bishop Gallagher on July 20, 1912, requesting
the return of the "beloved Sisters" to the Bernardo School.[29] St. Roch's
school was closed in 1913–14 but reopened from 1914 to 1916. It was
closed due to the small Catholic population in June, 1916.[30] This school
had seventy-three students in attendance in 1905–6 yet twenty-five
students in attendance in 1915–16. These schools were replaced by a
public school and became part of the Columbus Independent School
District.[31]

The German population was not singular in its desire for a priest of
its own nationality. The Polish settlement in Chappell Hill was equally
as vigorous in pursuit of a Polish priest. The community in Chappell
Hill originally attended Mass in Brenham. When Reverend J. Grabinger,
the pastor in Brenham, announced in 1888 that Chappell Hill needed
a church, the Catholics from that area assumed that a committee of
six people would assist Father Grabinger in collecting funds for it. The
parishioners explained the use of the committee by pointing out that
they had heard of the faithlessness of some priests up north. They said
this committee could "protect the priest in a case of some money difficulty and secondly to infuse more confidence and so induce to a greater
liberality." However, Father Grabinger would have nothing to do with
the elected committee. The committee went to Galveston to present
plans and a financial statement to Bishop Gallagher. The plans were
"perfected and approved by him." Bishop Gallagher further promised
that a Polish priest would visit the parish once or twice a year. In the
end $720.60 had to be borrowed. This committee believed that if the
pastor had worked with the committee, the entire cost of the church
would have been collected with no need for borrowing.[32] Father Laski
came to work with the congregation in Chappell Hill, replacing Father
Grabinger. Bishop Gallagher called forth Father Laski to bless the new
church. According to a parishioner, "At first, he [Father Laski] seemed to

try to do right with our people but this did not last long." Father Laski was from Russia. The community in Chappell Hill had been ruled by Germans but not Russians. According to these Poles, Father Laski saw them as ignorant Catholics.[33] Bishop Gallagher responded in a succinct fashion to the parishioners, "So long as you oppose the priest, you will be without one. The priest must have charge of the church and everything in it. I will not allow the church to be blessed until the priest has entire control."[34] The parishioners registered the complaints with the Archbishop of New Orleans, Francis Janssens,[35] who forwarded the correspondence to Bishop Gallagher, stating that he had told the parishioner he had "no power to act in such cases."[36] Father Laski served the people in Anderson from 1888 to 1890. He returned to Russian Poland soon afterward, where he continued his spiritual work among the people. Unfortunately, he was imprisoned by the Russians and martyred there.[37]

In 1916, more discord arose in Chappell Hill. On May 23, Father Dombroski wrote Bishop Gallagher stating that the congregation of Chappell Hill wanted no other priest than Father Domanski. He asked of the Bishop that he obtain the keys to the church and the priest's house and turn them over to Father Kirwin. Further, he requested of the Bishop that the people be admonished for their behavior.[38] A letter dated June 23 of that year to Bishop Gallagher from four parishioners at Chappell Hill stated how disappointed they were not to obtain Father Domanski. The parishioners pointed out that they had to borrow $350 to pay Father Domanski and the Sisters. Further, the people "will not pay a cent until they get a good Polish priest." The four parishioners wrote that they did not know what to do about the financial situation, in addition to a desire for a Polish priest: "Dear Father, you know, no doubt which one we want."[39]

A letter from seven parishioners in Chappell Hill dated July 14, 1916, continued their plea for Father Domanski:

To His Excellency:

Your letter was received on July 8, 1916, but we were not very much satisfied with it. You wrote that Rev. Nona [Francis J. Nona, served 1898–1915] was on the road to recovery, which we are very glad to hear and that he would soon be able to come to Chappell Hill. We can hardly believe that he would come here because when he left here he said that even though he may get well and live one thousand years, he would never come to Chappell Hill and if he should have to pass through Chappell Hill, he would rather go one hundred miles around to skip this parish.

Now we almost know that Rev. Nona is doing his best to keep us without a priest just so he could show us that he will do what he told us, that he will have a revenge on this Parish. For this we do not want Rev. Nona back in Chappell Hill. He will not be welcome here by anyone. Even the children hate him now but before he was loved by nearly every one of us.

We called a meeting Sunday and your letter was read but no one was satisfied. They all say that we are not treated right because at first we were promised to have Rev. Father Domanski but later he was sent to a much smaller parish and even later we asked and begged for him but our appeals were not granted. We must know real soon when we can have a priest, because we must notify the Sisters who have been teaching school for us, and if we do not have a priest here we may not get the Sisters back here to teach our next term and we want good teachers for our school.

Now we do not wish to write and ask for what we have asked many times, but we will ask you to come to Chappell Hill to see for yourself what is going on here. We would be glad to tell you, dear Father, in a personal way all about the condition we are in. We will pay all of your expenses. There must be a change made here real soon, because many of these people are turning the other way and losing confidence here.

Kindly let us know when you would be able to come here so we could gather the committee and trustees together so you would have a chance to understand this mixup.

Hoping that everything will soon be put in good shape we remain, Yours in Christ.[40]

Documentation from St. Stanislaus Church in Chappell Hill records that these Polish farmers migrated to America because of Bismarck's extermination policy and settled in Chappell Hill. They were served by Reverend James Grabinger of Brenham and then Father Adam Laski. The first resident priest was Reverend Theodore Jarron, May 1894–1897. His successors were the Reverend F. Pridal, January 1897–August

1898, and the Reverend Francis J. Nonna, 1898–1915. The 1900 storm destroyed the wooden church, which was rebuilt. At the time of the storm, the parish numbered 225 families, and 125 children attended the school. Father Nicodemus Thomas Domanski served from 1915 until May 1916. He was followed by the Reverend Michael Joseph Tabor, who served from 1916 until 1921.[41] Thus, Father Domanski did not return. During the time period of Father Tabor, who was living in Brenham, the Divine Providence Sisters left since there was not a resident pastor. Father Tabor's correspondence to Bishop Gallagher reveals that the county wished to borrow the school building, which had been serving 245 children. As it turned out, a layman and his sister taught double sessions.[42] The Sisters of Divine Providence returned in October 1918, teaching 220 children that year.[43] St. Stanislaus Church in Chappell Hill is listed today among the beautiful Polish churches in Texas.

Requests for a priest of the same nationality as the surrounding congregation are frequent in Bishop Gallagher's files. Language and culture were major components. St. Mary's Church in Taylor, Texas, was unusual in petitioning (forty-three signatures) for a priest who spoke English fluently. They expressed displeasure with the Holy Cross Fathers who were ministering in the parish and pointed to the need for CCD (Confraternity of Christian Doctrine) classes and a school.[44] The Holy Cross Fathers had been in Texas since 1870, as Bishop Dubuis requested them. They had served in a number of parishes around Austin. It would have been beyond the possibility of the number of priests Bishop Gallagher had in the Diocese to satisfy each of these requests.

When bearing in mind the above difficulties, one must understand the abuse of lay trusteeism that had preceded this era in American Catholic history. The causes were found in a lack of understanding of the roles of clergy and laity regarding Canon Law pertaining to the holding and administration of church property. Protestant neighbors had the dominant voice in ruling their congregations. Mounting antagonisms between clergy and laity had already been witnessed in this country.[45]

❧ 10 ❧

Shepherding the Flock

The third Bishop of the Diocese of Galveston, unlike the two preceding Bishops, possessed a desire to build a native clergy. Prior to this time period, many of the clergy and religious of this Diocese were foreign born, coming from France due to the country of origin of Bishop Odin and Bishop Dubuis.

Vocations

Religious vocations had always been a cherished goal for Bishop Gallagher. His pastoral letter on vocations twenty-one years into his episcopate addresses each of the three states in life. The Bishop begins by pointing out that each person is called to a particular state in life. One's vocation is governed by Divine Providence. It is through one's call that the individual "works out his salvation." St. Paul states that everyone abide by the vocation to which he is called (1 Cor. 7:17). God does provide the "special aids and graces for its fulfillment." The bishop lists the principal vocations as the married state, religious state, and holy priesthood, in addition to the single or unmarried state for those who are not called to one of the other states.[1]

Marriage represents the union of Christ with the Church. Those who marry in conformity with the will of God receive special graces to fulfill the duties of their state and save their souls.

The Providence of God extends to the choice of the individuals. He proclaims that "a prudent spouse is properly from the Lord." Those who feel called to this state should enter into fervent prayer that they may know and accept who the Lord intends as their lifelong companion. They should consult their parents for prudent advice, and their spiritual director for unbiased judgment. It is important that they bear in mind the laws of the Church. "Obedience to the laws of the Church is the best guarantee of a happy marriage."[2]

Bishop Gallagher describes the religious state as "the higher and holier Christian life" as it consists in the observance "not only of the laws of God and of the Church but also of the counsels of Jesus Christ . . . poverty, chastity and obedience." Referencing Matthew 19:29, the Bishop points out that the "singular happiness" guaranteed to good religious is the incentive to accept its crosses and to comply with the duties of that state in life. Religious vocations are found in the homes of parents who pray for them. Further, no child should expect to receive a religious vocation without having asked for it "by humble prayer."[3]

Referencing John 15:16, the Bishop writes that no one should expect to enter the priesthood who has not been invited by God. "The power and dignity of the priest surpass that of even the angels in Heaven, for to priests and not to angels was it given to change bread and wine into the Body and Blood of Jesus Christ." He points out that parents should make it their desire in prayer. "We shall, no doubt, see the good effects of their ardent petitions." Noting the children within the congregation, the shepherd requests that they ask of God light and grace that they each might know their vocation. The Council of Baltimore urged priests to seek out young men who are called to the ecclesiastical state.[4]

The Bishop expresses his great joy that there is a diocesan seminary. However, within the twenty-one years of his episcopate he had not received one vocation to priesthood from the diocese, Texas, or the South. Rather, the Bishop had been forced to go to other parts of the globe to find priests: England, Ireland, Germany, France, Italy, Poland, Bohemia, Switzerland, Canada, and the northern states of the United States. These distant lands cannot provide all the vocations needed. His urgent prayer is for diocesan vocations and a special blessing for the seminary.[5]

This pastoral was read to every congregation in the Diocese.

The Eucharist

Bishop Gallagher issued a letter to the clergy and faithful of the diocese on the feast of the Purification in 1911 addressing the document issued by Pope Pius X *Quam Singulari Christus Amore*, "On the First Communion of Children," issued August 2, 1910. The Pope of the Eucharist had previously written several documents regarding the mystery so central to the faith.[6]

In May 1905, the Pontiff issued a special prayer fostering frequent Communion. In December of that same year, he wrote a document detailing the disposition necessary for the worthy reception of Holy Communion: freedom from mortal sin and receiving with the right intention. This decree also said that anyone could receive Communion daily who fulfilled these conditions. In addition, he pointed out that it was the desire of the Church that the faithful receive Communion frequently, even daily. In February of the following year, Pope Pius X issued a document stating that all who received frequent and daily Communion would receive all their indulgences for which they were entitled without the necessity of weekly confession, which was formerly required for such indulgences. In that same year on December 7, the sick, who could not fast, were given permission to receive Communion twice a month after having taken some liquid food, presuming that the sickness had continued for a month. In April 1907, the Pope ordered a triduum of devotions in honor of the Eucharist to be held in every cathedral church within the octave of Corpus Christi. Through this prayer and instruction, the habit of frequent Communion was fostered.[7]

Quam Singulari was issued August 2, 1910, addressing the topic of the First Communion of children. All of the faithful who had reached the age of reason were called to confess their sins at least once a year and to receive Holy Communion at least at Easter. The age of reason was defined as the age of seven. Bishop Gallagher welcomed this decree for the faithful of the Diocese, proclaiming, "What a beautiful and edifying sight it will be, to see so many little ones, almost daily, flocking to the Holy Sacrifice and clustering around the Holy Table!"[8] The obligation to receive at the age of seven imposed on the parents the duty of instructing and preparing the children for the worthy reception of the sacrament. This obligation fell more on the mother than the father as she had more frequent contact with the child. "Surely the good Catholic mother can have no sweeter nor more sacred duty than to teach her darling little one to know the good God and to love Him, to love our dear Savior Jesus, and His dearest mother, Mary."[9] The obligation also rested with teachers, who shared the parental duty, even more so, if the parents failed or could not carry out their duty. The Bishop described the knowledge required of these children to receive these two sacraments:

> A knowledge of the mysteries of religion necessary for salvation, namely, that there is one God in three Divine Persons; that Jesus Christ died for our salvation, and that God will reward the good and punish the bad; also that they know the requisites for the worthy receiving of the Sacrament of Penance, namely: they must confess their sins with sorrow for offending God; and that they understand that in receiving Holy Communion not mere bread, but God Himself. Children should besides have a knowledge of the essential prayers of a Christian, namely the Our Father, Hail Mary, the Apostles' Creed, and the Acts of Faith, Hope, Charity and Contrition, and have a pious disposition to receive the Sacraments.[10]

It is the responsibility of the father of the family to judge the discretion of the child. Confessors are warned not to refuse absolution to children of tender age who are sufficiently disposed and not to refuse the sacraments of Penance, Holy Viaticum, and Extreme Unction for children who are in danger of death. Little children, it may be presumed, are not committing mortal sins. Confessors may give them permission to receive habitually without going to confession again "as long as they are not certain of having committed some mortal sin."[11]

Bishop Gallagher says further that the pastor will find great delight in preparing the "little lambs of his flock to receive worthily the Good Shepherd of their souls in Holy Communion . . . at least every Sunday, if not every day."[12] When the children have been prepared, they receive these sacraments privately or in groups if convenient. The Annual General Solemn First Communion is to be preceded by "some days of spiritual retreat."[13] This Solemn Communion is received by all children who have individually or collectively made their First Communion and are not over the age of twelve. These children are expected to learn all of the

Catechism at a later time. When the bishop visits the parish for Confirmation, all who have made their First Communion and have been duly instructed are presented for Confirmation.

The document *Quam Singulari Christus Amori* was to be read every first Sunday of Lent. This pastoral instruction was to be read on the first Sunday after its reception.[14]

The importance Bishop Gallagher gave to the document cannot be overestimated in emphasizing the practice of frequent communion. This was especially true since the beliefs encompassed in the heresy of Jansenism kept many away from the sacrament, presuming a personal unworthiness. The reception of First Communion at the age of seven eventually led to the fading of the practice of Solemn First Communion.

Lent

Bishop Nicholas Gallagher, in accord with the indult of Pope Leo XIII, faithfully issued the Lenten regulations each year. The following was issued in 1895

1. Every day, in Lent, except Sundays, is a fast day.

2. Only one full meal a day is allowed, which should be taken about noon (but when the full meal cannot be taken about noon, the order may be reversed, the collation may be taken in the morning, and the full meal in the evening).

3. A small refreshment, commonly called a COLLATION, may be taken in the evening.

4. A cup of coffee, tea, chocolate, or some similar drink with a bit of bread is allowed in the morning.

5. The use of flesh meat is allowed at any time on Sundays, and at the principal meal on Mondays, Tuesdays, Thursdays, and Saturdays, except on Ember Saturday and Holy Saturday.

6. Fish and flesh are not allowed at the same meal even on Sundays.

7. Those who are exempt from the obligation of fasting may eat meat at every meal on the days on which flesh meat is allowed.

8. Lard or fat may be used in preparing lawful food.

9. The use of eggs and white meats (Lacticinia) is allowed at the principal meal and collation.

10. Unless lawfully dispensed or exempted, all the faithful who are twenty-one years of age are bound to observe the fast of Lent.

11. The law of abstinence from meat is binding on ALL FROM SEVEN YEARS OF AGE.

The time within which the faithful must comply with their Easter duty extends from the first Sunday of Lent to Trinity Sunday.[15]

The Bishop went on to say that devotional exercises should be held in the Church on two days during the week. Permission was granted for Benediction of the Blessed Sacrament, which may be preceded by a rosary and an appropriate instruction or by the Stations of the Cross.

The Bishop also took the opportunity to make what he perceived to be noteworthy points of instruction. The Apostolic delegate Cardinal Francis Satolli had received the prescription from R. Archbishop Monaco in Rome, dated August 20, 1894, stating that any Catholic who was a member of the Odd Fellows, the Sons of Temperance, or the Knights of Pythias would be barred from receiving the sacraments.[16]

The prescription against membership in each of these societies was because they had a quasi-religious character and were of a secret nature. The Odd Fellows were formed in England in 1812 and came to America in 1819. In their manual they described the use of forms of worship. They taught the equality of Judaism, Christianity, and Mohammedanism; had chaplains, altars, high priests, ritual, order of worship, and funeral ceremonies. The Sons of Temperance, founded in New York in 1842, addressed not only temperance but also the manner of religious worship for both men and women. Regarding the Knights of Pythias, founded in 1864 by prominent Freemasons, the oath of secrecy, blind obedience, and the allegiance to the pagan Pythagoras rather than Christ illustrated its objectional nature.[17]

In his Lenten letters of 1898 and 1899, Bishop Gallagher chose to address the topic of marriage. He upheld the dignity of marriage by referencing relevant scripture: "What therefore God has joined together, let no man tear asunder" (Matt. 19:6) and reminded Catholics of the admonition that one may not marry a divorced person. The Church excommunicates any Catholic who attempts to marry a divorced person. He then went on to state that "the Church, for good reasons, has always detested mixed marriages. They tend to destroy that intimate union of mind and heart that should exist between husband and wife. They imperil the faith of a Catholic consort and of the children, and produce other baneful results." He pointed out that his attention at this time was toward present and future marriages rather those already in existence. He grieved at the loss of faith and piety these mixed marriages produce. He exhorted pastors to warn of the dangers of such marriages.[18]

Continuing with the importance of family, in his 1899 letter the Bishop urged that the diocese form the Association of the Holy Family in accord with the wishes of Pope Leo XIII in his encyclical of June 14, 1892. Referencing the Blessed Mother and Saint Joseph as models in the home, the purpose of the association was "to unite Christian families by a closer bond of piety to the Holy Family, or rather to consecrate them wholly to its service, with the intention that Jesus, Mary and Joseph may protect and cherish as their own the families consecrated to them. Members who are enrolled should gather within their households to perform exercises of piety before a picture of the Holy Family."[19]

It is quite evident that Bishop Gallagher was most fastidious in making known the responsibilities of each Catholic to their faith. He placed emphasis on the correct education of children and the example their parents brought forth. This was an age when there was no diocesan newspaper. Information disseminated from the pulpit had to be accurate and presented in such a way that families could make these practices part of their lives. Bishop Gallagher certainly realized the importance of his role here.

Figure 18. Bishop Nicholas A. Gallagher, 1902. Courtesy Catholic Archives of Texas, Austin, Texas.

✲ 11 ✲

Fiftieth Anniversary, Silver Jubilee of Bishop Gallagher

While the first years of Bishop Gallagher's tenure as Bishop of Galveston had many rocky turns, the celebration of his fiftieth birthday, February 19, 1896, and later his Silver Jubilee in 1907, brought no evidence of that. An ode written by P. McKenna and published in the *Southern Messenger* on the fiftieth anniversary of his birth proclaims:

This August, penitential day is a day we can enjoy.
A day of fast and abstinence, yet lit up with rays of joy;
Yea, pleasantly enjoyable is the incident this year,
That our Lenten season opens on a day to us so dear,
For endeared to all the clergy, and the faithful of the See
Of Galveston in Texas, is the eventuality
Of the Birth Day anniversary of one whom all revere,
The Bishop of this diocese; long may he the purple wear—
The Right Reverend N. A. Gallagher, whose honored ancestry,
were distinguished for their patriotic Irish loyalty,
Whose grandfather in penal days, of a hundred years ago,
Had assisted The Fitzgerald to oppose the common foe,
And to the Immortal Emmett did his largesses bestow.
Yet, those deeds of daring loyalty shall not forgotten be; Nay,
    while citizen and Christian live in close identity.
In by-gone years, long subsequent to that of "Ninety-Eight,"
His devoted parents journeyed to this land of vast estate,

To this bounteous Land of Liberty, renowned throughout this
   earth,
And Temperanceville, Ohio, claims our Bishops' place of birth.
There, the foundation of his cult was by his mother made,
And in due reward, her saintly cares have often repaid.
But another Alma Mater, Mount St. Mary's of the West,
Gave him in Holy Orders the Divine Affatus blest.
And when he assumed the purple, truthful chronicle relates
He was then the Junior Pontiff, in our Aggregate of States.
Hence above all other purposes, on this joyful day,
Long may our virtuous Bishop live, devotedly we pray.
P. McKenna[1]

In preparation for his Silver Jubilee as well as the sixtieth anniversary
of the Diocese, a number of changes were made in St. Mary's Cathedral.
Marble tiling was placed on the sanctuary floor and marble replaced the
wooden wainscoting. A marble foundation was put under the Bishop's
throne and the two side altars. A new main altar was erected that was
made of marble. Five memorial windows were installed as well as new
pews. The entire building, including the Bishop's residence, was stuccoed.[2] Two archbishops and twelve or more bishops were in attendance
for the consecration of the marble altar at St. Mary's Cathedral April
28, 1907, followed by two additional days of celebration, a gathering
of Catholic men in the opera house on Monday night and the jubilee
celebration on Tuesday.[3]

The *Galveston Tribune* painted a glorious first night celebration.

> Never in the history of Galveston, perhaps has there been such a pa-
> rade of Catholic men, and never in the history of the Grand Opera
> house has the playhouse been graced with such an assemblage of
> bishops, prelates and clergy as last night at the mass meeting held in
> honor of the silver jubilee anniversary of Bishop Gallagher. Higher
> tributes of love, veneration, esteem and well-wishes were never paid
> a man either as a dignitary of a church or a private citizen than were
> accorded Bishop N. A. Gallagher last night. Nearly 2000 men paraded
> the streets in his honor and joined in the eulogies to his name in the
> mass meeting assembled.[4]
>
> Few are the occasions where men have been made to feel so clearly
> the appreciation of the people among whom they have labored so

faithfully for years. Seldom do men assemble by hundreds to attest
in visible manner the love and esteem in which they hold a fellow
mortal, and the occasion last night, by its heartiness, sincerity and
every token of veneration, will doubtless live long in the memory of
Bishop Gallagher.[5]

A man, and a godly man, who has labored for twenty-five years in a
community, building and constructing, ministering to his people and
bringing honor to the city in which he resides, Bishop Gallagher was
forced to listen to words of praise and commendation from which he,
in his modesty, would have shrunk.[6]

The Honorable Charles J. Stubbs, speaking for the laity, referred to
those people Bishop Gallagher brought to the diocese: the "saintly
sisters . . . those angels of the poor . . . the beatitudes incarnate, the
corporal works of mercy, moving in forms of flesh." While there are
360 now, there were fifty twenty-five years ago. The Honorable Stubbs
went on to refer to the diocesan seminary, the increase in the number
of churches and chapels from twenty-five to ninety-one. There was one
hospital then and now seven. There were two parochial schools, now
thirty two. As he stated: "These are your works."

The Honorable Stubbs went on to bring further accolades to the Jubilarian Bishop. In closing,

> Long may you live and may honors be added to your years. And at
> Life's end, beyond the veil, may you rank among the heavenly hier-
> archy, and may every good deed of your life be a bright jewel in your
> crown. This is the wish of your laity to our well-beloved and illustri-
> ous bishop.[7]

Bishop Gallagher was certainly known beyond his immediate diocese of
Galveston. The *Daily Evening Blade* of Santa Ana, California, carried an
article on December 29, 1905, from Washington, DC, which stated that
in Catholic circles, the prevailing name mentioned to succeed the late
Archbishop Placide Louis Chapelle of New Orleans (1897–1905) was
Bishop Nicholas Gallagher. While this rumor did not become reality,
the article stated that "news of his appointment would be gratifying to
his many friends throughout the country."[8]

Figure 19. Fiftieth Anniversary celebration of Bishop Nicholas Gallagher, 1916, St. Mary's Orphanage, Galveston, Texas. Courtesy of The Archives of the Congregation of the Sisters of Charity of the Incarnate Word, Houston, Texas.

❧ 12 ❧

The Last Years of Bishop Nicholas Gallagher

The *Galveston Tribune* reported on February 18, 1911, that Bishop Gallagher would celebrate his sixty-fifth birthday in a religious manner. The article emphasized the tremendous growth of parishes, Catholic schools, and hospitals during the episcopate of Bishop Gallagher. The *Tribune* further pointed out that while many Galvestonians "trembled" at the future of the city after the 1900 storm, Bishop Gallagher "moved fearlessly ahead" in restoring the Catholic Church and helping to rebuild the city.[1] Bishop Gallagher made his ad limina visit to Rome in 1914. On returning, he received a testimonial of love from the laity.

In April 1917, Bishop Gallagher was honored with the celebration of the thirty-fifth anniversary of the episcopate. High Mass was offered at St. Mary's Cathedral at 9:00 a.m. on April 30. Monsignor Kirwin assisted Bishop Gallagher at this High Mass. Numerous other priests were present, in addition to members of the Knights of Columbus. A banquet was provided the night before through the services of the young ladies of Sacred Heart Academy. The *Galveston Daily News* reported a list of after-dinner speakers. Everyone went home with a silk American flag as a souvenir of the occasion.[2]

During World War I, Bishop Gallagher showed his loyalty to the country in a number of ways. The Bishop offered the services of Father Chataignon as chaplain to the Texas National Guard. He visited the camps and cantonments. On November 25, 1917, he celebrated a

Pontifical Mass at Camp MacArthur in Waco. He went to Houston to dedicate the Knights of Columbus building at Camp Logan and also to administer Confirmation. The correspondence of Bishop Gallagher dated December 4, 1917, from Reverend Lewis J. O'Hern, CSP, who represented the Catholic Army and Navy Chaplain Bureau, gives testimony to the fact that the Bishop was not able to supply priests for the army. As Father O'Hern stated: "I fully realize that there are many calls upon your Lordship, because of the many camps within your Diocese, and certainly appreciate your generosity in the past."[3]

However, on returning to Galveston, Bishop Gallagher became ill and retired to his bed. On January 16, 1918, he wrote to the Very Reverend James M. Kirwin, Vicar General and president of St. Mary's Seminary, in La Porte:

> Being of sound mind but very weak and in danger of death, I hereby appoint you Administrator of the Diocese of Galveston, Texas, side Vacante, with all the Authority as such until Rome makes the proper appointment.
>
> Signed in the presence of
> S. A. Zientek,
> N. T. Dommanshi
> John Joseph Keane[4]

Bishop Gallagher passed away peacefully on January 21, 1918. Galveston, in showing its respect for the Bishop, closed every establishment of business the morning of the funeral. His body was interred at the foot of the Blessed Mother's altar in St. Mary's Cathedral in accordance with his will on January 24, 1918.[5]

Rabbi Henry Cohen, who had long worked with Catholics on many projects, whether it be deterring the Ku Klux Klan or cleaning up the city with Father Kirwin after the great storm of 1900, gave the following eulogy for the Bishop at Temple B'nai Israel, where he had served since 1888:

> Judging by the life and work of Bishop Gallagher, Galveston has lost an incalculable power for good. Participating in every civic activity, bending the influence of his exalted position in furtherance of that

which was right and just in our everyday existence, the bishop will long be remembered as an exemplification of probity of the highest type. A simple modest kindly gentleman, a scholar, teacher and moral enthusiast, it was a privilege to share his human interest in all things. Notwithstanding his quiet carriage, he would rise to righteous wrath at an injustice, and would score sham and hypocrisy in no uncertain terms. He was particularly severe upon those who, born and reared of the faith in which he was so shining a light, tacitly repudiated their birthright by making overtures for social preferment to an alien faith. Talking to me of this defection he once averred that the people who sacrifice their spiritual belief on the altar of worldly fashion and who make light of their heritage for mundane things bring nothing to themselves but ridicule, for they are thoroughly understood by the very people whose good will they seek even at the loss of their self-respect.

We Jews owe Bishop Gallagher's memory a debt of gratitude. I recall that, in the interests of truth and justice, he was one of the first of this city in each instance to sign a protest to the French government upon the unfortunate Dreyfus affair; to the Russian government on the Kishineff massacre, and again the Russian government on the preposterous Beiliss blood accusation; and he voluntarily subscribed to whatever funds were collected for the relief of the victims of Russian persecution as well as to the Jewish war sufferers' fund. No narrow, partisan spirit could have done this!

A splendid example of consideration of other men's religious convictions and an ardent upholder and supporter of his own, Galvestonians can ill afford to lose so eminent a citizen. The Jewish people offer their sympathy to their Catholic brethren in their hour of trial. Bishop Gallagher numbered well his days and applied his heart to wisdom.[6]

The requiem Mass was celebrated at St. Mary's Cathedral on January 24, 1918, by Bishop Theophile Meerschaert of the Diocese of Oklahoma. He was the senior bishop of the New Orleans province. All bishops from the province were present.[7] As Bishop Gallagher had been recognized as the "Master Builder,"[8] Bishop Lynch of Dallas spoke of the tremendous growth of the Diocese of Galveston despite the fact that the Diocese of Dallas was carved from its original boundaries. In referring to the shepherd, he stated:

> The spiritual development is best told by the virtuous life of his faithful children as they obey the laws of God and man, as they are ever dutiful to church and state. God and his angels alone know the full measure of his spirit success. It will be revealed to the world on the day of judgment.
>
> Nicholas Aloysius, may your gentle soul find everlasting peace with the God you loved and served so well, for you have been in every true sense of the term a most devout Christian, a model priest, a zealous bishop, and a loyal citizen of our beloved country.[9]

Figure 20. Funeral of Bishop Nicholas Gallagher. Courtesy of the Archives of Galveston-Houston.

Figure 21. Grave of Bishop Nicholas A. Gallagher, St. Mary's Cathedral, Galveston, Texas.

Remember your prelates who have spoken to you the word of God; whose faith follow. Hebrews XIII. 7.

The Rt. Rev. Nicholas A. Gallagher, D. D.

Born February 19, 1846
Ordained Priest December 25, 1868
Consecrated Bishop April 30, 1882
Died January 21, 1918

Figure 22. Holy Card in honor of Bishop Gallagher's death. Courtesy of Catholic Archives of Texas, Austin, Texas.

❧ 13 ❧

Looking Back

In looking back one would have to say that Bishop Nicholas Gallagher was a surprise candidate to the episcopate for the Diocese of Galveston as the Holy Cross father, Father Peter Dufal, CSC, had been named coadjutor to Bishop Dubuis on May 14, 1878. He had been ordained a priest on September 8, 1852. He resigned from the Diocese of Galveston on April 18, 1880, due to ill health, returning to his congregation in Neuilly, France.[1]

Almost two years passed before Nicholas Gallagher was installed as Titular Bishop of Canopus, Africa, on January 10, 1882. Gallagher retained this position of Titular Bishop for ten years before Dubuis resigned as ordinary of the diocese, thus occasioning the insult of Bishop Brennan of Dallas, himself aspiring to be archbishop.

Bishop Gallagher celebrated the fiftieth anniversary of ordination to the priesthood of Bishop Dubuis June 10, 1894, at St. Mary's Cathedral in Galveston. The *Galveston News* reported that many who attended had entered the church and been confirmed during the episcopate of Bishop Dubuis. This bishop died less than a year later, at Vernaison, France, on May 21, 1895.[2]

Bishop Gallagher's desire to recruit only English-speaking clergy and religious for the Diocese of Galveston created much difficulty for the large number of immigrants moving into the diocese at the turn of the century. These immigrants were most accustomed to the Catholic faith taught and preached in their own language. This lack of foresight on the bishop's part created strife and tension in filling and maintaining pastorships of parishes. It would take at least another generation before immigrants could adjust to the American way of life in parishes. While James McMaster's call for a German Vicar General may not have been the answer, a greater abundance of priests from these immigrants' countries of origin would have alleviated many uneasy relationships and prevented the caustic questioning of authority of the bishop so readily found in parishioners' correspondence.

It cannot be denied that Bishop Gallagher was not the most prudent in dealing with people. His aloofness and uncommunicative style won him no support, yet he learned how to compensate for these seeming pitfalls. In studying the Galveston petition that so marked his episcopacy before the turn of the century, one may wonder why he so hesitated to reopen the Ursuline Convent to the public, an agreement made earlier with the Sisters by Bishop Dubuis. It appears that Gallagher thought his authority was in question. He had to be begged by the Archbishop of New Orleans and the Apostolic delegate before complying. Yet when Archbishop Janssens urged a front person, as found in Monsignor Kirwin, the bishop immediately acquiesced. Bishop Gallagher and Monsignor Kirwin made a successful team.

Bishop Gallagher's concern for the well-being of the Dominican Sisters, whom he personally brought to Texas, ultimately led to the realization, through Archbishop Janssens, that he needed to be more general in his shepherding. A bishop simply could not take on the role of confessor or chaplain for a religious community.

In a Sunday sermon preached at St. Mary's Cathedral in Galveston in August 1883, Bishop Gallagher chose to announce that no Catholic child attending the public schools would be allowed to receive their First Communion and Confirmation. The Catholic parents who sent their children to the public schools would not be allowed to receive the sacraments.[3] These prescriptions arose from the document issued by Propaganda in 1875, "Instruction to the Bishops of the United States concerning the Public Schools." The document referred to the grave danger to the faith and morals of the Catholic children in attending public schools. Parents have a serious obligation to send their children to Catholic schools unless it is not possible.[4] This message regarding the necessity of Catholic children attending Catholic schools was repeated at the Third Plenary Council of Baltimore held from November 9 to

December 7, 1884. Bishop Nicholas Gallagher was in attendance.[5] Title VI, addressing the Education of Catholic Youth, clarifies that pastors must establish Catholic schools and parents must send their children there unless the bishop has judged "the reason for sending them elsewhere" is sufficient. The council emphasized the need to strive for efficiency in these schools and the desire that they be free.[6]

When the Code of Canon Law was revised in 1917, Catholics were forbidden to send their children to non-Catholic schools. However, it pointed out that there must be a Catholic school within a reasonable distance. The bishop had the obligation of determining whether attendance at the public schools should be permitted. "Pastors of souls have the duty of arranging everything so that all the faithful have a Catholic education." By 1920, 35 percent of Catholic children were in Catholic schools, by 1959, 59 percent. The vision of the Third Plenary Council of Baltimore was never realized.[7]

The sermon did not win Bishop Gallagher popularity, especially in areas where Catholic schools were nonexistent or nearly nonexistent. While Bishop Gallagher chose the hard line here, his manifestation as shepherd became more apparent over time in his own pastorals, whether through the reception of frequent communion, one's state in life, or the fervor of a Lenten season.

According to Monsignor James Vanderholt, Bishop Gallagher had three "priorities" during his episcopate: native vocations, social justice, and a Catholic newspaper.[8] The establishment of a diocesan seminary was of major importance. He lived to see the beginning of native vocations. His ministry in the area of social justice is most evident in providing education for African Americans in various parts of the Galveston diocese. His desire for a Catholic diocesan paper did not reach the same fruition. He sent out a circular letter November 17, 1883, pointing out that:

> A Catholic Paper will be a messenger of good news and a means of conveying useful information to many; besides, it will exert a salutary influence on many who cannot be reached by other means. The establishing, therefore of a Catholic Paper here will surely be productive of much good.[9]

The Bishop requested attendance at a meeting, Wednesday, December 5 at 7:30 p.m. at the Bishop's residence. This letter was reprinted on February 12, 1884, and included the charter and by-laws, financial support, and business structure of the "Catholic Publishing Company of Texas." While an article printed in the *Austin Weekly Statesman* in December 1883, assured "the appearance of a first class Catholic weekly paper for Texas within a few weeks,"[10] there is no evidence that a diocesan Catholic newspaper was published during the episcopate of Bishop Nicholas Gallagher. The diocesan *Texas Catholic Herald* would actually commence publication on May 14, 1964, under the episcopate of John L. Morkovsky.[11]

It is certainly arguable that the most challenging role Bishop Gallagher met during his episcopate was the leadership and encouragement of Galvestonians after the 1900 storm. Bishop Gallagher and Monsignor Kirwin were called to minister to many who lost loved ones during the disaster. Two of the five Catholic churches in Galveston were almost leveled, and the other three suffered extensive damage. St. Mary's Orphanage was lost. Nine other churches in the diocese were also destroyed, including the historic St. Joseph Church in Brazoria. While Father Kirwin was involved in the saving of lives and reconstruction, Bishop Gallagher sought and obtained funds to repair and rebuild. One of his immediate efforts was rebuilding the orphanage. Certainly, this was an immediate need. One cannot help but surmise the Bishop's regret in not having the vision and perhaps the means to move the orphanage location sooner with an approaching "storm of the century." It is through his shepherding, however, that many of these diocesan facilities and houses of prayer were reconstructed. To a great extent, Monsignor Kirwin aided the process in spurring the flock on in these rebuilding efforts. It must be admitted, however, that this natural disaster was the first in a series of events that would direct the economic thrust away from Galveston and toward Houston.[12]

Bishop Gallagher's passion seemed to be the fostering of education in various realms. He envisioned the growth of religious vocations through the establishment and expansion of St. Mary's Seminary in La Porte in 1901. Two years later he pointed out in his pastoral on vocations that he had not received one candidate for the priesthood from the diocese.

Yet, fifteen years later he was credited with building the native clergy in southeast Texas.[13] He further established a diocesan school board and teachers' institute. The First Teachers' Institute was held in Galveston in December 1910.[14] The third area in education was the establishment of Newman Centers at the University of Texas and Texas A&M. Bishop Gallagher, in 1884, donated the land and buildings of the University of St. Mary's in Galveston to the New Orleans Jesuits. The Jesuits kept the school through the administration of Bishop Gallagher. It was closed in the mid-1920s due to a lack of funds and enrollment.[15] This four-pronged effort does not consider the growth of Catholic schools in the parishes and the religious orders invited to teach in them.

Bishop Gallagher is remembered for his missionary efforts among African American Catholics. This was evident in the establishment of Holy Rosary Parish in Galveston, the first parish established especially for a Catholic African American congregation in Texas. The bishop established St. Nicholas parish in Houston for black Catholics in October 1887. He invited the Josephite Fathers and Holy Family Sisters to work among these communities. Blessed Sacrament Parish in Beaumont (1914) and Sacred Heart Parish in Port Arthur (1915) were established by the Josephite Fathers. Bishop Gallagher received personnel and financial support from Mother, now Saint, Katherine Drexel in this endeavor. Bishop Gallagher further invited the Oblate Fathers to establish Immaculate Conception Parish in 1911 and Our Lady of Guadalupe Parish in 1912 to serve predominantly Spanish-speaking Catholics in Houston.[16] The bishop further obtained two grants for the establishment of schools for Spanish-speaking children in Galveston and Austin.[17]

In 1905, Bishop Gallagher made an appeal to the Catholic Church Extension Society for the southern and western parts of the United States. Bishop Gallagher's correspondence reveals that he received a $500 check from the Catholic Church Extension Society for the mission church in Rosebud, Texas.[18] The following year, the pastor of St. Anne's Church in Rosebud, Father P. C. Pfiffner was provided an application form from this society to request $1,000 for a "school for Mexicans."[19] Through the efforts of this society, chapels and Mass stations were established in Alvin, Missouri City, Rosenberg, Texas City, Velasco, and Manor.[20]

Bishop Gallagher was ahead of his times in working with members of other faiths, especially members of the Jewish community. This was most evident after the 1900 storm, his jubilee celebration, and many recollections after his passing.

Bishop Gallagher survived all the priests who were living at the time of his episcopal ordination. The number of priests and laity in the diocese more than doubled: 105 priests, 120 churches and missions, and 70,000 Catholics.[21] He was a master builder, and in a certain sense a master designer, for the future. Christopher Byrne would build on his legacy, as he was "challenged to address the spiritual needs of a population that was becoming increasingly diverse, better educated, more willing to speak out on its own behalf and to support causes that were of national import as often as they were of local interest."[22]

One may pause in wonder in hearing that from three children in the Gallagher family, twelve priests and religious vocations came. Seven of these vocations followed Bishop Nicholas Gallagher to Galveston in becoming members of the Dominican Sisters of the Sacred Heart.

Despite the fact that Bishop Nicholas Gallagher came from a large family, he possessed a reserved nature that did not always serve him well, yet it must have been bound in a deep humility. He was not one who needed to be in the forefront of any event. For nearly a generation, Monsignor James Kirwin spoke at practically every episcopal event within the diocese. Monsignor. Kirwin earned a reputation as a great orator, and Bishop Gallagher readily recognized his giftedness. It was Bishop Gallagher's activation of his role as shepherd that was key. He brought this message forth to his niece: "If people praise and flatter you, do not think yourselves so exceptionally good. You must be good to do good, but without the blessing of God, you will accomplish little. Pay little attention to the praises of others, but in true humility . . . have confidence in God's help."[24] In a certain sense, these few words represent his pathway to the laity, but likewise his pathway to the next life. The laity certainly recognized the uniqueness of each of these prelates.

A stained glass window of St. Nicholas built in honor of the memory of Bishop Nicholas Gallagher is found in the sacristy of Annunciation Church in Houston. Monsignor James Golasinski, former pastor of Annunciation, believes the stained glass windows were added one by one as individuals donated funds for their establishment. Archbishop Fiorenza, former archbishop of the Archdiocese of Galveston-Houston, renamed the administration building at St. Mary's Seminary in honor of Bishop Nicholas Gallagher in November 2001.[25] This edifice was built in 1954, replacing the structure in La Porte.

In the end, a solemn city populace stood at rest in closing every business to pay tribute to a Yankee bishop adopted as a gentle shepherd amid a growing and divergent flock. It appears that, at that moment, the prophecy of James A. McMaster had become reality:

> If Dr. Gallagher will accept, and will disentangle a knot on a most beautiful chord, he will not only have a great crown in Heaven, but his success on earth will render him blessed, very widely.[26]

Evidence of this blessedness directed toward Bishop Gallagher was found among the seminarians Bishop Gallagher fostered over a century ago, yet also today. The students in Second Year Theology at St. Mary's Seminary celebrated the first annual Founder's Day February 26, 2015. Now located in Houston for over sixty years, St. Mary's is the oldest Catholic seminary in the South that has been in continual existence. As one of the seminarians stated, Bishop Gallagher simply wished to encourage vocations for the rapidly growing state of Texas. That legacy continues on, leading to ever-growing service for the Catholic Church in Texas.[27]

Figure 23. St. Mary's Seminary in Houston. Established 1954. Administration Building named in honor of Bishop Nicholas Gallagher by Archbishop Joseph Fiorenza, November 2001.

Figure 24. Stained glass of St. Nicholas in honor of Bishop Nicholas Gallagher, Annunciation Church, Houston, Texas. Courtesy of Elizabeth J. Kimes.

Figure 25. Medallion of Bishop Nicholas Gallagher located at bottom of stained glass window, Annunciation Church, Houston, Texas. Courtesy of Elizabeth J. Kimes.

Notes

Chapter 1

1. Patrick Foley, *Missionary Bishop: Jean-Marie Odin in Galveston and New Orleans* (College Station: Texas A&M University Press, 2013), 132.

2. Carlos E. Castañeda, *The Church in Texas since Independence, 1836–1950*, vol. 7 of *Our Catholic Heritage in Texas, 1519–1936* (Austin, TX: Von Boeckmann-Jones, 1958), 110–11.

3. The term *suffragan bishop* refers to the relationship between the Bishop and his Archbishop or Metropolitan. The Bishop may be called forth to a synod by the Archbishop and he would there give his "suffrage." See F. L. Cross and E. A. Livingstone, eds., *Oxford Dictionary of the Christian Church*, 1997 ed., s.v., "suffragan bishop."

4. Castañeda, *Church in Texas since Independence*, 110–11.

5. Leo Vincent Jacks, *Claude Dubuis, Bishop of Galveston* (Saint Louis: B. Herder, 1946), 200.

6. Castañeda, *Church in Texas since Independence*, 131–34.

7. James Talmadge Moore, *Through Fire and Flood: The Catholic Church in Frontier Texas, 1836-1900* (College Station: Texas A&M University Press, 1992), 200–203.

8. McMaster experienced a lengthy and colorful publishing career. Having purchased the *Freeman's Journal* from Bishop Hughes of New York in 1848, he took on the job as editor. He was involved in the political controversies prior to and during the Civil War as a states-rights Democrat and antiabolitionist. His attacks on Lincoln and his administration landed him in jail for eleven months at the beginning of the war. He resumed publication on April 19, 1862. He took a milder stance on national politics following the Civil War. He was a strong advocate of the papacy and Catholic education. In later years, his personal journalistic style began to decrease his readership. He died in 1886. Two of his three children became religious, one a Carmelite and another a Sister of the Holy Child. See *The Catholic Encyclopedia*, 1910, s.v. " James Alphonsus McMaster," accessed December 28, 2014, www.newadvent.org/cathen/09506a.htm, and Jay P. Dolan, *The American Catholic Experience: A History from Colonial Times to the Present* (New York: Doubleday/Image, 1985), 270.

9. James A. McMaster, "Bishop Administrator for Galveston," *New York Freeman's Journal*, December 31, 1881, 4.

10. Even though Abraham Lincoln issued the Emancipation Proclamation in September 1862, taking effect January 1, 1863, the document applied only to the Confederate states that had broken away yet were back under the control of the Union army. The effect of the Emancipation Proclamation was felt in Texas in June 1865, when slavery became unconstitutional and illegal according to the Thirteenth Amendment. Less than a generation of time had elapsed before Nicholas Gallagher became Bishop of Galveston. See "The Texas Emancipation Proclamation (June 19, 1865)," *Black Past.org*, accessed October 30, 2014, www.blackpast.org/primarywest/texas-emancipation-proclamation-1865.

11. Bulletin of the Catholic Record Society, Diocese of Columbus, 14, 1 (January 1989), 103.

12. Bulletin of the Catholic Record Society, Diocese of Columbus, 103–4.

13. *Catholic Telegraph*, 1859, quoted in *Diamond Jubilee, 1847–1922, of the Diocese of Galveston and St. Mary's Seminary*, compiled by Priests at the Seminary (Galveston, TX: Knapp Brothers, 1922), 112.

14. Sheila Hackett, OP, *Dominican Women in Texas: From Ohio to Galveston and Beyond* (Houston, TX: Sacred Heart Convent, 1986), 56.

15. Initially referred to as St. Francis Xavier Seminary and now as the Athenaeum of Ohio.

16. *Diamond Jubilee, 1847–1922, of the Diocese of Galveston and St. Mary's Seminary*, 112.

17. Tonsure was seen in the past as an introductory ceremony by which a layman became a cleric. It was not considered a part of the Sacrament of Holy Orders. Within the ceremony, the bishop or his delegate cut or snipped small portions from the hair of the candidate: front, back, two sides, and crown. The candidate was invited to accept the Lord as "his portion." See Robert C. Broderick, comp., *The Catholic Encyclopedia* (Nashville: Thomas Nelson, 1975), s.v. "tonsure."

18. *Diamond Jubilee, 1847–1922, of the Diocese of Galveston and St. Mary's Seminary*, 113.

19. Bulletin of the Catholic Record Society, Diocese of Columbus, 103–4.

20. Bulletin of the Catholic Record Society, Diocese of Columbus, 104.

21. A *titular bishop* is a bishop in partibus infidelium. He is ordained to a diocese that existed at one time but because of the loss of faith in that part of the world, it no longer exists as a distinct diocese. He is thus a titular bishop. See Broderick, *Catholic Encyclopedia* s.v. "titular bishop."

22. Bulletin of the Catholic Record Society, Diocese of Columbus, 104.

23. Hackett, *Dominican Women in Texas*, 57.

24. Father Louis Chaland to Bishop Nicholas Gallagher, January 6, 1882, Catholic Archives of Texas.

25. Circular Letter of Nicholas A. Gallagher to the Clergy of the Diocese of Galveston, March 3, 1882, Archives of the Archdiocese of Galveston-Houston.

26. Bulletin of the Catholic Record Society, Diocese of Columbus, 104. Bishop Edward M. Fitzgerald from Limerick, Ireland, served as bishop of Little Rock for forty-one years, beginning his episcopate on February 3, 1867. He was one of two bishops who voted against the dogma of papal infallibility at Vatican I. This led to the phrase "Big Rock versus the Little Rock." The bishop later explained that he voted as he did because he believed that affirming papal infallibility would hinder his

efforts to convert non-Catholics in Arkansas. See "Bishop Edward M. Fitzgerald," accessed February 1, 2015, www.dolr.org/former-bishops-fitzgerald.

27. Hackett, *Dominican Women in Texas*, 59.

28. Castañeda, *Church in Texas since Independence*, 479.

29. *Diamond Jubilee, 1847–1922, of the Diocese of Galveston and St. Mary's Seminary*, 113.

Chapter 2

1. Bishop Nicholas Gallagher to Bishop John A. Watterson, July 18, 1882, Archives of the Diocese of Columbus, quoted in the Bulletin of the Catholic Record Society, Diocese of Columbus, 14, 1 (January 1989), 105.

2. James Talmadge Moore, *Through Fire and Flood: The Catholic Church in Frontier Texas, 1836–1900* (College Station: Texas A&M University Press, 1992), 210–11.

3. Toby Terrar, "Catholic Socialism: The Reverend Thomas McGrady," *Dialectical Anthropology* 7 (1983), 211–13.

4. Thomas McGrady, "How I Became a Socialist," *Comrade* 2 (1902), quoted in Terrar, "Catholic Socialism," 214.

5. Terrar, "Catholic Socialism," 214.

6. James Hennessey, SJ, *American Catholics: A History of the Roman Catholic Community in the United States* (New York: Oxford University Press, 1981), 213–14.

7. *Los Angeles Herald*, September 5, 1904. California, Digital Newspaper Collection.

8. Terrar, "Catholic Socialism," 215–29.

9. Rev. Paul Ryan, *History of the Diocese of Covington, Kentucky on the Occasion of the Centenary of the Diocese, 1853–1953*, accessed December 10, 2014, www .nkyviews.com/campbell/text/newport_text_ryan_stanthony.htm.

10. "Thomas McGrady," in *Eugene Debs, His Life Writings and Speeches*, by Bruce Rogers and Stephen Marion Reynolds (Girard, KS: Appeal to Reason, 1908), 277–82.

11. Patrick Foley, *Missionary Bishop: Jean-Marie Odin in Galveston and New Orleans* (College Station: Texas A&M University Press, 2013), 136.

12. Foley, *Missionary Bishop*, 136–41.

13. Sister Loyola Hegarty, CCVI, *Serving with Gladness: The Origin and History of the Congregation of the Sisters of Charity of the Incarnate Word, Houston, Texas* (Houston, TX: Bruce Publishing in cooperation with the Sisters of Charity of the Incarnate Word, Houston, Texas, 1967), 139–40.

14. Leo Vincent Jacks, *Claude Dubuis, Bishop of Galveston* (Saint Louis: B. Herder, 1946), 169–72.

15. Hegarty, *Serving with Gladness*, 146.

16. Hegarty, *Serving with Gladness*, 145.

17. Jacks, *Claude Dubuis, Bishop of Galveston*, 202.

18. A case in point was the situation of the School Sisters of St Francis, a German order, responding to the invitation of Bishop Thomas Langdon Grace, to establish a motherhouse in the diocese of St Paul. The Sisters already staffed twelve parish schools in southern Minnesota by 1884. Archbishop John Ireland demanded of the superior that the order accept no more postulants from Europe, that all Sisters teaching attend an American normal school and that the order become a diocesan community. Mother Alexia accepted only the normal school requisite and moved

on to the more friendly neighboring diocese of Milwaukee to establish her mother-house. See Marvin R. O'Connell, *John Ireland and the American Catholic Church* (Saint Paul: Minnesota Historical Society Press, 1988), 197.

19. Correspondence from Bishop Claude Dubuis to Bishop Nicholas Gallagher, October 28, 1882, courtesy of the Archives of the Congregation of the Sisters of Charity of the Incarnate Word, Houston, Texas. Not to be reproduced without proper authorization of the archives.

20. Bulletin of the Catholic Record Society, Diocese of Columbus, 104.

21. Sheila Hackett, OP, *Dominican Women in Texas: From Ohio to Galveston and Beyond* (Houston, TX: Sacred Heart Convent, 1986), 47–52.

22. Hackett, *Dominican Women in Texas*, 50–51.

23. Bishop N. A. Gallagher to the Right Reverend John A. Watterson, July 23, 1882, as quoted by Hackett, *Dominican Women in Texas*, 53.

24. Hackett, *Dominican Women in Texas*, 52–55.

25. *Annals*, 46, Sacred Heart Dominican Convent Archives, Houston, Texas.

26. An acute infectious disease characterized by sudden onset, headache, racking joint pain, and a rash and caused by a virus transmitted by mosquitos of the genus *Aedes* chiefly in tropical and semitropical regions; also called breakbone fever; see *Webster's Third New International Dictionary of the English Language,* unabridged (Springfield, MA: G. & C Merriam Company, 1971), s.v., "dengue." A tropical disease often referred to as dandy fever; see Albert and Loy Morehead, eds., *The Penguin Webster Handy College Dictionary*, 3rd ed., Philip D. Morehead (New York: Penguin Books, 2003), s.v., "dengue."

27. Hackett, *Dominican Women in Texas*, 66.

28. Hackett, *Dominican Women in Texas*, 118.

29. Carlos E. Castañeda, *The Church in Texas since Independence, 1836–1950*, vol. 7 of *Our Catholic Heritage in Texas, 1519–1936* (Austin, TX: Von Boeckmann-Jones, 1958), 336–37 and Hackett, *Dominican Women in Texas*, 120.

30. Castañeda, *Church in Texas since Independence*, 337–38.

31. Hackett, *Dominican Women in Texas*, 64–65.

32. Hackett, *Dominican Women in Texas*, 70.

33. Castañeda, *Church in Texas since Independence*, 337–38.

34. Hackett, *Dominican Women in Texas*, 71.

35. Father Andrew Fruhwirth, Master General of the Order of Preachers to Bishop Nicholas Gallagher, June 23, 1902, Archives of the Dominican Sisters of Houston, Texas; and Hackett, *Dominican Women in Texas*, 162–63.

36. Pontifical institutes refer to those institutes of consecrated life that fall directly under the jurisdiction of the papacy as different from institutes that are diocesan and fall directly under the supervision of a bishop. Pontifical institutes share in common the living of the evangelical counsels, following of Christ under the guidance of the Spirit, the striving for the perfection of charity. These institutes have an eschatological significance in that they are a reminder that this life is lived as a preparation for the next. All constitutions of pontifical institutes are necessarily approved by the Vatican. For further information, see John P. Beal, James A. Coriden, and Thomas J. Green, eds., *The New Commentary on the Code of Canon Law* (New York: Paulist Press, 2000), cc. 589.

37. Hackett, *Dominican Women in Texas*, 170.

38. Bishop Nicholas Gallagher to Sister M. Agnes, September 22, 1909, Catholic Archives of Texas.

39. Hackett, *Dominican Women in Texas*, 75.

40. Bishop Nicholas Gallagher to Sister M. Agnes, July 1, 1914, Catholic Archives of Texas.

41. Castañeda, *Church in Texas since Independence*, 337.

42. Hackett, *Dominican Women in Texas*, 176–90.

Chapter 3

1. Carlos E. Castañeda, *The Church in Texas since Independence, 1836–1950*, vol. 7 of *Our Catholic Heritage in Texas, 1519–1936* (Austin, TX: Von Boeckmann-Jones, 1958), 228–29; and Aníbal González, "St. Mary's University, Galveston," *Handbook of Texas Online*, accessed December 28, 2014, https://tshaonline.org/handbook/on line/articles/kbs62.

2. Bishop Nicholas A. Gallagher to Very Reverend George M. Searle, CSP, Superior General, 1908, Archives of Texas, quoted in Castañeda, *Church in Texas since Independence*, 239.

3. Pope Pius X, *A Cerbo Nimis*, 1905, accessed December 1, 2014, http://w2.vatican .va/content/pius-x/en/encyclicals/documents/hf_p-x_enc_15041905_acerbo-ni-mis.html

4. Castañeda, *Church in Texas since Independence*, 240.

5. Sheila Hackett, OP, *Dominican Women in Texas: From Ohio to Galveston and Beyond* (Houston, TX: Sacred Heart Convent, 1986),178–79.

6. *Memoirs of Monsignor J. M. Kirwin* (Houston, TX: Standard Printing and Lithographing, 1928), not paginated.

7. Bishop Nicholas A. Gallagher to Rev. Mother M. of Loretto, Provincial G. S. Saint Louis, Missouri, September 9, 1905, Archives of the Good Shepherd Sisters, Saint Louis, Missouri.

8. Bishop Nicholas A. Gallaher to Rev. Mother M. of Loretto, Provincial G. S. Saint Louis, Missouri, September 29, 1906, Archives of the Good Shepherd Sisters, Saint Louis, Missouri.

9. Bishop Nicholas A. Gallaher to Rev. Mother M. of Loretto, Provincial G. S. Saint Louis, Missouri, July 14, 1907, Archives of the Good Shepherd Sisters, Saint Louis, Missouri.

10. Bishop Nicholas A. Gallaher to Rev. Mother M. of Loretto, Provincial G. S. Saint Louis, Missouri, January 14, 1914, Archives of the Good Shepherd Sisters, Saint Louis, Missouri.

11. Sister Mary of Loretto, Provincial to Bishop Nicholas Gallagher, January 17, 1914, Archives of the Good Shepherd Sisters, Saint Louis, Missouri.

12. Bishop Nicholas A. Gallaher to Rev. Mother M. of Loretto, Provincial G. S. Saint Louis, Missouri, February 6, 1914, Archives of the Good Shepherd Sisters, Saint Louis, Missouri.

13. Bishop Nicholas A. Gallaher to Rev. Mother M. of Loretto, Provincial G. S. Saint Louis, Missouri, February 21, 1914, Archives of the Good Shepherd Sisters, Saint Louis, Missouri.

14. Nicholas Gallagher to the Priests of the Diocese of Galveston, January 28, 1916, Archives of the Diocese of Galveston-Houston.

15. Castañeda, *Church in Texas since Independence*, 239, 414–15.

16. "Cornerstone of St. Basil's College to be Laid—Prominent Clergy to Attend," *Waco Times Herald*, April 6, 1902.

17. R. E. Lamb, CSB, "St. Basil's College," *Handbook of Texas Online*, accessed October 28, 2014, https://tshaonline.org/handbook/online/articles/kbs65.

18. Father Raphael O'Laughlin, *Basilian Leaders from Texas* (Houston, TX: Wings Press, 1991), 23–25.

19. Father Nicholas J. Murphy, OSA, to Bishop Nicholas A. Gallagher, June 26, 1915, Archives of the Archdiocese of Galveston-Houston.

20. Mother M. Albertine to Rt. Rev. Bishop Nicholas Gallagher, July 29, 1915, Archives of the Sisters of St. Mary of Namur, Fort Worth, Texas.

21. Father A. Antoine, OMI, Provincial, to R. Rev. N. A. Gallagher, August 2, 1916, Archives of the Archdiocese of Galveston-Houston.

22. Father Ed A. Kelley to Father J. M. Kirwin, VG, Diocese of Galveston, December 24, 1915, Archives of the Archdiocese of Galveston-Houston, and R. E. Lamb, CSB, "St. Basil's College," *Handbook of Texas Online*, accessed June 16, 2015, https://tshaonline.org/handbook/online/articles/kbs65.

23. Sister Louise Smith, SSMN, Archives for the Sisters of St. Mary of Namur, Fort Worth, Texas, letter to author, November 19, 2014.

24. V. Marijon, CSB, Provincial of Community of St. Basil, Toronto, June 14, 1899, Archives of Galveston-Houston, and Priests of St. Basil vs. Christopher Byrne, Bishop, No. 404-3751 (Comm'n of Appeals, November 15, 1923).

25. Most Reverend John Bonzano, DD, Apostolic Delegate, Washington, DC, to Rev. Edward A. Kelly, Waco, Texas, June 18, 1916, Archives of the Archdiocese of Galveston-Houston.

26. Most Reverend John Bonzano, DD, Apostolic Delegate, Washington, DC, to Rt. Rev. N. A. Gallagher, DD, Bishop of Galveston, March 13, 1917, Archives of the Archdiocese of Galveston-Houston.

27. Bishop Nicholas Gallagher, Last Will and Testament, November 14, 1911, Archives of the Diocese of Austin.

28. *Community of Priests of St. Basil*, No. 404-3751.

29. Reverend James Vanderholt, *Lone Star Catholicism: A Measure of Faith; From the Spanish Missions to the Golden Anniversary of the Diocese of Austin* (Austin, TX: Diocese of Austin, 1997), 32.

30. Father Victorin Marijon, CSB, Provincial of the Basilians in North America to Bishop Nicholas Gallagher, January 15, 1900, Archives of St. Thomas High School, Houston, and Archdiocese of Galveston-Houston.

31. Father Victorin Marijon, CSB, to Bishop Nicholas Gallagher, February 6, 1900, Archives of the Archdiocese of Galveston-Houston.

32. A copy of this deed may be found in the Archives of St. Thomas High School and the Archives of Galveston-Houston. See also Betty Fischer, Connie Voss, et al., *St. Thomas High School in the Twentieth Century* (St. Thomas High School, 2000), 3.

33. T. Thomas College ad, *Houston Daily Post*, September 17, 1900, p 10. Archives of St. Thomas High School.

34. Fischer, Voss, et al., *St. Thomas High School in the Twentieth Century*, 4.

35. "St. Thomas College," *Houston City Directory, 1902–03*, Archives of St. Thomas High School, Houston, Texas.

36. Fischer, Voss, et al., *St. Thomas High School in the Twentieth Century*, 4.

37. Fischer, Voss, et al., *St. Thomas High School in the Twentieth Century*, 3–8.

38. Castañeda, *Church in Texas since Independence*, 343.

39. Sister Mary Ursula Thomas, "The Catholic Church in the Oklahoma Frontier, 1824–1907" (PhD diss., Saint Louis University, 1938), 111.

40. Sister Mary Sebastian McHugh, IWBS, "History of the Order of the Incarnate Word and Blessed Sacrament in Houston, Texas" (unpublished thesis, University of Houston, 1950), 24–29, Archives of Incarnate Word Convent, Houston, Texas.

41. McHugh, "History of the Order of the Incarnate Word and Blessed Sacrament," 28.

42. McHugh, "History of the Order of the Incarnate Word and Blessed Sacrament," 29–32.

43. McHugh, "History of the Order of the Incarnate Word and Blessed Sacrament," 46–48.

44. McHugh, "History of the Order of the Incarnate Word and Blessed Sacrament," 48–49, and Sister Agatha Sheehan, CVI, "Sisters of the Incarnate Word and Blessed Sacrament, Houston, TX" (unpublished manuscript, 1962), 34. Archives of Incarnate Word Convent, Houston, Texas.

45. McHugh, *History of the Order of the Incarnate Word and Blessed Sacrament*, 51–53.

46. Sister Mary Xavier Holworthy, IWBS, *Diamonds for the King* (privately printed, n.p., 1945), 94.

47. McHugh, *History of the Order of the Incarnate Word and Blessed Sacrament*, 54–55.

48. *Diocese of Galveston-Houston, 1847–1997* (Dallas, TX: Taylor Publishing), 139.

49. Sheehan, "Sisters of the Incarnate Word and Blessed Sacrament," 6.

50. Robert C. Giles, *Changing Times: The Story of the Diocese of Galveston Houston in Commemoration of Its Founding, 125th Anniversary of the Diocese of Galveston-Houston, 1847–1972* (Texas Catholic Herald Production Staff, Most Reverend John L. Morkovsky, STD), 36.

51. Giles, *Changing Times*, 36.

52. Sheehan, "Sisters of the Incarnate Word and Blessed Sacrament," 7–9.

53. *Diocese of Galveston Centennial, 1847–1947*, 58–59, and Giles, *125th Anniversary of the Diocese of Galveston-Houston*, 110–11.

54. *Diocese of Galveston Centennial, 1847–1947*, 59.

55. *Diocese of Galveston Centennial, 1847–1947*, 61

56. Giles, *Changing Times*, 129.

57. Vanderholt, *Lone Star Catholicism*, 25.

58. Giles, *Changing Times*, 115.

59. "All Saints Catholic Community," accessed September 12, 2014, ttp://allsaintsheights.com/history.

60. Sister M. Agatha Sheehan, CVI, *The History of Houston Heights from Its Foundation in 1891 to Its Annexation in 1918* (Houston, TX: Premier Printing, 1956), 64–65.

61. Giles, *Changing Times*, 91; and *Diocese of Galveston-Houston, 1847–1997*, 121.

62. Vanderholt, *Lone Star Catholicism*, 33.

63. *Diocese of Galveston-Houston, 1847–1997*, 129.

64. *Diocese of Galveston-Houston, 1847–1997*, 130.

65. The painted churches of Texas, built by Czech, German, and Polish immigrants at the turn of the twentieth century are known for their Gothic revival windows, and facades clad in white frame siding or sometimes in stone. The wooden interiors of these churches are covered with bright painting. Inscriptions on the walls are written in the mother tongue of those who built these churches. See "The Painted Churches of Texas: Echoes of the Homeland," accessed February 1, 2015, www.klru.org/paintedchurches/.

66. Vanderholt, *Lone Star Catholicism*, 33.

67. *Diocese of Galveston Centennial, 1847–1947*, 92–93.

68. Giles, *Changing Times*, 102–3.

69. Castañeda, *Church in Texas since Independence*, 239, 341–42.

70. Sister Agatha Sheehan, CVI, "St. Nicholas Parish," *Early Church in Houston*, Archives of the Sisters of the Incarnate Word and Blessed Sacrament, Houston, Texas (unpublished manuscript, 1961), 38–40, and McHugh, *History of the Order of the Incarnate Word and Blessed Sacrament*, 53–54.

71. Castañeda, *Church in Texas since Independence*, 232.

72. Sheehan, "St. Nicholas Parish," *Early Church in Houston*, 38–40.

73. Castañeda, *Church in Texas since Independence*, 232.

74. Mother Katherine Drexel was canonized a saint in the year 2000 by Pope, now Saint, John Paul II.

75. Mother Katherine Drexel to Bishop Nicholas Gallagher, March 13, 1917, Archives of the Diocese of Beaumont.

76. Father James Vanderholt, Carolyn B. Martinez, and Karen A. Gilman, *The Diocese of Beaumont: the Catholic Story of Southeast Texas* (Diocese of Beaumont: East Texas Catholic, 1991), 108.

77. Rt. Rev. L. M. Fink, Leavenworth, Kansas, to Bishop Nicholas Gallagher, December 19, 1888; Bishop Nicholas Gallagher to Rt. Rev. L. M. Fink, December 19, 1888, and Msgr. James Vanderholt, "The Catholic Experience at Old Washington-on-the Brazos, Washington County, Texas: The Oldest Black Catholic Community in Texas" (unpublished manuscript, March 2, 1995), 14–15.

78. One may wonder why the orphans disappeared over a seven-year period. While some would have grown to adulthood, reports were found in the local newspapers accusing Father Huhn of mistreatment of the children. When boys escaped and were found in a nearby town, they did not wish to go back. As the matter of the accusations of maltreatment was brought to court, physical examination of the boys revealed that they had been whipped. The orphans were supposed to have five hours of schooling and spend five hours picking cotton. There was little evidence of school work done at the orphanage. At one point, Father Huhn was fined $1,000 so that he would give sufficient care to the orphans entrusted to him. When Bishop Gallagher visited the locale and became aware of such reports, it stands to reason that he would have demanded that the orphans be moved to a safer environment. See "Bishop Gallagher's Visit," *Brenham Weekly Banner*, August 27, 1891; "Fr. Huhn's Case," *Fort Worth Gazette*, August 20, 1891; and "An Inhuman Priest," *Fort Worth*

Gazette," August 27, 1891. In extant correspondence of Bishop Gallagher to Father Huhn in a much later time period, the bishop expressed the belief that the priest is spending too much time farming, that he should concentrate on his priestly duties. See "Bishop Nicholas Gallagher to Fr. Huhn, January 15, 1912, Archives of the Archdiocese of Galveston-Houston. Five months later, the Bishop granted Father Huhn a month's leave of absence due to his health. See Bishop Nicholas Gallagher to Fr. Huhn, May 23, 1912.

79. Father Huhn was buried at the parish in Brenham as there was no Catholic cemetery in Independence. No marker identifies his grave. The *Brenham Daily Banner* reported that the "state of Texas loses one of its's most spectacular personages . . . the decedent established for himself a reputation for uniqueness of character that placed himself in the category of eccentric." See "Fr. Huhn," *Brenham Daily Banner*, February 15, 1915. Monsignor James Vanderholt reported that an editorial in the Brenham newspaper stated, "Those who knew him loved him for his kind heart and many noble qualities, and his earnest work for the welfare of his church. He had retired from active service as a priest, but continued in a quiet way, to labor for his church. Fr. Huhn was widely known for his charities and benevolent work, and gave very liberally to Catholic charitable enterprises." See Vanderholt, "The Catholic Experience at Old Washington-on-the Brazos," 15. The *Southern Messenger* reported that the orphanage he started for "colored children was 'quite successful' for a few years. . . . The greatest obstacle to success was the isolation of the town of Independence, there being fifteen miles of muddy road to its nearest railroad station." See "The Death of Rev. F. M. Huhn," *Southern Messenger*, February, 1915. Did the populace have a very short memory of events barely a dozen years earlier or did Father Huhn's charity blossom forth in a more benevolent way in the last years of his life?

80. Sister Mary Brendan O'Donnell, CVI, "Annunciation Church: Catholic Motherchurch of Houston" (master's thesis, University of Houston, 1965), 62–65.

81. Sister Nora Marie Coffey, CCVI, *Remember, Rejoice, Renew, 1887–1987: A Centennial Celebration of St. Joseph Hospital, Houston, TX* (Houston, TX: Charles P. Young, 1987), 17–25.

82. Coffey, *Remember, Rejoice, Renew*, 25.

83. Coffey, *Remember, Rejoice, Renew*, 26.

84. Coffey, *Remember, Rejoice, Renew*.

85. Coffey, *Remember, Rejoice, Renew*, 27.

86. Coffey, *Remember, Rejoice, Renew*.

87. Sister Loyola Hegarty, CCVI, *Serving with Gladness: The Origin and History of the Congregation of the Sisters of Charity of the Incarnate Word, Houston, Texas* (Houston, TX: Bruce Publishing in cooperation with the Sisters of Charity of the Incarnate Word, Houston, Texas, 1967), 335–36.

88. Hegarty, *Serving with Gladness*, 340.

89. Coffey, *Remember, Rejoice, Renew*, 38–41.

90. Hegarty, *Serving with Gladness*, 339, and Coffey, *Remember, Rejoice, Renew*, 38.

91. Coffey, *Remember, Rejoice, Renew*, 42.

92. Coffey, *Remember, Rejoice, Renew*, 46.

93. Hegarty, *Serving with Gladness*, 355–56.

94. Hegarty, *Serving with Gladness*, 348.

95. Hegarty, *Serving with Gladness*, 349–50.

96. Hegarty, *Serving with Gladness*, 342–43, 350.

97. It is believed that Bishop Dubuis made the separation between the Sisters of Charity of the Incarnate Word, San Antonio Texas and the Sisters of Charity of the Incarnate Word, Houston, Texas official when he returned from the First Vatican Council in 1870. This thinking was in line with the parent Order of the Incarnate Word and Blessed Sacrament, specifically that each house become independent as soon as it was able to be self-supporting. The distance between Galveston and San Antonio in addition to the creation of new dioceses certainly entered into the decision. See Hegarty, *Serving with Gladness*, 217.

98. Sister M. Loyola Hegarty, CCVI, "Catholic Health Care," *Handbook of Texas Online*, accessed December 19, 2014, www.tshaonline.org/handbook/online/articles/smc01.

99. Hegarty, *Serving with Gladness*, 351.

100. Castañeda, *Church in Texas since Independence*, 398–99.

101. Castañeda, *Church in Texas since Independence*, 399.

102. The influenza pandemic of 1918, more commonly known as the "Spanish flu" or "La grippe" killed more people than were killed in World War I or by the Black Death, bubonic plague, from 1347 to 1351. An estimated 675,000 Americans died of the influenza. The name "Spanish flu" comes from the large number of those afflicted and who succumbed to it in Spain in 1918. See "The Influenza Pandemic of 1918," accessed February 3, 2015, https://virus.stanford.edu/uda/.

103. Castañeda, *Church in Texas since Independence*, 399.

104. Castañeda, *Church in Texas since Independence*, 400.

105. Charter, Sisters of Charity of Hotel Dieu El Paso, Texas, quoted in Casteñada, *Church in Texas since Independence*, 393.

106. Castañeda, *Church in Texas since Independence*, 392–93.

107. Debbie Vasquez and Guadalupe Dominguez, "Sisters of Charity Began Hotel Dieu Hospital," accessed December 12, 2014, http://epcc.libguides.com/content.php?pid=309255&sid=2583686.

108. Castañeda, *Church in Texas since Independence*, 401–4.

109. *Diamond Jubilee, 1847–1922, of the Diocese of Galveston and St. Mary's Cathedral*, 113.

110. Stephen Fox, "Nicholas Joseph Clayton as a Catholic Architect," *Journal of Texas Catholic History and Culture* (1991): 54–55; and Barrie Scardino and Drexel Turner, *The Architecture of Nicholas J. Clayton and His Contemporaries*, foreword by Peter Brink, afterword by Stephen Fox (College Station: Texas A&M University Press, 2000), 30–31.

111. Fox, "Nicholas Joseph Clayton as a Catholic Architect," 56–58.

112. Fox, "Nicholas Joseph Clayton as a Catholic Architect," 56–58.

113. Scardino and Turner, *Architecture of Nicholas J. Clayton*, 204–11.

114. Howard Barnstone, *The Galveston That Was*, photographs by Henri Cartier-Bresson and Ezra Stoller, foreword by James Johnson Sweeney (Houston, TX: Museum of Fine Arts, 1966), 193.

115. Fox, "Nicholas Joseph Clayton as a Catholic Architect," 60–61.

116. David B. Harris, Annunciation Catholic Church, 1871, 1884–1895 (unpublished manuscript, n.d.). n.p.

117. Fox, "Nicholas Joseph Clayton as a Catholic Architect," 60–61; and Scardino and Turner, *Architecture of Nicholas J. Clayton*, 217–18.

118. Robert A. Nesbitt, *The Legend of Nicholas Clayton* (Port Galveston, No. 6, 1974), n.p.

119. Barnstone, *Galveston That Was*, 155–56.

120. Barnstone, *Galveston That Was*, 89, and "Married," *Galveston Daily News*, July 7, 1891, 10.

121. Nesbitt, *Legend of Nicholas Clayton*, n.p.

122. "Clayton's Artwork Is Featured," *Galveston Daily News*, January 4, 1989, 10.

123. Fox, "Nicholas Joseph Clayton as a Catholic Architect," 63–64.

124. Scardino and Turner, *Architecture of Nicholas J. Clayton*, 134.

125. Scardino and Turner, *Architecture of Nicholas J. Clayton*, 134.

126. John Murphy, "Galveston Is Home to Many Texas Firsts," *Galveston Daily News*, June 17, 1998, 14.

127. Nesbitt, *Legend of Nicholas Clayton*, n.p.

128. Barnstone, *Galveston That Was*, 89.

Chapter 4

1. Howard Barnstone, *The Galveston That Was*, photographs by Henri Cartier-Bresson and Ezra Stoller, foreword by James Johnson Sweeney (Houston, TX: Museum of Fine Arts, 1966), 138.

2. James Tucek, *A Century of Faith: The Story of the Diocese of Dallas* (Dallas: Taylor Publishing, 1990), 26.

3. Carlos E. Castañeda, *The Church in Texas since Independence, 1836–1950*, vol. 7 of *Our Catholic Heritage in Texas, 1519–1936* (Austin, TX: Von Boeckmann-Jones, 1958), 138-–39.

4. Pope Leo XIII, *Romani Pontificis*, July 15, 1890.

5. Castañeda, *Church in Texas since Independence*, 139.

6. John Edward Fitzgerald, "Departures of the Forgotten Bishop: Thomas Francis Brennan (1855–1916) of Dallas and St. John's," *CCHA Historical Studies* 71 (2005): 60–63.

7. Fitzgerald, "Departures of the Forgotten Bishop," 63.

8. Tucek, *A Century of Faith*, 29.

9. Castañeda, *Church in Texas since Independence*, 138–40.

10. James Talmadge Moore, *Through Fire and Flood: The Catholic Church in Frontier Texas, 1836-1900* (College Station: Texas A&M University Press, 1992), 225.

11. Tucek, *A Century of Faith*, 30.

12. Tucek, *A Century of Faith*, 31.

13. Castañeda, *Church in Texas since Independence*, 141.

14. Castañeda, *Church in Texas since Independence*, 142–43.

15. Bishop Brennan to Bishop Gallagher, July 10, 1891, Archives of the Diocese of Austin.

16. Bishop Brennan to Bishop Gallagher, January 15, 1892, Archives of the Diocese of Austin.

17. Fitzgerald, "Departures of the Forgotten Bishop," 66.

18. Tucek, *A Century of Faith*, 35.

19. Tucek, *A Century of Faith*, 38–39.

20. Tucek, *A Century of Faith*, 40.

21. Tucek, *A Century of Faith*, 40.

22. Tucek, *A Century of Faith*, 40.

23. Bishop Brennan [in Rome] to Bishop Gallagher, September 20, 1892, Archives of the Diocese of Austin.

24. Bishop John Neraz to Bishop Nicholas Gallagher, October 2, 1892, Archives of the Archdiocese of Galveston-Houston.

25. The phrase translates literally as "to the thresholds of the Apostles." Pilgrimages to the tombs of the apostles Peter and Paul were very common during medieval times, and since the thirteenth century all bishops have been required to make a visit to the tombs of Peter and Paul and report on the affairs of their diocese. The *1983 Code of Canon Law* mandates that this visitation be done every five years, canon 400. See *Oxford Dictionary of the Christian Church*, "ad Limina Apostolorum."

26. Tucek, *A Century of Faith*, 37, 40.

27. Archbishop Janssens to Bishop Gallagher, October 13, 1892, Archives of the Archdiocese of Galveston-Houston.

28. Father Joseph Blum to the Congregation of Propaganda, [undated], Archives of the Diocese of Austin, Texas. The Congregation of Propaganda was often referred to as Propaganda Fide. This Roman congregation was concerned with missionary activity in areas of the world where there was not yet an established hierarchy. It originated in the latter half of the sixteenth century when missionary activity was quite prevalent. The Apostolic Constitution of June 28, 1988, renamed it the Congregation for the Evangelization of the Nations. See *Oxford Dictionary of the Christian Church*, "Propaganda Fide, Congregation of."

29. See Sister Madeleine Grace, CVI, "John Ireland and Michael Corrigan: A Varied Mixing of the Old Sod within American Soil," *The Priest* (September 2009), for more information on this topic.

30. Fitzgerald, "Departures of the Forgotten Bishop," 67.

31. What officially happened to Bishop Brennan remains rather elusive. While Castañeda maintains that he was transferred to the see of Saint John's, Newfoundland, after his *ad limina* visit to Rome on February 1, 1893, Tucek maintains that he was made titular bishop of Utilla and auxiliary to Bishop T. J. Power of Saint John's, Newfoundland, yet his tenure in Newfoundland was brief for he was sent to Rome "for cause." In 1894, he stayed at the Grotta Ferrata Monastery until his death on May 21, 1916. He was seen by others at Castel Gandolfo and other places in Rome. There is some musing in correspondence that he would be sent as a university professor to Constantinople, but that did not occur. Fitzgerald provides a much fuller account of Brennan in Newfoundland. Refused by Thomas Labrecque of Chicoutimi, Quebec, for the position of vice-prefect apostolic, he served under the elderly Irish-born Thomas Joseph Power (1830–1893). On Power's death, Brennan campaigned for the see of Saint John's. However, division already existed between Brennan and the priests of the diocese. A local candidate Michael Francis Howley was chosen by Rome for the see. Brennan continued to lobby the Vatican for a see. Ultimately, he spent his last years in Rome at the Monastery at Grotta Ferrata. An elderly monk who remembered the bishop said nothing other than "he was a holy

man." See Castañeda, *Church in Texas since Independence*, 144; Moore, *Through Fire and Flood*, 235–36; Tucek, *A Century of Faith*, 43–44; and Fitzgerald, "Departures of the Forgotten Bishop," 60–78.

32. Fitzgerald, "Departures of the Forgotten Bishop," 69, 77.

33. Tucek, *A Century of Faith*, 49; and Moore, *Through Fire and Flood*, 236–37.

34. Tucek, *A Century of Faith*, 38.

35. Castañeda, *Church in Texas since Independence*, 145–47.

36. James Talmadge Moore, *Acts of Faith: The Catholic Church in Texas, 1900–1950* (College Station: Texas A&M University Press, 2002), 37–38.

37. Mother M. Patricia Gunning, *To Texas with Love: A History of the Sisters of the Incarnate Word and Blessed Sacrament* (Corpus Christi, TX: Printers Unlimited, 2003), 110.

38. Sister Mary Xavier Holworthy, "History of the Diocese of Corpus Christi, Texas" (unpublished thesis, St. Mary's University,1939), 63–65, Archives of Incarnate Word Convent, Houston, Texas, and Castañeda, *Church in Texas since Independence*, 149.

39. Castañeda, *Church in Texas since Independence*, 140.

40. Castañeda, *Church in Texas since Independence*, 150.

41. Castañeda, *Church in Texas since Independence*, 153–54.

Chapter 5

1. James F. Vanderholt, ed., "Chapters in the Life of Nicholas A. Gallagher, Third Bishop of Galveston, 1882–1918" (unpublished manuscript, 1989), 10, Cardinal Beran Library, St. Mary's Seminary, Houston, Texas.

2. Mother Aloysia Chambodut, OSU, and Monsignor James F. Vanderholt, "Father [C. L. M.] Chambodut, "The First Secular Priest Ordained for Texas, Biographical Sketch" (unpublished manuscript, n.d.); Mother Aloysia Chambodut, OSU, the niece of Father Chambodut, wrote a five-page biography of her uncle, Father C. L. M. Chambodut. Monsignor James Vanderholt expanded her work. The material included here is taken from both works.

3. Americanism was a movement propagated among American Roman Catholics in the last decade of the nineteenth century. It had as its focus the adaptation of the external life of the Church to supposed modern cultural ideals. A biography of Father Thomas Hecker, published in France, also influenced the movement. Stress was laid on the active virtues. Subjection to authority was depreciated. Members of this movement believed that requirements for converts should be minimized. They also perceived little value in cloistered religious orders. Leo XIII addressed the issue in his encyclical *Testem benevolentiae*, issued January 22, 1889. See *The Oxford Dictionary of the Christian Church*, s.v., "Americanism."

4. Petition of Catholic Laymen of Galveston: J. Z. H. Scott of the Law Firm of Scott, Levi and Smith and other Individuals to Cardinal Satolli, February 15, 1896, Archives of the Archdiocese of Galveston-Houston, and Raymond C. Mensing Jr., "A Papal Delegate in Texas: The Visit of His Eminence Cardinal Satolli in 1896," *East Texas Historical Journal* (Fall 1982): 23.

5. Cardinal Francesco Satolli to Bishop Nicholas Gallagher, March 20, 1896, Archives of the Archdiocese of Galveston-Houston.

6. Bishop Nicholas Gallagher to Cardinal Francesco Satolli, March 26, 1896, Archives of the Archdiocese of Galveston-Houston.

7. Mensing, "Papal Delegate in Texas," 21–22.

8. Archbishop Francis Janssens to Bishop Nicholas Gallagher, April 2, 1896, Archives of the Archdiocese of Galveston-Houston.

9. Archbishop Francis Janssens to Bishop Nicholas Gallagher, April 4, 1896, Archives of Archdiocese of Galveston-Houston.

10. Cardinal Francesco Satolli to Bishop Nicholas Gallagher, April 15, 1896, Archives of Archdiocese of Galveston-Houston.

11. Bishop Nicholas Gallagher to Cardinal Satolli, April 28, 1896, Archives of Archdiocese of Galveston-Houston.

12. Archbishop Janssens to Bishop Nicholas Gallagher, May 2, 1896, Archives of Archdiocese of Galveston-Houston.

13. Bishop Nicholas Gallagher to Mother M. Joseph, February 24, 1894, Archives of the Ursuline Sisters, Saint Louis, Missouri.

14. Mensing, "Papal Delegate in Texas," 21.

15. Petitioners regarding Ursuline Chapel to Bishop Nicholas Gallagher, January 25, 1895, Archives, Archdiocese of Galveston-Houston.

16. Bishop Nicholas Gallagher to Mother M. Joseph, February 24, 1894, Archives of the Ursuline Sisters, St. Louis, Missouri.

17. S. M. Johnston, *A Light Shining: The Life and Letters of Mother Mary Joseph Dallmer* (Chicago: Benziger, 1937), 1–31.

18. Johnston, *A Light Shining*, 1–31.

19. Cardinal Francesco Satolli to Mother Joseph, March 15, 1896, Archives of the Ursuline Sisters, Saint Louis, Missouri.

20. Cardinal Mazzella to Mother Joseph, April 9, 1896, Archives of the Ursuline Sisters, Saint Louis, Missouri.

21. Cardinal Francesco Satolli to Sister M. Joseph, April 15, 1896, Archives of the Ursuline Sisters, Saint Louis, Missouri.

22. Bishop Janssens to Bishop Nicholas Gallagher, May 5, 1896, Archives of Archdiocese of Galveston-Houston.

23. Bishop Janssens to Bishop Nicholas Gallagher, June 5, 1896, Archives of the Archdiocese of Galveston-Houston.

24. Father Hennessey, Pastor of Annunciation Church, Houston to Bishop Gallagher, June 13, 1896, Archives of the Archdiocese of Galveston-Houston.

25. Bishop Nicholas Gallagher to Reverend Mother Sister Joseph, Superior of the Ursuline Convent, Galveston, Texas, June 15, 1896, Archives of the Archdiocese of Galveston-Houston.

26. Bishop Nicholas Gallagher to Reverend Mother Sister Joseph, Superior of the Ursuline Convent, Galveston, Texas, June 15, 1896, Archives of the Ursuline Sisters, Saint Louis, Missouri.

27. Cardinal Francesco Satolli to Mother Joseph, June 22, 1896, Archives of the Ursuline Sisters, Saint Louis, Missouri

28. Hegarty, *Serving with Gladness*, 397.

29. Document concerning St. Mary's Orphanage, Bishop C. M. Dubuis and Mother St. John Pradinaud, March 31, 1875, Courtesy of the Archives of Congregation of the Sisters of Charity of the Incarnate Word, Houston, Texas. Not to be reproduced without proper authorization of the Archives.

30. Hegarty, *Serving with Gladness*, 241.

31. Hegarty, *Serving with Gladness*, 241.

32. St. Mary's Infirmary, Galveston, Texas, March 16, 1896. Courtesy of the Archives of the Congregation of the Sisters of Charity of the Incarnate Word. Houston, Texas. Not to be used without proper authorization of the Archives.

33. Archbishop Janssens to Bishop Gallagher, June 5, 1896, Archives of Archdiocese of Galveston-Houston.

34. Archbishop Janssens to Bishop Gallagher, June 5, 1896, Archives of Archdiocese of Galveston-Houston.

35. Hegarty, *Serving with Gladness*, 314–16.

36. Archbishop Janssens to Bishop Gallagher, June 5, 1896, Archives of Archdiocese of Galveston-Houston.

37. Mensing, "Papal Delegate in Texas," 14.

38. Archbishop Janssens to Bishop Gallagher, June 5, 1896, Archives of Archdiocese of Galveston-Houston.

Chapter 6

1. See *New Commentary on the Code of Canon Law*, Canon 470, Power of Vicars.

2. Mother Aloysia Chambodut, OSU, and Father James Vanderholt, "Biography of Fr. CLM Chambodut" (unpublished manuscript, n.d.), 1.

3. Chambodut and Vanderholt, "Biography of Fr. CLM Chambodut," 2–5.

4. Chambodut and Vanderholt, "Biography of Fr. CLM Chambodut," 7; and Carlos E. Castañeda, *The Church in Texas since Independence, 1836–1950*, vol. 7 of *Our Catholic Heritage in Texas, 1519–1936* (Austin, TX: Von Boeckmann-Jones, 1958), 212, 262–66.

5. Chambodut and Vanderholt, "Biography of Fr. C. L. M. Chambodut," 7–9.

6. Chambodut and Vanderholt, "Biography of Fr. C. L. M. Chambodut," 11.

7. Chambodut and Vanderholt, "Biography of Fr. C. L. M. Chambodut," 11–12.

8. L. V. Jacks, *Claude Dubuis, Bishop of Galveston* (Saint Louis: B. Herder, 1947), 169.

9. Sister Loyola Hegarty, CCVI, *Serving with Gladness: The Origin and History of the Congregation of the Sisters of Charity of the Incarnate Word, Houston, Texas* (Houston, TX: Bruce Publishing in cooperation with the Sisters of Charity of the Incarnate Word, Houston, Texas, 1967), 148, 165, 396.

10. Patrick Foley, *Missionary Bishop: Jean-Marie Odin in Galveston and New Orleans* (College Station: Texas A&M University Press, 2013), 157.

11. *Diocese of Galveston-Houston, 1847–1997*, 24.

12. Hegarty, *Serving with Gladness*, 204.

13. Hegarty, *Serving with Gladness*, 207–8.

14. *Flake's Semi-Weekly Bulletin*, August 7, 1869, quoted in Hegarty, *Serving with Gladness*, 208–9.

15. *Flake's Semi-Weekly Bulletin*, August 7, 1869, quoted in Hegarty, *Serving with Gladness*, 209.

16. *Flake's Semi-Weekly Bulletin*, August 7, 1869, quoted in Hegarty, *Serving with Gladness*, 150–51, 232

17. Chambodut and Vanderholt, "Biography of Fr. C. L. M. Chambodut," 13.

18. *Galveston News*, December 8, 1880, quoted in Hegarty, *Serving with Gladness*, 273.

19. *Galveston News*, December 8, 1880, quoted in Hegarty, *Serving with Gladness*, 275.

20. Chambodut and Vanderholt, "Biography of Fr. C. L. M. Chambodut, 14."

21. "Handsome Marble Altar at Sacred Heart Church Is to Be Consecrated on Sunday Morning," *Galveston Daily News*, December 17, 1909.

22. Monsignor James Vanderholt, Pastor Emeritus of Saint Mark's Church, Silsbee, Texas, interviewed by Sister Madeleine Grace, CVI, June 18, 2014.

23. Archbishop Janssens to Bishop Gallagher, June 5, 1896, Archives of Archdiocese of Galveston-Houston.

24. Rev. Steven F. Brown, "Monsignor James M. Kirwin," in *Memoirs of Monsignor J. M. Kirwin*, ed. Father George T. Elmendorf (Houston, TX: Standard Printing and Lithographing., 1928), unpaginated. Father Brown was a student of the monsignor.

25. Brown, "Monsignor James M. Kirwin."

26. Brown, "Monsignor James M. Kirwin."

27. Brown, "Monsignor James M. Kirwin."

28. Brown, "Monsignor James M. Kirwin."

29. Brown, "Monsignor James M. Kirwin."

30. Brown, "Monsignor James M. Kirwin."

31. "Corner Bar Rooms—Home Protective League Full of Earnestness in Its Efforts to Weed Out Saloons," *Galveston Daily News*, November 6, 1907.

32. Brown, "Monsignor James M. Kirwin."

33. Brown, "Monsignor James M. Kirwin."

34. "[Monsignor James Kirwin] Declares Socialism Is an Idle Dream," *Galveston Daily News*, March 12, 1911.

35. Rev. James Kirwin, "The Church and the Flag," *Memoirs of Monsignor J. M. Kirwin*, unpaginated.

36. Rev. James Kirwin, "The Christian Soldier," *Memoirs of Monsignor J. M. Kirwin*, unpaginated.

37. Brown, "Monsignor James M. Kirwin."

38. Rev. Thomas Ryan, "A Foot Soldier of Jesus Christ," *Memoirs of Monsignor J. M. Kirwin*, unpaginated.

39. Ryan, "A Foot Soldier of Jesus Christ," *Memoirs of Monsignor J. M. Kirwin*, unpaginated.

40. Robert C. Giles, *Changing Times: The Story of the Diocese of Galveston Houston in Commemoration of Its Founding, 125th Anniversary of the Diocese of Galveston-Houston, 1847–1972* (Texas Catholic Herald Production Staff, Most Reverend John L. Morkovsky, STD), 42.

41. Brown, "Monsignor James M. Kirwin."

42. "Father Kirwin's Silver Jubilee of Ordination," *Memoirs of Monsignor J. M. Kirwin*, unpaginated.

43. Castañeda, *Church in Texas since Independence*, 273.

44. In 1947 Father Louis Reicher was appointed by Pope Pius XII as the first bishop of the recently established Diocese of Austin.

45. Sheila Hackett, OP, *Dominican Women in Texas: From Ohio to Galveston and Beyond* (Houston, TX: Sacred Heart Convent, 1986), 139, and "The Great Priest Passes," *Memoirs of Monsignor J. M. Kirwin*, unpaginated.

46. Brown, "Monsignor James M. Kirwin."

47. "St. Mary of the Immaculate Conception Catholic Church, LaPorte, TX," accessed June 13, 2015, http://stmaryslaporte.com/history-of-st-marys-church.

Chapter 7

1. Patricia Bellis Bixel and Elizabeth Hayes Turner, *Galveston and the 1900 Storm: Catastrophe and Catalyst* (Austin: University of Texas Press, 2000), 1–4.

2. Bixel and Turner, *Galveston and the 1900 Storm*, 4–5, 10.

3. John Edward Weems, *A Weekend in September* (New York: Henry Holt, 1957), 34.

4. Weems, *Weekend in September*, 34.

5. Bixel and Turner, *Galveston and the 1900 Storm*, 18.

6. Bixel and Turner, *Galveston and the 1900 Storm*, 18–20; Susan Wiley Hardwick, *Mythic Galveston: Reinventing America's Third Coast* (Baltimore: Johns Hopkins University Press, 2002), 97, and Erik Larson, *Isaac's Storm: A Man, a Time, and the Deadliest Hurricane in History* (New York: Crown, 1999), 257.

7. Clarence Ousley, ed., *Galveston in Nineteen Hundred* (Atlanta, GA: William C. Chase, 1900), 100.

8. Ousley, *Galveston in Nineteen Hundred*, 100–103.

9. Ousley, *Galveston in Nineteen Hundred*, 104.

10. Ousley, *Galveston in Nineteen Hundred*, 107.

11. Sheila Hackett, OP, *Dominican Women in Texas: From Ohio to Galveston and Beyond* (Houston, TX: Sacred Heart Convent, 1986), 108–10.

12. Ousley, *Galveston in Nineteen Hundred*, 107–8.

13. Ousley, *Galveston in Nineteen Hundred*, 109–11.

14. Weems, *Weekend in September*, 122.

15. S. M. Johnston, *A Light Shining: The Life and Letters of Mother Mary Joseph Dallmer* (Chicago: Benziger, 1937), 119.

16. Sister Loyola Hegarty, CCVI, *Serving with Gladness: The Origin and History of the Congregation of the Sisters of Charity of the Incarnate Word, Houston, Texas* (Houston, TX: Bruce Publishing in cooperation with the Sisters of Charity of the Incarnate Word, Houston, Texas, 1967), 322–23; Larson, *Isaac's Storm*, 233–34; and Hardwick, *Mythic Galveston*, 101.

17. Ousley, *Galveston in Nineteen Hundred*, 114–15.

18. Hegarty, *Serving with Gladness*, 324–27.

19. Murat Halstead, *Galveston: The Horrors of a Stricken City* (Chicago: American Publishers' Association, 1900), 168.

20. Hegarty, *Serving with Gladness*, 324–27.

21. Bixel and Turner, *Galveston and the 1900 Storm*, 31.

22. Weems, *Weekend in September*, 145.

23. Gary Cartwright, *Galveston: A History of the Island* (New York: Maxwell Macmillan International, 1991), 179.

24. Bixel and Turner, *Galveston and the 1900 Storm*, 7, 9–82.

25. Halstead, *Galveston: The Horrors of a Stricken City*, 93.

26. Hegarty, *Serving with Gladness*, 330–34.

27. *Diocese of Galveston-Houston, 1847–1997*, 34.

28. Ousley, *Galveston in Nineteen Hundred*, 98, 120.

29. Bixel and Turner, *Galveston and the 1900 Storm*, 89.

30. Hardwick, *Mythic Galveston*, 113.

31. Hegarty, *Serving with Gladness*, 329.

32. Hardwick, *Mythic Galveston*, 116–18.

33. *Diocese of Galveston Centennial, 1847–1947*, 58.

34. "Church of the Annunciation, Houston," accessed December 29, 2014, www.tshaonline.org/handbook/online/articles/ivc01.

35. Sister Mary Brendan O'Donnell, CVI, "Annunciation Church: Catholic Mother Church of Houston" (master's thesis, University of Houston, 1965), 72–73.

36. In the early 1840s, a group of German immigrants settled in Brazoria. Father Jacob Wiser, with the aid of some Irish plantation owners, built a small frame church and dedicated it to St. Joseph. Shortly after, a brick church and rectory were established. See Giles, *125th Anniversary: Diocese of Galveston-Houston, 1847–1972*, 82–83.

37. Bixel and Turner, *Galveston and the 1900 Storm*, ix.

38. Bixel and Turner, *Galveston and the 1900 Storm*, 33, 41, 43.

39. Terry MacLeod, "Galveston Remembers Terror of a Hurricane," *Texas Catholic Herald*, September 8, 1964, 8.

Chapter 8

1. I am indebted to Monsignor James Vanderholt for the thorough research he has done in "The History of Saint Mary's Seminary: La Porte, Texas, 1901–1954" (unpublished manuscript, n.d.), Cardinal Beran Library, St. Mary's Seminary, Houston, Texas.

2. Bishop Nicholas Gallagher to the Priests and Laity of the Diocese of Galveston, December 17, 1883, Archives of the Archdiocese of Galveston-Houston.

3. Bishop Nicholas Gallagher, "Lent" (unpublished manuscript, 1892), n.p., Archives of the Archdiocese of Galveston-Houston.

4. *Diary of Bishop Nicholas Gallagher* (1892), n.p., Archives of the Archdiocese of Galveston-Houston.

5. *Diocese of Galveston Centennial 1847–1947*, 122.

6. Vanderholt, "The History of St. Mary's Seminary," 2.

7. Monsignor Joseph Valente, "The Beginning" (unpublished manuscript, n.d.), in Vanderholt, "The History of St. Mary's Seminary," n.p.

8. Vanderholt, "The History of St. Mary's Seminary," 2.

9. Vanderholt, "The History of St. Mary's Seminary," 8.

10. Vanderholt, "The History of St. Mary's Seminary," 9.

11. "St. Mary's Seminary, La Porte, Texas," *Houston Post*, September 1, 1902, 10.

12. "Bishop Gallagher Returned," *Galveston Daily News*, November 1, 1904, 3.

13. Monsignor Joseph Valenta, "The Beginning" (unpublished manuscript, n.d.), in *The History of St. Mary's Seminary*.

14. Vanderholt, "The History of St. Mary's Seminary," 10–11, 13.

15. Vanderholt, "The History of St. Mary's Seminary," 12–13.

16. "A Second Victory: The Houston High School Won from St. Mary's Seminary," *Houston Post*, May 20, 1906, 16.

17. "Students of St. Mary's Hold Commencement: Bishop Gallagher Attended from Galveston—Many Visitors from Houston," *Houston Post*, June 18, 1905, 9.

18. "Another Scholarship Secured," *Houston Post*, May 24, 1906, 2.

19. Vanderholt, "The History of St. Mary's Seminary," 14–15.

20. An ongoing problem at the seminary was found in the diversity of the student body, which required the teaching of a variety of courses. The Basilians expected to teach college and postcollege students, yet Bishop Gallagher included lower academic levels to promote vocations and ensure reasonable value for diocesan money. In the summer of 1908, Father Thomas Gignac, CSB, stated that the workload of the teachers was excessive and needed to be changed. While a meeting with Bishop Gallagher followed, no satisfactory agreement could be reached. Ultimately, Bishop Gallagher was not pleased with the leadership in the seminary and demanded a change. See Raphael O'Laughlin, CSB, *Basilian Leaders from Texas* (Houston, TX: Wing Press, 1991), 28, and Archbishop Joseph A. Fiorenza, "St. Mary's Seminary, 1901–2011," address given at St. Mary's Seminary, Houston, 2011.

21. Bishop Nicholas Aloysius Gallagher to the Priests of the Diocese of Galveston, July 26, 1911, Archives of the Archdiocese of Galveston-Houston.

22. Vanderholt, "The History of St. Mary's Seminary," 23.

23. Bishop Nicholas Gallagher to Very Rev. D. Brosnan, February 9, 1913, Archives of Archdiocese of Galveston-Houston.

24. Vanderholt, "The History of St. Mary's Seminary," 25.

25. Vanderholt, "The History of St. Mary's Seminary."

26. Vanderholt, "The History of St. Mary's Seminary," 26.

27. Vanderholt, "The History of St. Mary's Seminary," 27.

28. Vanderholt, "The History of St. Mary's Seminary," 28.

29. Vanderholt, "The History of St. Mary's Seminary," 29.

30. Vanderholt, "The History of St. Mary's Seminary," 27.

31. Vanderholt, "The History of St. Mary's Seminary," 30–31.

Chapter 9

1. Thomas Meehan, "James Alphonsus McMaster," *Catholic Encyclopedia* (New York: Robert Appleton Company, 1910), accessed October 3, 2014, www1000.newadvent.org/cathen/09506a.htm.

2. James A. McMaster to Bishop Nicholas Gallagher, January 6, 1882, Catholic Archives of Texas.

3. James A. McMaster to Bishop Nicholas Gallagher, January 7, 1882, Catholic Archives of Texas.

4. Adam Giesinger, *From Catherine to Khrushchev: The Story of Russia's Germans* (Battleford, SK: Marian Press, 1974), 1.

5. Giesinger, *From Catherine to Khrushchev*, 56.

6. Dona B. Reeves-Marquardt and Lewis R. Marquardt, "Catholic Germans from Russia in Texas," *Journal of Texas Catholic History and Culture* 4 (1993): 27–28.

7. Giesinger, *From Catherine to Khrushchev*, 202–3, 211.

8. Reeves-Marquardt and Marquard, "Catholic Germans from Russia in Texas," 32.

9. Reeves-Marquardt and Marquardt, "Catholic Germans from Russia in Texas," 27–28.

10. "Fr. Joseph Klein," *Southern Messenger*, June 10, 1920, Catholic Archives of Texas.

11. Robert C. Giles, *Changing Times: The Story of the Diocese of Galveston Houston in Commemoration of Its Founding, 125th Anniversary of the Diocese of Galveston-Houston, 1847–1972* (Texas Catholic Herald Production Staff, Most Reverend John L. Morkovsky, STD), 109.

12. Reeves-Marquardt and Marquardt, "Catholic Germans from Russia in Texas," 27–28, 34.

13. Grimes County Historical Commission, *History of Grimes County: Land of Heritage and Progress* (Dallas: Taylor Publishing, 1982), 116.

14. Betty Markey, "History of Catholicism in the Vicinity of Plantersville, Grimes County, TX," *PGST [Polish Genealogical Society of Texas] News* 9, no. 2 (Summer 1992): 1–3.

15. Markey, "History of Catholicism," 2.

16. Markey, "History of Catholicism," 3.

17. Bishop Nicholas Gallagher to Parishioner, August 20, 1911, Catholic Archives of Texas.

18. Bishop Nicholas A, Gallagher to Rev. Father Weisneroski, November 9, 1911, Archives of the Archdiocese of Galveston-Houston.

19. Giles, *Changing Times*, 109.

20. Trustees to Bishop Gallagher, July 29, 1912, Catholic Archives of Texas.

21. Bishop Gallagher to Parishioners in Plantersville, August 6, 1912, Archives of Archdiocese of Galveston-Houston.

22. Markey, "History of Catholicism," 3.

23. Parishioners from Dobbin, Texas, to Bishop Nicholas Gallagher, July 11, 1917, Catholic Archives of Texas.

24. Father George Apel to Bishop Nicholas Gallagher, July 22, 1917, Catholic Archives of Texas.

25. Sharon Sicinski Skeans, *Church of the Nativity of the Blessed Virgin Mary, St. Mary's Visitors' Guide-2011, Plantersville, TX* (Montgomery, TX: Thomas Printing and Publishing, n.d.), n.p.

26. Parishioners of St. Roch's Church, Mentz, Texas, to Bishop Nicholas Gallagher, October 23, 1912, Archives of Diocese of Austin, Texas.

27. George Berberich, "Golden Jubilee at Mentz Church: Historical Sketch of Congregation," *Eagle Lake Headlight*, 1920.

28. Sister Charlotte Kitowski, CDP, archivist, letter to author, December 9 2014.

29. Jas. I. Klein, Mentz, Texas, to Bishop Nicholas Gallagher, July 20, 1912, Archives of the Diocese of Austin, Texas.

30. Sister Charlotte Kitowski, CDP, archivist, letter to author, December 9, 2014.

31. Arliss Treybig, "Bernardo, TX," *Handbook of Texas Online*, accessed December 06, 2014, www.tshaonline.org/handbook/online/articles/hnb29.

32. Parishioners of Chappell Hill to Archbishop Janssens of New Orleans, August 2, 1890, Archives of the Diocese of Austin, Texas.

33. Parishioners of Chappell Hill to Bishop Nicholas Gallagher, March 3, 1890, Catholic Archives of Texas.

34. Bishop Nicholas A. Gallagher to Parishioners of Chappell Hill, Texas, April 16, 1890, Archives of the Diocese of Austin, Texas.

35. Parishioners of Chappell Hill to Archbishop Francis Janssens of New Orleans, August 2, 1890, Catholic Archives of Texas.

36. Archbishop Francis Janssens to Bishop Nicholas Gallagher, August 11, 1890, Catholic Archives of Texas.

37. "History of St. Stanislaus Kostka Church Anderson," Archdiocese of Galveston-Houston, accessed October 30, 2014, www.polish-texans.com/2007/06/history-of-st-stanislaus-kostka-church-anderson/reference.

38. Father N. T. Domanski to Bishop Nicholas Gallagher, May 23, 1916, Archives of the Diocese of Austin, Texas.

39. Parishioners of Chappell Hill to Bishop Nicholas Gallagher, June 28, 1916, Catholic Archives of Texas.

40. Parishioners in Chappell Hill to Bishop Nicholas Gallagher, July 14, 1916, Catholic Archives of Texas.

41. Virginia Felchak Hill, "History of St. Stanislaus Catholic Church, Chappell, Texas," accessed November 30, 2014, www.bishop-accountability.org.

42. Father Michael Joseph Tabor to Bishop Nicholas Gallagher, October 4, 1916, Archives of the Sisters of Divine Providence, San Antonio, Texas.

43. "History of St. Stanislaus Catholic Church, Chappell Hill, TX," accessed June 15, 2015, www.polish-texans.com/2007/07/ii-57/2/.

44. Parishioners of Saint Mary's Church, Taylor, Texas, to Bishop Nicholas Gallagher, February 20, 1891, Catholic Archives of Texas.

45. For more information on this topic, see "Lay Trusteeism in New York, January 25, 1786," and "The Abuse of Lay Trusteeism at Norfolk, Virginia, June–September, 1819," in *Documents of American Catholic History*, ed. John Tracy Ellis (Lexington, KY: Forgotten Books, 2013), 150–54 and 220–27.

Chapter 10

1. Bishop Nicholas Gallagher, "Vocation" (unpublished manuscript, 1903), 5, Archives of the Archdiocese of Galveston-Houston.

2. Gallagher, "Vocation," 5–6.

3. Gallagher, "Vocation," 6–7.

4. Gallagher, "Vocation," 7–8.

5. Gallagher, "Vocation," 9–10.

6. Bishop Nicholas Gallagher, "The Decree of Our Holy Father Pius X *Quam Singulari Christus Amore*, On the First Communion of Children" (unpublished manuscript, February 2, 1911), 1–3, Archives of the Archdiocese of Galveston-Houston.

7. Gallagher, "The Decree of Our Holy Father Pius X," 2–3.

8. Gallagher, "The Decree of Our Holy Father Pius X," 4.

9. Gallagher, "The Decree of Our Holy Father Pius X," 4.

10. Gallagher, "The Decree of Our Holy Father Pius X," 5.

11. Gallagher, "The Decree of Our Holy Father Pius X," 5.

12. Gallagher, "The Decree of Our Holy Father Pius X," 6.

13. Gallagher, "The Decree of Our Holy Father Pius X," 6.

14. Gallagher, "The Decree of Our Holy Father Pius X," 7.

15. Bishop Nicholas Gallagher, "Lenten Letter," 1895, Archives of the Archdiocese of Galveston-Houston.

16. Gallagher, "Lenten Letter."

17. It is worthy of note that the decree of January 18, 1896, permitted a nominal

membership in these three societies provided that in the judgment of the Apostolic delegate, four conditions were met: the society was entered in good faith, there is no scandal, grave temporal injury would result from withdrawal, there is no danger of perversion. The Apostolic Delegate, in granting the dispensation, requires that the individual not attend meetings, or frequent the lodge rooms, that dues be sent in by mail or by a third party, that in the event of death, the society will have nothing to do with the funeral. See William Fanning, "Secret Societies," *Catholic Encyclopedia* (New York: Robert Appleton, 1912), accessed November 28, 2014, www.newadvent.org/cathen/14071b.htm.

18. Bishop Nicholas Gallagher, "Lenten Letter," 1898, Archives of the Archdiocese of Galveston-Houston.

19. Bishop Nicholas Gallagher, "Lenten Letter," 1899, Archives of the Archdiocese of Galveston-Houston.

Chapter 11

1. P. McKenna, "Ode on the Fiftieth Anniversary of Rt. Rev. Bishop Gallagher," *Southern Messenger*, March 19, 1896, 5.

2. *Diocese of Galveston, Centennial, 1847–1947,* 42

3. "Silver Jubilee of Bishop Gallagher," *Houston Daily Post,* April 28, 1907, Archives of Rosenberg Library, Galveston, Texas.

4. *Galveston Tribune,* 1907, quoted in *Diamond Jubilee 1847–1922* of the Diocese of Galveston and St. Mary's Cathedral as Compiled by the Priests of the Seminary, 114.

5. *Galveston Tribune,* 1907, quoted in *Diamond Jubilee 1847–1922* of the Diocese of Galveston and St. Mary's Cathedral as compiled by the Priests of the Seminary, 114.

6. *Galveston Tribune,* 1907, quoted in *Diamond Jubilee 1847–1922 of the Diocese of Galveston and St. Mary's Cathedral* as compiled by the Priests of the Seminary, 114.

7. *Galveston Tribune,* 1907, quoted in *Diamond Jubilee 1847–1922 of the Diocese of Galveston and St. Mary's Cathedral,* 115.

8. "[Bishop Gallagher] May Succeed Archbishop Chapelle," *Daily Evening Blade,* December 29, 1905.

Chapter 12

1. "The Bishop's 65th Anniversary," *Galveston Tribune,* February 18, 1911, 8.

2. "Bishop Gallagher's Anniversary Honored," *Galveston Daily News,* May 1, 1917.

3. Rev. Lewis J. O'Hern, CSP, to Bishop Nicholas Gallagher, December 4, 1917, Catholic Archives of Texas.

4. Bishop Nicholas Gallagher to Very Reverend James M. Kirwin, VG, June 16, 1918, Catholic Archives of Texas.

5. Bishop Nicholas Gallagher, Last Will and Testament, Catholic Archives of Texas, *Diamond Jubilee 1847–1922 of the Diocese of Galveston and St. Mary's Cathedral,* 116, and "Will of Bishop is Filed for Probate," *Galveston Daily News,* February 28, 1918.

6. *Diamond Jubilee 1847–1922 of the Diocese of Galveston and St. Mary's Cathedral,* 116–17.

7. James Talmadge Moore, *Acts of Faith: The Catholic Church in Texas, 1900–1950* (College Station: Texas A&M University Press, 2002), 62.

8. Carlos E. Castañeda, *The Church in Texas since Independence, 1836–1950,* vol. 7 of *Our Catholic Heritage in Texas, 1519–1936* (Austin, TX: Von Boeckmann-Jones, 1958), 162.

9. *Diamond Jubilee 1847–1922 of the Diocese of Galveston and St. Mary's Cathedral,* 117–18.

Chapter 13

1. *New Catholic Encyclopedia,* 2004 ed., s.v. "Diocese of Galveston" by Thomas Meehan.

2. Sister Loyola Hegarty, CCVI, *Serving with Gladness: The Origin and History of the Congregation of the Sisters of Charity of the Incarnate Word, Houston, Texas* (Houston, TX: Bruce Publishing in cooperation with the Sisters of Charity of the Incarnate Word, Houston, Texas, 1967), 305.

3. Sheila Hackett, OP, *Dominican Women in Texas: From Ohio to Galveston and Beyond* (Houston, TX: Sacred Heart Convent, 1986),65.

4. Pope Pius IX, *Instruction to the Bishops of the United States,* 1875, accessed October 20, 2014, www.catholicessentials.net/christianeducation.htm.

5. Bishop Gallagher is listed as bishop administrator among the bishops who attended the Council in the Lives of American Prelates. As it states: "Right Reverend Nicholas A. Gallagher was born at Temperanceville, Belmont County, Ohio, February 19, 1846. He made his classical, philosophical and theological studies at Mt. St. Marty's Seminary, Cincinnati, and was ordained December 25, 1868, at Columbus. He was appointed administrator of the Diocese of Columbus, October 8, 1878, and transferred to the administration of Galveston, Texas, January 10, 1882, being consecrated April 30, 1882." See *The Memorial Volume: A History of the Third Plenary Council of Baltimore November 9–December 7, 1884* (Baltimore: Baltimore Publishing, 1885), 92–93. According to a letter written by Bishop Gallagher to Archbishop James Gibbons, Bishop Gallagher asked for a theologian for the Third Council of Baltimore and received Father William F. Clarke. See Archbishop James Gibbons to Bishop Nicholas Gallagher, August 30, 1884, Archives of Archdiocese of Galveston-Houston.

6. "The Third Plenary Council of Baltimore, Title VI," accessed October 20, 2014, www.newadvent.org/cathen/02235a.htm.

7. *The 1917 or Pio-Benedictine Code of Canon Law: In English Translation with Extensive Scholarly Apparatus,* foreword by John J. Myers, translation by editor and curator Edward N. Peters (San Francisco; Ignatius Press, 2001), canon 794, #2 and Dolan, 397.

8. Monsignor James Vanderholt, "The History of Saint Mary's Seminary: La Porte, Texas, 1901–1954" (unpublished manuscript, n.d.), Cardinal Beran Library, Saint Mary's Seminary, Houston, Texas, 1.

9. Bishop Nicholas Gallagher to Individuals within Diocese of Galveston, November 30, 1883, Archives of the Archdiocese of Galveston-Houston.

10. "Galveston, December 8 [1883]," *Austin Weekly Statesman*, December 13, 1883, 7.

11. Robert C. Giles, *Changing Times: The Story of the Diocese of Galveston Houston in Commemoration of Its Founding, 125th Anniversary of the Diocese of Galveston-Houston, 1847–1972* (Texas Catholic Herald Production Staff, Most Reverend John L. Morkovsky, STD), 29 and 50.

12. *Diocese of Galveston-Houston, 1847–1997*, 34–36.

13. Father James Vanderholt, Carolyn B. Martinez, and Karen A. Gilman, *The Diocese of Beaumont, the Catholic Story of Southeast Texas* (Diocese of Beaumont: East Texas Catholic 1991), 32.

14. "First Diocesan Teachers' Institute," *Southern Messenger*, December 29, 1910, and James F, Vanderholt, ed., "Chapters in the Life of Nicholas A. Gallagher, Third Bishop of Galveston, 1882–1918" (unpublished manuscript, 1989), 120–22.

15. Vanderholt, "Chapters in the Life of Nicholas A. Gallagher," 85.

16. Giles, *Changing Times*, 29, and Vanderholt, "Chapters in the Life of Nicholas A. Gallagher," 82–93.

17. *Diocese of Galveston-Houston, 1847–1997*, 36.

18. Father E. B. Ledvina to Bishop Nicholas Gallagher, January 22, 1916, Catholic Archives of Texas.

19. Father E. B. Ledvina to Father B. C. Pfiffner, July 6, 1917, Catholic Archives of Texas.

20. *Diocese of Galveston-Houston, 1847–1997*, 36.

21. Giles, *Changing Times*, 29.

22. *Diocese of Galveston-Houston, 1847–1997*, 39.

24. Bishop Nicholas Gallagher to his Niece [Sr. M. Agnes], September 22, 1909, Catholic Archives of Texas.

25. Lisa May, archivist for the Archdiocese of Galveston-Houston, letter to author, December 9, 2014.

26. James A. McMaster, "Bishop Administrator for Galveston," *New York Freeman's Journal*, December 31, 1881, 4.

27. Reverend Mr. Rich Wilson, "Looking Back to Look Ahead," *Regina Cleri ora pro nobis* (Spring 2015).

Bibliography

Archives, Collections, and Manuscripts

Annals. Vol. 46. Sacred Heart Dominican Convent Archives. Houston, Texas.

Archives of the Archdiocese of Galveston-Houston, Texas.

Archives of the Congregation of Divine Providence, San Antonio, Texas.

Archives of the Congregation of the Mission, Western Province, Chicago, Illinois.

Archives of the Congregation of the Sacred Heart, Houston, Texas.

Archives of the Congregation of Saint Basil, Toronto, Canada.

Archives of the Congregation of Saint Ursula, Saint Louis, Missouri.

Archives of the Diocese of Beaumont, Texas.

Archives of the Good Shepherd Sisters, Saint Louis, Missouri.

Archives of the Sisters of Charity of the Incarnate Word, Houston, Texas.

Archives of the Sisters of the Incarnate Word and Blessed Sacrament, Houston, Texas.

Archives of the Sisters of Saint Mary of Namur, Fort Worth, Texas.

Archives of the University of Notre Dame, Notre Dame, Indiana.

Beal, John P., James A. Coriden, and Thomas J. Green, eds. *The New Commentary on the Code of Canon Law.* New York: Paulist Press, 2000.

Bulletin of the Catholic Record Society, Diocese of Columbus. 14th year, 1st edition. January 1989.

Catholic Archives of Texas.

Chambodut, Mother Aloysia, OSU, and Msgr. James F. Vanderholt. "Father [CLM] Chambodut: The First Secular Priest Ordained for Texas, Biographical Sketch." Unpublished manuscript, n.d.

Drexel, Mother Katherine. Correspondence. Diocese of Beaumont, Texas.

Gallagher, Bishop Nicholas. Correspondence. Archives of the Archdiocese of Galveston-Houston, Texas.

———. Correspondence. Catholic Archives of Texas.

———. "The Decree of Our Holy Father Pius X *Quam Singulari Christus Amore,* On the First Communion of Children." Unpublished manuscript. February 2, 1911. Archives of the Archdiocese of Galveston-Houston, Texas.

———. *Diary of 1892.* Archives of the Archdiocese of Galveston-Houston, Texas.

———. "Last Will and Testament," November 14, 1911. Catholic Archives of Texas.

———. "Lent." Unpublished manuscript. 1892. n.p. Archives of the Archdiocese of Galveston-Houston, Texas.

———. "Vocation." Unpublished manuscript. 1903. Archives of the Archdiocese of Galveston-Houston, Texas.

Harris, David B. "Annunciation Catholic Church, 1871, 1884–1895." Unpublished manuscript, n.d.

Holworthy, Sister Mary Xavier. "History of the Diocese of Corpus Christi, Texas." Unpublished thesis. St. Mary's University, 1939. Archives of Incarnate Word Convent, Houston, Texas.

Kirwin, Monsignor James. Correspondence. Archives of the Archdiocese of Galveston-Houston, Texas.

McHugh, Sister Mary Sebastian, IWBS. "History of the Order of the Incarnate Word and Blessed Sacrament in Houston, Texas." Unpublished thesis, University of Houston, 1950. Archives of Incarnate Word Convent, Houston, Texas.

Nesbitt, Robert A. *The Legend of Nicholas Clayton.* Port Galveston, No. 6, 1974.

O'Donnell, Sister Mary Brendan, CVI. "Annunciation Church: Catholic Motherchurch of Houston." Master's thesis, University of Houston, 1965.

Sheehan, Sister Agatha, CVI. "St. Nicholas Parish," *Early Church in Houston.* Unpublished manuscript, 1961. Archives of the Sisters of the Incarnate Word and Blessed Sacrament, Houston, Texas.

———. "Sisters of the Incarnate Word and Blessed Sacrament, Houston, TX." Unpublished manuscript, 1962. Archives of Incarnate Word Convent, Houston, Texas.

Thomas, Sister Mary Ursula. "The Catholic Church in the Oklahoma Frontier, 1824–1907." PhD diss., Saint Louis University, 1938.

Valente, Monsignor Joseph. "The Beginning." Unpublished manuscript. n.d. in *The History of St. Mary's Seminary.*

Vanderholt, Monsignor James. "The Catholic Experience at Old Washington-on-the Brazos, Washington, County, Texas: The Oldest Black Catholic Community in Texas." Unpublished manuscript, March 2, 1995.

———. "The History of Saint Mary's Seminary: La Porte, Texas, 1901–1954." Unpublished manuscript, n.d. Cardinal Beran Library, Saint Mary's Seminary, Houston, Texas.

Vanderholt, Monsignor James F., ed. "Chapters in the Life of Nicholas A. Gallagher, Third Bishop of Galveston, 1882–1918." Unpublished manuscript, 1989. Cardinal Beran Library, Saint Mary's Seminary, Houston, Texas.

Books and Articles

"Another Scholarship Secured." *Houston Post,* May 24, 1906, 2.

Barnstone, Howard. *The Galveston That Was.* Photographs by Henri Cartier-Bresson and Ezra Stoller. Foreword by James Johnson Sweeney. Houston: Museum of Fine Arts, 1966.

Begnaud, Sister St. John, SSMN. *A Little Good: The Sisters of St. Mary in Texas.* Foreword by Monsignor Joseph Schumacher. Eugene, OR: Wiff and Stock, 2011.

Berberich, George. "Golden Jubilee at Mentz Church: Historical Sketch of Congregation." *Eagle Lake Headlight*, 1920.

"[Bishop Gallagher] May Succeed Archbishop Chapelle." *Daily Evening Blade*, December 29, 1905.

"Bishop Gallagher Returned." *Galveston Daily News*, November 1, 1904.

"Bishop Gallagher's Anniversary Honored." *Galveston Daily News*, May 1, 1917.

"Bishop Gallagher's Visit." *Brenham Weekly Banner*, August 27, 1891.

"The Bishop's 65th Anniversary." *Galveston Tribune*, February 18, 1911, 8.

Bixel, Patricia Bellis, and Elizabeth Hayes Turner. *Galveston and the 1900 Storm: Catastrophe and Catalyst*. Austin: University of Texas Press, 2000.

Cartwright, Gary. *Galveston: A History of the Island*. New York: Maxwell Macmillan International, 1991.

Castañeda, Carlos E. *The Church in Texas since Independence, 1836–1950*, vol. 7 of *Our Catholic Heritage in Texas, 1519–1936*. Austin, TX: Von Boeckmann-Jones, 1958.

Catholic Encyclopedia. Robert C. Broderick, comp. Nashville: Thomas Nelson, 1975.

"Clayton's Artwork Is Featured." *Galveston Daily News*, January 4, 1989, 10.

Coffey, Sister Nora Marie, CCVI. *Remember, Rejoice, Renew, 1887–1987: A Centennial Celebration of St. Joseph Hospital, Houston, TX*. Houston: Charles P. Young, 1987.

"Cornerstone Laying of Catholic College Tomorrow." *Waco Evening Telegraph*, April 5, 1902.

"Cornerstone of St. Basil's College to Be Laid—Prominent Clergy to Attend." *Waco Times Herald*, April 6, 1902.

"The Death of Rev. F. M. Huhn." *Southern Messenger*, February, 1915.

Diamond Jubilee, 1847–1922, of the Diocese of Galveston and St. Mary's Seminary. Compiled by Priests at the Seminary. Galveston: Knapp Brothers, 1922.

Diocese of Galveston Centennial, 1847–1947. Foreword by Christopher Edward Byrne, Bishop of Galveston. Houston: Centennial Book Committee, 1947.

Diocese of Galveston-Houston, 1847–1997. Foreword by Bishop Joseph A. Fiorenza. Dallas, TX: Taylor Publishing, 1997.

Elmendorf, Monsignor George. *Memoirs of Monsignor J. M. Kirwin*. Houston, TX: Standard Printing and Lithographing, 1928.

"First Diocesan Teachers' Institute." *Southern Messenger*, December 29, 1910.

Fischer, Betty Connie Voss et al. *St. Thomas High School in the Twentieth Century*. Houston, TX: Wetmore Printing/Curtis Weeks, 2000.

Fitzgerald, John Edward. "Departures of the Forgotten Bishop: Thomas Francis Brennan (1855–1916) of Dallas and St. John's." *CCHA Historical Studies* 71 (2005): 60–78.

Foley, Patrick. *Missionary Bishop: Jean-Marie Odin in Galveston and New Orleans*. College Station: Texas A&M University Press, 2013.

Fox, Stephen. "Nicholas Joseph Clayton as a Catholic Architect." *Journal of Texas Catholic History and Culture* (1991): 54–78.

"Fr. Huhn." *Brenham Daily Banner*, February 15, 1915.

"Fr. Huhn's Case." *Fort Worth Gazette*, August 20, 1891.

"Galveston, December 8 [1883]." *Austin Weekly Statesman*, December 13, 1883, 7.

Giesinger, Adam. *From Catherine to Khrushchev: The Story of Russia's Germans*. Battleford, SK: Marian Press, 1974.

Giles, Robert C. *Changing Times: The Story of the Diocese of Galveston Houston in Commemoration of Its Founding, 125th Anniversary of the Diocese of Galveston-Houston, 1847–1972*. Forewords by Bishop Wendelin J. Nold and Bishop John L. Morkovsky. Houston: Texas Catholic Herald Production Staff, Most Reverend John L. Morkovsky, STD, 1972.

"Good Lecture to Large Crowd." *Los Angeles Herald*. September 5, 1904. California: Digital Newspaper Collection.

Grace, Sr. Madeleine, CVI. "John Ireland and Michael Corrigan: A Varied Mixing of the Old Sod within American Soil." *The Priest* (September 2009): 40–49.

———. "A New Beginning in a New Land: A Recasting of a Treasured Heritage." *Catholic Southwest: A Journal of History and Culture* 23 (2012): 69–79.

Grimes County Historical Commission. *History of Grimes County: Land of Heritage and Progress*. Dallas: Taylor Publishing, 1982.

Gunning, Mother M. Patricia. *To Texas with Love: A History of the Sisters of the Incarnate Word and Blessed Sacrament*. Corpus Christi, TX: Printers Unlimited, 2003.

Hackett, Sheila, OP. *Dominican Women in Texas: From Ohio to Galveston and Beyond*. Houston, TX: Sacred Heart Convent, 1986.

Halstead, Murat. *Galveston: The Horrors of a Stricken City*. Chicago: American Publishers' Association, 1900.

Hardwick, Susan Wiley. *Mythic Galveston: Reinventing America's Third Coast*. Baltimore: Johns Hopkins University Press, 2002.

Hegarty, Sister Loyola, CCVI. *Serving with Gladness: The Origin and History of the Congregation of the Sisters of Charity of the Incarnate Word, Houston, Texas*. Houston: Bruce Publishing in cooperation with the Sisters of Charity of the Incarnate Word, Houston, Texas, 1967.

Hennessey, James, S.J. *American Catholics: A History of the Roman Catholic Community in the United States*. New York: Oxford University Press, 1981.

"An Inhuman Priest." *Fort Worth Gazette*, August 27, 1891.

Jacks, L.V. *Claude Dubuis, Bishop of Galveston*. Saint Louis: B. Herder, 1947.

Johnston, S. M. *A Light Shining: The Life and Letters of Mother Mary Joseph Dallmer*. Chicago: Benziger, 1937.

Larson, Eric. *Isaac's Storm: A Man, a Time, and the Deadliest Hurricane in History*. New York: Crown, 1999.

"Lay Trusteeism in New York, January 25, 1786," and "The Abuse of Lay Trusteeism at Norfolk, Virginia, June–September, 1819." In *Documents of American Catholic History*, edited by John Tracy Ellis (Lexington, KY: Forgotten Books, 2013), 150–54 and 220–27.

Leo XIII, Pope. *Romani Pontificis,* July 15, 1890.

MacLeod, Terry. "Galveston Remembers Terror of a Hurricane." *Texas Catholic Herald,* September 8, 1964.

Markey, Betty. "History of Catholicism in the Vicinity of Plantersville, Grimes County, TX." *PGST [Polish Genealogical Society of Texas] News* 9, no. 2 (Summer 1992): 1–4.

"Married, [Nicholas Clayton and Mary Ducie]." *Galveston Daily News,* July 7, 1891.

McKenna, P. "Ode on the Fiftieth Anniversary of Rt. Rev. Bishop Gallagher. *Southern Messenger,* March 19, 1896, 5.

McMaster, James A. "Bishop Administrator for Galveston." *New York Freeman's Journal* (December 31, 1881).

The Memorial Volume: A History of the Third Plenary Council of Baltimore, November 9–December 7, 1884. Baltimore: Baltimore Publishing, 1885.

Mensing, Raymond C., Jr. "A Papal Delegate in Texas: The Visit of His Eminence Cardinal Satolli in 1896." *East Texas Historical Journal* (Fall 1982): 18–27.

Moore, James Talmadge. *Acts of Faith: The Catholic Church in Texas, 1900–1950.* College Station: Texas A&M University Press, 2002.

———. *Through Fire and Flood: The Catholic Church in Frontier Texas, 1836–1900.* College Station: Texas A&M University Press, 1992.

Murphy, John. "Galveston Is Home to Many Texas Firsts." *Galveston Daily News,* June 17, 1998, 14.

New Catholic Encyclopedia. 2004 edition. s.v. "Diocese of Galveston," by Thomas Meehan.

O'Connell, Marvin R. *John Ireland and the American Catholic Church.* Saint Paul: Minnesota Historical Society Press, 1988.

O'Laughlin, Father Raphael, *Basilian Leaders from Texas.* Houston, TX: Wings Press, 1991.

Ousley, Clarence, ed. *Galveston in Nineteen Hundred.* Atlanta: William C. Chase, 1900.

The Oxford Dictionary of the Christian Church, F. L. Cross and E. A. Livingstone, eds. 1996 edition.

Reeves-Marquardt, Dona B., and Lewis R. Marquardt. "Catholic Germans from Russia in Texas." *Journal of Texas Catholic History and Culture* 4 (1993): 25–44.

Rogers, Bruce, and Stephen Marion Reynolds. *Eugene Debs: His Life Writings and Speeches.* Girard, KS: Appeal to Reason, 1908.

Scardino, Barrie, and Drexel Turner. *The Architecture of Nicholas J. Clayton and His Contemporaries.* Foreword by Peter Brink. Afterword by Stephen Fox. College Station: Texas A&M University Press, 2000.

"A Second Victory: The Houston High School Won from St. Mary's Seminary." *Houston Post,* May 20, 1906, 16.

Sheehan, Sister M. Agatha, CVI. *The History of Houston Heights from Its Foundation in 1891 to Its Annexation in 1918.* Houston, TX: Premier Printing, 1956.

"Silver Jubilee of Bishop Gallagher." *Houston Daily Post*, April 28, 1907. Archives of Rosenberg Library, Galveston, Texas.

Skeans, Sharon Sicinski. *Church of the Nativity of the Blessed Virgin Mary, St. Mary's Visitors' Guide—2011: Plantersville, TX.* Montgomery, TX: Thomas Printing and Publishing, n.d.

"Students of St. Mary's Hold Commencement: Bishop Gallagher Attended from Galveston—Many Visitors from Houston." *Houston Post*, June 18, 1905, 9.

Terrar, Toby. "Catholic Socialism: The Reverend Thomas McGrady." *Dialectical Anthropology* 7 (1983): 209–35.

"Thomas McGrady." In *Eugene Debs, His Life Writings and Speeches*. Girard, KS: The Appeal to Reason, 1908.

Tucek, James. *A Century of Faith: The Story of the Diocese of Dallas*. Dallas, TX: Taylor Publishing, 1990.

Vanderholt, Father James, Carolyn B. Martinez, and Karen A. Gilman. *The Diocese of Beaumont, the Catholic Story of Southeast Texas*. Diocese of Beaumont: East Texas Catholic, 1991.

Vanderholt, Reverend James. *Lone Star Catholicism: A Measure of Faith; From the Spanish Missions to the Golden Anniversary of the Diocese of Austin*. Austin, TX: Diocese of Austin, 1997.

Weems, John Edward. *A Weekend in September*. New York: Henry Holt, 1957.

"Will of Bishop Is Filed for Probate." *Galveston Daily News*, February 28, 1918.

Wilson, Reverend Mr. Rich. "Looking Back to Look Ahead." *Regina Cleri ora pro nobis* (Spring 2015).

Websites

"All Saints Catholic Community." Accessed September 12, 2014. http://allsaint sheights.com/history.

"Bishop Edward M. Fitzgerald." Accessed February 1, 2015. www.dolr.org/former-bishops-fitzgerald.

Catholic Encyclopedia, 1910, s.v., "James Alphonsus McMaster." Accessed December 28, 2014. www.newadvent.org/cathen/09506a.htm.

"Church of the Annunciation, Houston." Accessed December 29, 2014. www .tshaonline.org/handbook/online/articles/ivc01.

Fainning, William. "Secret Societies." *Catholic Encyclopedia*. New York: Robert Appleton, 1912. Accessed November 28, 2014. www.newadvent.org/cathen/ 14071b.htm.

González, Aníbal A. "St. Mary's University, Galveston." *Handbook of Texas Online*. Accessed December 28, 2014. www.tshaonline.org/handbook/online/ articles/kbs62.

Hegarty, Sister M. Loyola, CCVI. "Catholic Health Care." *Handbook of Texas Online*. Accessed December 19, 2014. www.tshaonline.org/handbook/online/ articles/smc01.

Hill, Virginia Felchak. "History of St. Stanislaus Catholic Church, Chappell, Texas." Accessed November 30, 2014. www.bishop-accountability.org.

"History of St. Stanislaus Kostka Church Anderson." Archdiocese of Galveston-Houston. Accessed October 30, 2014. www.polish-texans.com/2007/06/history-of-st-stanislaus-kostka-church-anderson/reference.

"History of St. Stanislaus Catholic Church, Chappell Hill, TX." Accessed June 15, 2015. www.polish-texans.com/2007/07/ii-57/2/.

"The Influenza Pandemic of 1918." Accessed February 3, 2015. https://virus.stanford.edu/uda/.

Lamb, R. E., CSB. "St. Basil's College." *Handbook of Texas Online*. Accessed October 28, 2014. www.tshaonline.org/handbook/online/articles/kbs65.

Meehan, Thomas. "James Alphonsus McMaster." *Catholic Encyclopedia*. New York: Robert Appleton, 1910. Accessed October 3, 2014. http://www1000.newadvent.org/cathen/09506a.htm.

"The Painted Churches of Texas: Echoes of the Homeland." Accessed February 1, 2015. www.klru.org/paintedchurches/.

Pius IX, Pope. *Instruction to the Bishops of the United States*. 1875. Accessed October 20, 2014. www.catholicessentials.net/christianeducation.htm.

Pius X, Pope. *Acerbo Nimis*, 1905. Accessed December 1, 2014. www.vatican.va/holy_father/pius_x/encyclicals/documents/hf_p-x_enc_15041905_acerbo-nimis_en.html.

Ryan, Reverend Paul. "History of the Diocese of Covington, Kentucky, on the Occasion of the Centenary of the Diocese, 1853–1953." Accessed December 10, 2014. www.nkyviews.com/campbell/text/newport_text_ryan_stanthony.htm.

"St. Mary of the Immaculate Conception Catholic Church, La Porte, TX." Accessed June 13, 2015. http://stmaryslaporte.com/history-of-st-marys-church.

"The Texas Emancipation Proclamation (June 19, 1865)." Black Past.org. Accessed October 30, 2014. www.blackpast.org/primarywest/texas-emancipation-proclamation-1865.

"The Third Plenary Council of Baltimore, Title VI." Accessed October 20, 2014. www.newadvent.org/cathen/02235a.htm.

Treybig, Arliss. "Bernardo, TX." *Handbook of Texas Online*. Accessed December 6, 2014. www.tshaonline.org/handbook/online/articles/hnb29.

Vasquez, Debbie, and Guadalupe Dominguez. "Sisters of Charity Began Hotel Dieu Hospital." Accessed December 12, 2014. http://epcc.libguides.com/content.php?pid=309255&sid=2583686.

Index

www.ingramcontent.com/pod-product-compliance
Lightning Source LLC
Chambersburg PA
CBHW071858090426
42811CB00004B/651